The Bordens of Burkesville

A Romantic Historical Fiction
By

Barbara Dumas Ballew

The Bordens of Burkesville

**This novel is a work of fiction. However, several
names, descriptions, entities and incidences included in
the story may be based on the lives of real people.**

Author's Note:

I hope you've enjoyed reading the Borden Family Series of books as much as I've enjoyed writing them. They are a fictitious family. The places are real and are beautiful little towns that I have visited in the past. I fell in love with each while I was there.

The Bordens and other characters in this series are from my imagination. They are all characters I would liked to have known. To me, they are as Americans should be and as I imagined they were.

Credits:

Editor-Marsha Welsh
Cover design-Joe Ballew
Cover photos-istockphotos.com
Printing-Createspace

The Bordens of Burkesville

Chapter One

Daniel sat there in stunned silence. With the puzzlement still on his face, he asked Sarah, "Would you say that again, please?"

Her bright blue eyes were dancing as she began to laugh.

"That just slipped out in the devilment of the moment. It's really too soon for me to be saying anything to anyone, but you know how timely I always am. This month I'm running late and I think all of this excitement just made what I said pop out. I meant to keep it to myself for another month or so."

She looked in Daniel's direction and continued, "I want our first child to be on its way so badly that I couldn't contain the news."

Daniel stood, went to her, and encircled her in his arms.

"Oh, Sarah, this is the greatest news. I'm glad you told me because I want to share every moment of this with you."

She looked into his eyes and replied, "Let's keep this our secret for another month or so just to be sure."

"Okay, but then I want to have a get-together for the whole family and make an announcement. Next to marrying you, this is the biggest event in my life."

All of a sudden he acted as though she might break.

"How are you feeling? You need to be careful and slow down."

"Daniel, I feel wonderful. Now don't worry. This is a normal, natural function in my life. I'm not sick. Hopefully I'm just with child. Life will continue as usual for us, at least for the next few months. Then things will change and our lives will be more complete and exciting than it has ever been. Let's just enjoy the moment."

Daniel and Sarah Borden had been married almost two years. Daniel was twenty-two years old, and Sarah was twenty. He was a very good-looking young man. Daniel stood straight, and was of medium height with dark brown hair that was slightly curled. His eyes were hazel with golden flecks that made them appear to twinkle. There was a prominent dimple on his right cheek which lent itself to his rugged, good looks. He was a smart, pleasant, and a fun-loving young man.

Sarah was a beautiful young lady. She was very well-built with blond hair which hung in ringlets most of the time. Her eyes were a clear, soft, sky blue-so soft and blue you could see no end to their depth. Her smile could melt your heart. Together they were a stunning couple, and one instantly knew they were meant for each other. That was the strength of their marriage.

They had been living in their new home in Burkesville, Kentucky for only a few months. Sarah taught in her privately owned school, and Daniel was getting his own furniture factory established. Both of their businesses were located conveniently on their acreage.

The couple moved to Kentucky with two of Daniel's brothers and three of their nephews. They were all married and some had children. The clan had built along the same road about two miles out of town on the Cumberland River Road.

Sarah sniffed the air.

"I smell food cooking. I believe it's fried fish and fresh bread. Jetty must be cooking supper. It's been a busy afternoon, and I'm getting hungry. How about you?"

"It *does* smell good. Ollie must have gone fishing while we were working on Miss Purdy's Palace," Daniel said and laughed.

"I'll go out, check on Jetty, and tell her we're back with our undertaking completed."

Sarah headed toward the kitchen.

6

"We're back, Jetty. Miss Purdy's Palace is back in its rightful place. All's right with the world again."

Sarah chuckled a bit.

"Can you believe that when Allen and Joel started to remove the home-made sign, Miss Purdy asked them to leave it? She liked the whimsy it added over the privy door."

When Jetty rolled her dark eyes toward the ceiling, Sarah caught her breath. At that moment Jetty reminded her so much of Dolly and how Dolly laughed and roll her eyes. She must remember to tell Daniel, for he'd like that thought of the resemblance.

Jetty and Ollie were a middle-aged, black couple who hadn't been working for Daniel and Sarah very long. Ollie was a freeman and they had moved from Massachusetts along with their older son, Ansell, and his wife, Effie. Ansell found work in town at the blacksmith shop and livery.

"Jetty, I'll set the table for me and Daniel. With all the excitement this afternoon, I can't settle down and just sit."

"Miss Sarah, I almost forgot. Miss Mary came up and said she closed up the school this afternoon, and she couldn't find Mittens. Later, Ollie said he noticed Mittens out at the barn poking around."

She continued with concern in her voice.

"He petted her and she rubbed against his leg, but he didn't think much about it. I called her, but she didn't come."

"After we eat, Daniel and I'll take some fish out to the barn and look for her. That cat loves fish, and it should draw her out of her hiding place. I don't think she'll go far."

Once supper was finished, Sarah and Daniel went to the kitchen, and Jetty already had a small bowl of fish crumbled for Mittens.

"The very smell should bring her running. Supper was delicious, Jetty."

7

Sarah picked up the bowl, and the two of them headed for the barn. While Sarah was *calling* Mittens, Daniel started *looking* for her. The cat caught Daniel's eye as she jumped off the shelf under the wagon and down onto the step he had build for her.

"Here she is, Sarah. She's been taking a nap in her old home."

Sarah took the bowl of fish to her and set it on the ground. Mittens lapped up the fish as though she was starved.

"Do you suppose she wants to move back to her old home?"

"Well, I'm sure the school gets very quiet, especially on the weekends. Why don't I go get her washbasin and her rabbit skin and put it on the wagon shelf again? Tomorrow I can build her a shelf here in the barn."

"Perhaps she'd like it better outside again. She could follow Ollie around in the garden and be nearer to us. Between the three of us, one of us is outside a great deal of the time. They both seem to like her and can help tend to her some, too. Let's try it."

Daniel went to fetch the basin and skin. When he returned, he placed it on the wagon shelf. Mittens watched, but instead of going to it, she followed them to the porch.

"Let's sit here in the rockers for a while and see what she does."

Mittens curled up on the edge of the porch. She seemed to be content watching the birds while they looked for their last few bites of food before roosting. The two sat for about thirty minutes.

Finally, Daniel said, "It'll be dark shortly. Why don't we go inside and watch her out the window?"

They stood watching toward the barn, and in only a few seconds after going in, they saw Mittens head back toward the barn and probably the wagon.

Early the next morning, Daniel could hear Jetty already out in the kitchen. Smelling the coffee on the fire, he slipped out of bed and pulled on his breeches. When he got to the kitchen, Jetty had already gotten the cool milk out of the bucket in the well, and she was pouring some into a small bowl.

"Mittens met me on the porch this morning, and I thought I'd give her some milk," Jetty said.

"Oh, she'll like that. Miss Sarah and I decided she might like it better to be outside again and nearer to all of us."

"I'll have coffee ready in just a few minutes. I have some teacakes and I'll fix you and Miss Sarah a little tray if you like."

"Jetty, it'd be a treat for us and very much like back home. I used to take hot coffee and teacakes on occasion to wake Miss Sarah up when we lived in North Carolina. We'd sit in rockers in front of our bedroom fireplace and visit to start our day."

While the coffee finished brewing, Jetty got a pair of scissors and went out the back door. She came back carrying a couple of sprigs of rosemary and a few fern leaves.

"I don't have any flowers this time of year, but the rosemary'll smell fresh and good. We need to tell Ollie to plant some roses and flowers come next spring."

Jetty got a small, silver vase out of a chest, fixed a green bouquet, and placed it in the center of the tray. She poured their coffee into pretty china cups and placed four teacakes on a matching saucer.

Daniel sweetened the coffee with fresh honey and poured a bit of milk into each cup.

"Thank you, Jetty. Sarah will love this little surprise."

As he stepped into their bedroom, Sarah rolled over saying, "I smell coffee."

"Yes, look what Jetty fixed for us. Doesn't this remind you of home and other mornings we've had?"

9

"This is wonderful. Hand me my robe, and I'll join you."

Daniel looked in the armoire and found one of Sarah's robes.

As they sat in the rockers, Daniel told her, "I wanted to tell Jetty we're expecting a baby, so she'll know and will take care of you."

Sarah thought for a minute before answering.

"I believe she and Ollie can keep our secret until we announce it, so I guess it's all right."

"Okay. We'll tell her when we go to breakfast."

The smell of hickory-smoked bacon frying drifted into the room.

"Did you want to dress or just go to the dining room for breakfast in your robe?"

"I'll slip on one of my skirts and waists this morning."

"I'm going on to the kitchen and I'll tell Jetty you'll be ready soon."

They both arose from their chairs. One headed for the kitchen and the other to the armoire to retrieve her dress.

Jetty had set the dining table and was making hot cakes for breakfast. While they were eating, Jetty came into the dining room to pour more hot coffee.

"Jetty, we've something to tell you."

Daniel hesitated for a moment to allow Jetty to finish pouring the coffee.

"Miss Sarah thinks we're going to have a baby. If she's correct, it'll be here some time next May. I want you to help look after her over these next few months."

Jetty almost dropped the coffee pot when she heard the news.

"Lordy me! That's wonderful news for you and Miss Sarah. I've been a midwife for a long time, so I can be lots of help."

Daniel quickly answered, "That's good. I think I'm going to talk to Dr. Wade and have him examine Miss Sarah in about a month. I'll want him to be here when this first baby comes, but I'll want you right there to assist him."

"I'll watch over Miss Sarah and this baby just like a mammy."

"Good! Then I know we can depend on you."

Sarah spoke up saying, "Jetty, we're telling you, and you can tell Ollie, but we want to wait awhile longer to tell anyone else. I want to be sure this is it before we really spread the news to anyone else."

Jetty turned and looked directly in Sarah's eyes.

"This *is* it, Miss Sarah. I can tell by your eyes that you're with child. I don't doubt it a minute."

Smiling, Jetty walked back to the kitchen.

"While you're building a barn shelf for Mittens this morning, I think I'd like to get Ollie started on a path through the herb garden. I'd like to bring it from the turn-around to the back porch and then wind it through the garden."

Daniel stood up from the table as he commented, "I noticed the last few days that Ollie has started piling some good sandstone from the quarry to make paths. I'll go out and check with him. He'll want your input and directions, I'm sure."

Daniel talked to Ollie about the path and then went by the barn and got a hand cart. While walking to the factory to get the boards and tools he needed, he planned how to build a little square house on the shelf for Mittens.

With hay on the bottom and the rabbit skin on top of that, it would make a warmer, cozier place for her to sleep. In warmer weather, she could sleep on the shelf.

Sarah went out and she and Ollie discussed how the paths should look. Ollie began to haul river sand for the base. It was obvious that the paths would be a long-term project.

Daniel made quick work of the shelf and the little house for Mittens. He returned the tools, and next he joined Sarah and Ollie to work on the paths from then until noon.

The family ate dinner, and later in the afternoon Daniel suggested, "Why don't we walk down to George's farm and visit with him and Charity. I'd like to see how he's doing with his horses. We've never taken time to walk over his horse farm, and I know he's proud of it."

"It's such a beautiful afternoon, and I could certainly use the exercise. I think I'll wear a cape, and you may want to wear a light jacket."

"I believe my long sleeve shirt is plenty for me," Daniel responded.

As they leisurely walked the road to George's house, Sarah looked at the colorful trees and marveled at how many different kinds there were.

"You know, some of the kids walk this road in the mornings, and I never think about it being quite this far."

"Are you tired already?"

"Oh, no. It's just a little farther than I imagined. I always think about George being just across the road. He's really not that close."

The couple finally turned off the main road and started on the lane toward the house.

"I noticed you can't see James' or George's house from the main road."

"You can barely see ours, Sarah. You notice the school when you come down the road because it's in a clearing with only few trees around it."

"I guess I've noticed more while we are walking than I do when we're in the carriage. It's been nice walking it for the first time."

Arriving at George's door, Daniel knocked and George answered.

"Well, look who we have here. Do come in."

"Sarah and I decided that it was such a nice afternoon, we'd walk."

As they entered, they continued talking, "We've never been out around your barn or pastures, and we wanted to see your horses. Do you feel like showing us around?"

"Sure, I'd enjoy it. Let's see if Charity will join us."

They found his wife in the kitchen, and after greetings were exchanged, George remarked, "Sarah and Daniel have walked down to visit and want to go look at some of our property and horses. Do you want to walk with us?"

"Certainly. Let me get a shawl and I'll be right with you."

The four stopped at the barn first. Sarah was amazed. "George, I don't think I've ever seen a larger barn."

"A horse ranch calls for a big barn, and I'll probably have to build another one before long. I plan to have a lot of horses before I'm through. I only have about thirty-five in my herd presently. I don't have a certain goal in mind, but it'll be a lot more horses than I have now."

"There're some beauties in the herd, and it looks like you'll be having some foals next spring."

"We can hardly wait," Charity said.

Sarah chimed in, "I'll want to come back to see the little ones when they come. Let us know."

They spent a long time walking and talking, and it was beginning to get dusk.

"Sarah, we'd better start home. We've stayed longer than I intended," Daniel observed.

"Daniel, it may be dark before you get home, so let me light a lantern for you to take. I can pick it up later."

Sarah laughed as she replied, "We'll take you up on that."

With the lighted lantern in hand, Sarah and Daniel started down the lane. They *had* visited longer than they intended, and it was beginning to get dark.

"Isn't this romantic? Walking through the woods with just a dim light to guide our way."

Daniel was holding Sarah's hand and carrying the lantern in the other. After they reached the main road, Daniel heard a wolf howl not too far away. He didn't say anything; they just kept walking. In a minute, another wolf joined in chorus with the first one and then Sarah noticed

13

their howls. In another few minutes, they could tell there were at least three voices, if not more.

Daniel and Sarah picked up their pace. The wolves were getting a little nearer, and Daniel could tell that there were several.

"Sarah, can you walk a little faster? I don't like the sound of that pack. Their howls are getting nearer, and they're on the hunt. Right now I wish I had my flintlock or at least my pistol. Remind me to stick my pistol in my belt the next time we go walking at night."

"Daniel, are you scared?"

"Well, I don't feel too good about this. I'm not able to fight a whole pack of wolves. They're vicious animals. Do you think you can trot? I guess what I'm asking is, if you're pregnant, will it hurt anything?"

"I'm not that far along if I *am* pregnant. It shouldn't hurt, and if you think we should, let's go. The wolves could be worse than even losing our baby."

Daniel took Sarah's arm in his hand and was almost pulling her along. Soon they turned off the road and toward Sarah's school.

"I've got a key to the door in my pocket. Let's stop there for a few minutes. At least that'll give me a chance to listen better and for us to rest."

They made it to the school, and Daniel had hardly let Sarah's feet touch the steps. He fished the key from his pocket and held the lantern so he could see. After opening the door and going inside, he shut the door, and Sarah melted on a bench.

"Are you all right?"

"I can hardly breathe. I'm gasping for breath."

"Just be quite for a moment and you'll recover. Nothing else is bothering, is it?"

Sarah shook her head *no*. Daniel opened the top section of one of the Dutch doors, and he stood very still and listened.

14

"Sarah, I can see the pack on our road. The wolves are close. They're sniffing and circling, and I can count six of them. We made it here just in time. Let's wait them out before we go to the house."

Sarah shivered.

"Are you cold?"

"No, still just a little frightened."

"It's a little chilly in here, so I think I'll start a fire. There's plenty of wood and kindling. Before we head for the house, I might try to make a torch. They're afraid of fire, and we'd have a better chance with a torch of some kind."

"Let's stay here long enough for them to leave."

Sarah was *not* in a hurry to leave the safety of the school.

"We will."

Daniel suddenly had a new thought.

"Sarah, you know, I'm thinking I might get another flintlock and put it down here in the school. You could keep it in one of the chests, and it'd be here if you ever needed it. Who knows when a bear or what else might show up. Well, like tonight we could use one. You could at least scare something. "

Sarah ignored his last remark. Right now she was more interested in getting home rather than what might happen in the future.

"Daniel, I'm thinking we should make two torches before we start to the house just in case I had to fight, too. I know there's one broomstick in the corner by the fireplace. I have some old rags and some twine string."

"That would do. We can even wrap some of the rags around the poker if there's nothing else. They only have to burn long enough to get us to the house. There's plenty of lamp oil here for the flares."

Daniel made their torches but didn't put oil on them yet. He stood watching and listening to determine if the wolf pack had retreated back to the woods.

15

After waiting for almost an hour, he said, "I haven't heard or seen them for a while. It should be clear. Can you run again? I'll leave the lantern here. We won't need it. The torches will light our way. We can run faster holding them instead of a swinging lantern."

"Yes, I can run with no problem. Do you think it's clear now?"

Sarah, too, had heard no howls for some time.

"I think it is. I'm not going to lock the door so we can get back in quickly just in case. If they come after us, go to the nearest building for protection. If they attack, they'll circle us. Turn your back to me, punch the torch at them, and holler loudly. Move sideways to the nearest building and keep your back to me. Think about our plan. Are you clear on it? "

"I'm ready. Let's go."

Daniel doused the torch rags with lamp oil and lit them in the fireplace.

Daniel warned, "Stay beside me. I don't want to get ahead. Let's go!"

With flares in hand, the couple ran for their home. When they got there, they quickly opened the door and went inside. Daniel put their torches in the fireplace, and then he held Sarah in his arms as tightly as he could. The danger was now over, but it had come too close.

The weekend had passed quickly with all the excitement. When Sarah got to the school Monday morning, she stopped and rang the school bell. When Mary heard the clang, she stuck her head out of one of the Dutch doors. Sarah wrapped the bell rope back around the peg and started up the path to the porch.

"I love to hear that bell. I almost rang it this morning, but I didn't want you to think I was rushing you. You're always here first."

"You've beat me this morning."

16

"Yes, I came to start the fire, but when I got here, it was already going. I was expecting you to be here, but I guess Daniel started it before he went to the factory. It still seems kind of strange with you not living in the school anymore. That means it's cold in the building on Monday mornings."

"Yes, I'm glad Daniel thought of the fire this morning, as it's very cool."

Sarah removed her cloak and hat and hung them on a peg. By the time she was settled, the children began to come. The students removed their coats and hung them beside Mary's and Sarah's.

After the Lord's Prayer had been recited and the hymn had been sung, Mary asked Rose Stewart for a favor.

"Would you please go to the box in the back corner near the fireplace and bring some parchment paper and graphite pencils?"

It was such a treat to be asked to perform a special task that Rose was glad to do it. She felt that it was a reward for being a good student as they were the ones who were usually asked to do little special duties.

She went to the corner to get the paper and pencils while the rest of the class was busy preparing for today's lessons. She lifted the lid to the box and stuck her hand in to find the pencils which most probably were on the bottom of the box.

Suddenly she let out a loud, frightening scream. Then another as she jumped back from the box and started to run to the front of the room. More tears and screams followed before Sarah could calm Rose down enough for the girl to tell what was happening.

Half sobbing, she said, "It almost scared me to death!"

"What almost scared you to death?"

"A little mouse was in the box."

"Mouse? I didn't see a mouse. Are you sure it was a mouse?"

"Yes ma'am. It was in the box and it ran up my arm. Then it ran over to the other corner of the room."

By now Allen Burke had grabbed the only broom in the classroom. He approached the box with caution and the broom at the ready.

"I think it went behind the scrap lumber bag. Where else could it be hiding but there?"

Aaron Holder slowly wiggled the bag and the poor little mouse went scampering around under the benches. All the girls and Mary were squealing and climbing up on the benches. The scared, confused mouse, trying to find safety once more, ran behind the box.

"Joel, if you'll slide the box out from the corner, I'll whack it with the broom."

Allen was ready. Joel slowly and cautiously began to slide the box away from the wall. The gray mouse popped out again.

"Get him!" shouted Joel to Allen, the boy with the solitary broom.

"I see him. There he goes!"

There was a great rush of boys to the opposite corner of the room as the mouse scurried out through a very small crack in the log cabin.

Joel, the oldest boy, exclaimed, "You missed him, darn it."

Sarah decided there had been enough confusion, so she told the boys, "That's too bad, but you scared him out. I'll get Ollie to come put a patch over the mouse hole. If the rascal comes back, he won't get in through the same place."

Sarah then explained to the class that this was the time of year when all of the smaller animals searched for a warm, comfortable place for the winter, and the field mouse was no exception. In fact, they were probably the worst winter home invaders with the squirrels a close second. Then she remembered that Mittens moved out of the school over the weekend and wasn't surprised they had been invaded by a mouse.

It had taken Rose a bit longer to settle down, for she was the one with the close encounter. The very thought of it having touched her was almost more than she could bear.

"Let's go out for an early recess. The fresh air will do us good," Sarah told the class.

She thought, *This should help get their minds off the mouse.*

The children chose sides and had a rousing game of *Red Rover*. When they returned to the classroom, all thoughts of the mouse seemed to have disappeared, and they had a very productive morning with no more interruptions.

As usual, school was dismissed at midday, and Sarah and Mary walked to the house for dinner. Sarah was pleasantly surprised to see that Ollie had finished the sandstone path from the turnaround in front of the house to the front steps. He had now started working on the path that would lead to the back porch. There was Mittens out with Ollie, seeing the path well built.

Sarah told Ollie about the mouse hole and asked if he could repair it.

"I'll fix it right after we eat dinner."

Daniel came in from the factory to join the ladies for dinner. Mary and Sarah had to tell Daniel all about the mouse incidence. They laughed about Mary climbing up on a bench for safety.

"Well, I certainly didn't want it running up my arm like it did Rose's."

"That's right, but running up your arm would be much better than running up your skirt."

They laughed until tears rolled down their cheeks.

When Daniel recovered, he asked, "I'm going into Creel's General Store after we eat. Would you ladies like to ride in with me? I have to pick up a few bags of slaked lime for the milk paint. We can ride in the carriage, and the lime can go in the luggage storage."

"How long will we be gone? There're still a few things to do for tomorrow."

19

"Sarah, I'll take that work home with me and do it later. Let's go and look around," Mary insisted.

"Okay, we need some fun time ourselves anyway. I *do* need to show Ollie the mouse hole, though."

Daniel got up and went in the kitchen.

"Ollie, would you hitch up the carriage? I'm taking the women into town. If you'll meet us down at the school, Miss Sarah'll stop by and show you the mouse hole."

"Yes sir, I'll get right on that."

The ladies were ready to leave, and Daniel helped them into the carriage. As they were driving toward the school, they saw Ollie go in the front door. Sarah went in to show him where the mouse had run out between a log and the floor.

"I'll do the best I can to fix it, but you know these little ole mice can get in through next to nothing."

"I know Ollie, but try your best."

As the three continued their trip into town, they decided to go by John P.'s office and say "hello."

Daniel noticed John's new sign beside his door. It read, *John P. Crim, Attorney at Law.* Mary opened his office door and stuck her head in. There was no one with him, and he looked up from his reading.

"What are you doing in town?" John questioned.

He was very surprised to see her.

Mary opened the door wider, and John could see his Uncle Daniel along with Sarah standing there. Although Daniel was John's uncle, Daniel was a little younger than his nephew; John therefore, never referred to him as Uncle Daniel.

"Well, come on in. You haven't been to my office since I first opened it. I'm glad you took time to stop by."

John jumped up and pulled up another chair.

"Have a seat. By the way, I've wanted to talk you, Sarah. I'm glad you're here."

"Talk to *me*, John?"

"Yes, I need some advice."

20

"What on earth can *I* advise you about?"

"I'm considering getting a young male apprentice for my office. I've given thought that perhaps one of your bright, young students would be what I need. He must not only be a good student, but perhaps has the best potential and temperament to become a lawyer and would enjoy the work."

Sarah thought for a moment.

"Hands down, your cousin, Rice. He's very smart, catches on to things quickly, and is neat in his work."

Sarah turned to Mary, "What's your opinion?"

"You're right on the button." Mary smiled at John. "Your cousin, Rice, is the answer. He's a natural, and it runs in the family."

John laughed.

"That's wonderful. I thought I'd ask him to work in the office for awhile, and then I'll encourage him to attend William and Mary College to get a law degree. I'll even help finance his schooling. When he returns, he'll eventually become a partner in this office. "

Daniel spoke up saying, "That's a great idea, John. It not only will please your Uncle George but Rice should be pleased, also. That'll give the boy a goal in life. His brother, Clay, will inherit the horse ranch one day. This will give Rice a future as well."

Daniel stood up as he continued to talk.

"Heck, this pleases me, too. I'd like to see Rice stay in this area. He's a good kid. Oh, by the way, I like your new sign. It's very impressive."

He turned to Mary and Sarah.

"Don't you think we'd better be going, so John can get back to his reading?"

The two ladies rose as did John, and he kissed Mary on the cheek.

"By the way, drive down in front of our new tavern on your way out of town. There's been a new addition put up just this morning. I want you to see it."

21

John grinned knowing that he had managed to peak everyone's interest.

Daniel and the ladies drove on to Creel's Store, and Daniel got the slaked lime. Sarah and Mary found skirt and waist fabric and notions that they wanted for new outfits.

"Sarah, you'll help me make my new outfit, won't you?"

"Oh, sewing together will be fun. Carolina and I used to have such good times sewing. She taught me so much."

They paid for their purchases and left. As they drove down the street, Daniel guided the horse in front of the tavern. When they looked up at the roof of the building, there was a big sign that read, *The Palace.* Daniel laughed and slapped his knee.

"Can you believe that?"

Laughing, Sarah said, "I just wonder what Miss Purdy thinks about it. You know everyone connects that name with her. That is *sooo* funny! She's so prim and proper."

Daniel circled the horse around and headed back out the road toward home.

A few evenings later, John and Mary drove to George and Charity's home. When George looked out, he was a little surprised to see them. He stepped out on the porch to welcome them.

"Come in. It's good to see you. It's been a while."

"I hope this is a convenient time to come visiting. We'd like to talk to you, Charity, and Rice."

"It's always a good time for your visit. Is something wrong or do you need help?"

John smiled and said, "Nothing's wrong, and I hope we can help each other. Can we sit around your table? We bring a proposition, and I think we'll all have input to what I have to ask."

As they entered the house, George said, "Charity, I think this calls for some coffee or cider."

After greeting the guests, Charity went to the kitchen to get Alma to serve coffee and cider in the dining room. When they were all seated, they chatted about the horses and what had been going on in the families.

Alma served them, and then John said, "I came this evening to make an offer to Rice. I asked Sarah for her recommendation, and, out of all her male students, she suggested Rice. Mary agreed with her, too."

Now that he had their attention, he continued, "I'm looking for a law apprentice to work in my office. I plan to start teaching him the ins and outs of law. I need a bright young man and Sarah assures me that Rice is a quick learner and dependable."

John thought it was time to pause and let some of this startling information sink in. He looked around the table and saw nothing but blank, surprised faces at that point. He could imagine what was running through their minds right now. He continued.

"If Rice accepts, I'd like for him to start working three afternoons a week after school. When the school term is over, I'd like for him to work full time in my office for a year. Then I'll help him go to William and Mary College in Virginia for two years. When he can meet the Kentucky state requirements, I'd like for Rice to come back and be a full-fledged lawyer in my office. One day, if it all works out, he could become a full partner in the office."

Rice's eyes were big, and he was taking in every word before he answered his cousin.

"John, may I have time to talk to papa and mama before I answer. The thought of being a lawyer is exciting, but it hasn't soaked in as to what all of this could mean to us."

"Certainly, Rice, I want all of you to discuss it before you answer. This is just one direction you can take in your life."

"Would it be possible to come to your office for a few afternoons before I answer? I have some idea of what a lawyer does, but I'm sure I don't have the full picture. I don't want to waste your time, but I do want to be sure before I answer."

"Come in anytime and look things over and ask questions. I like your answer, and I believe Sarah's given me a good recommendation. You *are* a bright young man."

George could hold his opinion no longer.

"John, this is a surprise to all of us. You don't realize how proud this makes me and Charity. Why don't I bring Rice to your office tomorrow after dinner? Could you give him a ride back as far as your house when the office closes?"

"That works for me if it works for you and Rice."

"We'll be there tomorrow as soon after class as we can."

John reached over to shake hands with Rice. By this time the refreshments had been consumed by all.

"Mary, I guess we better get home. It'll soon be dark, and I'm sure George still has work to do."

Mary pushed her chair back, stood, and hugged Charity, Rice, and George.

"I'll see you at school in the morning, Rice."

There would be plenty to discuss around the supper table at the George Borden home that night.

Chapter Two

Almost a month had passed, and November was presenting a mixture of weather. One day would be nice and comfortable with just a shawl. The next day might be wet and a heavy cloak was needed.

Daniel realized that Tom was right about the Franklin stove in the school. It burned a lot less wood and put out a lot more heat than the fireplace. Most days a fire in the stove by itself did a good job heating the school.

The Rumford fireplaces at the furniture factory were doing excellent. Each took much less wood and the two kept the whole building comfortable for the working men. Tom had made good choices.

Rice was working for John at the law office in the afternoons now. After trying it for awhile, Rice was taken with the idea of becoming a lawyer. George and Charity were happy that Rice would be staying in the area even when he was older. John's helping out with the boy's education was also appreciated very much by Rice's family.

John and Rice got along wonderfully well for they had so much in common. They were more like brothers, rather than cousins. John was not paying Rice much salary right now, but there were a lot of gifts of very nice clothing and leather luggage. John was getting him ready to attend *The College of William and Mary*. All were very proud of and for Rice.

Sarah thought the time had come for them to make their announcement to the family about having a baby. She and Daniel decided it was time for a party and the baby announcement. They invited just the family members and, of course, the Stewarts and Noah Wade. The get-together was to be at the school.

They planned to line the benches around the wall for people to sit, and the floor would be clear for dancing. Food could be kept warm in the school fireplace, but it

25

would be cooked at the house, and Daniel would take it down to the school in the wagon. The invitation was for a party on Saturday afternoon. Mary and John would have to be told early, because the pair was needed for planning and work.

When they issued the invitations, little did the two know that Noah would decide what a great opportunity a family get-together would be to announce his engagement to Susan. Noah had bought Susan a ring, and he planned to give it to her in front of the family. They had discussed marriage but had not made it formal. Now it would be.

There was a great deal of excitement the afternoon of the party. Green boughs and fruits decorated the table. Jetty, Sarah, and Mary had been cooking and baking for the party. Daniel had the lanterns setting all around just waiting for dark so he could light them. The school was warm and festive looking.

Sarah looked radiant and especially pretty as she welcomed the guests, and Daniel was attentive but a little nervous. He knew a secret that the guests did not know. Jetty and Ollie were there to serve and tend the guests. The brothers had played a couple of tunes but no one was dancing yet.

At dusk, Noah had a glass of cider in his hand. He took a spoon and tapped on the glass for attention. The conversation in the room dropped, and he had everyone's eyes on him. He held his hand out for Susan to come to his side.

Noah raised his voice so all could hear and said, "I need your attention, please. I have something very important to announce."

Noah looked at Susan and took her left hand in his.

"You all know that Susan and I've been seeing each other for several months now. I want Susan to know that I love her very much. Susan, will you do me the honor of becoming my wife?"

As he said this, he reached in his coat pocket and pulled out a beautiful ring.

Susan was shocked almost speechless but she managed to say, "Yes, Noah, you know I will."

He slipped the ring on her finger, gave her a gentle kiss, and everyone clapped. George, James, and Daniel began to play a lively tune while everyone offered congratulations. The brothers played a waltz and Noah asked Susan to dance. It made for a very romantic setting. Daniel decided to ask Sarah to dance. He wanted to talk to her about telling of the coming baby.

"What do we do now? I believe we've been preempted. I hate to horn in on their big moment."

Sarah said, "We need to make our announcement anyway because, if we don't, there won't be an announcement to make. I'll be showing and everyone'll know I'm having a baby and wonder why we hadn't said something. Besides, I don't want to give another party so soon."

"Well, what do you want to do?"

"Wait a little while and then we'll tap on a glass and you tell our secret. That'll just be double joy for everyone."

After a few more tunes, Daniel told James and George, "Play *Rock-A-Bye Baby.*"

"What?"

They couldn't believe Daniel wanted them to play that song.

"You heard me."

Daniel poked James in the ribs with his elbow. Then he nodded for Sarah to meet him up at the front table. This time the musicians didn't hesitate--they played the song. Everyone looked at James and George and wondered why on earth they were playing that old nursery rhyme? Daniel picked up a spoon and a glass and tapped on it.

"Excuse me everyone, but Sarah and I have an announcement to make, too."

Silence again fell over the group.

Daniel continued, "We're having a baby in May."

Everyone gasped, a murmur went through the room, and then they began to clap. James and George struck up *Rock-A-Bye Baby* again. Daniel laughed and asked Sarah to dance. When the dance was complete, he walked back to the table and tapped on the glass again.

"Does anyone else in the family have more surprises to be announced this evening?"

Everyone began to laugh and hollered, "NO," in unison.

After all had settled down, Noah and Susan went to Sarah and Daniel.

"We're so sorry. I never thought about you having anything that important to tell, or I would have never proposed to Susan at this time."

Sarah took Susan's hand.

"Oh, Susan, there's no worry. We don't mind that you did. It was fun, and, just think, it'll be a family tale for generations to come. Daniel knew I had to tell soon or I'd be showing, and everyone would wonder why we hadn't said something."

Daniel added, "We're so happy for you and Noah and we certainly don't mind sharing the evening."

"Well, Uncle Daniel, you did make the whole thing fun and rather funny. We couldn't have planned it better."

When the party ended, there was very little food left. With six of them working, it didn't take long to put the school back in order. The few leftovers were loaded in Daniel's wagon, and Jetty and Ollie drove the wagon to the house.

John and Mary were in their carriage, and Sarah and Daniel rode up to the house with them. The rest of the food was put up and the kitchen cleaned.

"We had a delightful evening. Everything turned out so nice, and everyone enjoyed it. We're sure we shall see you at church in the morning."

Mary and John hugged Sarah and Daniel and took their leave.

The following morning, Sarah and Daniel readied themselves for church. Jetty and Ollie were given time off until late afternoon on Sundays. This gave the couple a chance to go to church with their son, Ansell, and his wife, Effie. Ollie and Jetty usually took food to their son's house and had Sunday dinner there. That made for a nice day for both families.

Daniel and Sarah sat with the other family members at the services. The group filled a large section of the church. Molly and Caleb Creel melded in with the Borden clan.

After the service was over, Caleb talked to Daniel about bringing more benches to the store on Monday morning. The benches were selling like they were going out of style and there would be no more.

"Daniel, I'm really thinking you should go to the general stores in the nearby areas and take a few of your benches to show. I know you'd get orders for them. As fast as I'm selling them, there must be customers in other areas that'd want them. I know some of my customers are from out of town."

"I'll get some to you first thing in the morning. I'll take your suggestion and call on a few other stores. That's a good idea. I could surely use another painter or find someone Nichols Findley can train. You know what kind of men I like to hire. Be on the lookout and send them out, and I'll consider them."

They shook hands.

"I'll see you in the morning."

When Caleb and Daniel finished talking, James came up to Daniel.

"Lucy and I want you and Sarah to follow us home for dinner. We didn't get to talk much to you yesterday at the party. We want to hear more about having this baby."

"That sounds good because Jetty is off on Sunday, so there's no dinner waiting for us. I'll get Sarah and follow you."

Sarah was pleased when Daniel told her, "I've accepted an invitation from James for dinner at their house."

When they went to get their carriage, Anna and Eli were waiting beside it.

"May we ride with you? We've wanted to ride in your carriage."

"We'd enjoy having you. Hop in and we'll follow behind your papa."

Daniel helped Sarah in while the children were getting settled in the rear seat.

"Aunt Sarah, have you ever seen a piano?"

"No, Anna, I can't say that I've ever seen one."

"I saw a newspaper the other day at Amy Holder's house. There was a picture of one in the paper. Amy let me cut the article out, and I brought it home for my papa and mama to see. I'm thinking I'd like to have one. Papa said it was expensive. Do you know what one costs?"

"No, I have no idea. Your Grandmother Carolina has a spinet harpsichord. She can play it beautifully. I understand that the piano is somewhat like a harpsichord, but the sound is different. Do you still have the article?"

"Yes ma'am. I saved it. Someday when I get older, I'll have one even if I have to save a long time."

"Papa is teaching me to play his banjo," Eli added.

"I'm glad to hear that, Eli. Someday perhaps you can play as well as your papa and Uncle Daniel."

By this time they were pulling up to James' house. Daniel drove his carriage around to the back to offer his horse, Midge, a drink of water. James went to the barn to unhitch his team. After Midge drank, Daniel pulled her back around in front of the house and then went inside.

Anna got the article and picture of the piano and was showing it to Sarah.

"I'd love to hear one. I wish I could play one. Amy told me that Miss Purdy has a piano and that she gives lessons on it."

Sarah was surprised at that revelation.

"I know Miss Purdy, but I didn't know she taught piano. That's interesting. I might be able to get her to play it for us someday."

"Oh, Aunt Sarah, that'd be exciting."

Lucy called, "Dinner's ready," and everyone came to the table.

"Let's eat, and I'll talk to Miss Purdy soon."

While they were eating, James brought up the subject of the expected baby.

"The baby's due in May?"

"I think sometime around the middle of May."

Lucy was helping Eli fill his plate.

"Have you discussed names yet?"

"Yes, and we've come up with two that we both like. For a boy, we are thinking about Beau James Borden. We like the sound of Beau Borden. You know Beau is Daniel's middle name. The James part is hard to explain."

Sarah cut her eyes at James and laughed.

"If it's a girl, we like Kate Caroline Borden. The Caroline is for Carolina with the slight change."

"I like your choices, especially the boy's name," James said with a grin. "He's bound to be good-looking being named after the two best looking men in America."

Daniel laughed and changed the subject.

"Ollie's been rearranging our root cellar better than I had it fixed. You know, that fellow just does things without being asked. I like that in him."

"He's a good man. I ran into him down at the spring house the other day. He was showing me how he had separated out a section for your food. He said that gave a better idea of what was for you, and what he was free to take."

"Ollie's honest, there's no doubt."

"I told him he's welcome to pick or to dig as much of the crops as he thought you all needed. If he wants to fill up my space, too, he's welcome. He brings us fresh herbs when he has them, dried if he doesn't. He keeps the springhouse clean and neat, too."

The meal was finished, and they moved into the parlor.

"Did you know Ollie caught more than enough fish for you the other day, so he cleaned and brought us a mess for supper?"

"He considers fishing his time off. Ollie loves it, and Jetty can *fry those fish.* I go out on the dock to visit and see what he's catching. He sits there with a big smile on his face pulling fish in left and right. Ollie has the touch. I keep watching and trying to learn from him."

"Daniel, I hate to break this up but I think we better get home," Sarah urged.

Daniel pulled out his pocket watch and checked the time.

"You're right. The afternoon's gone by fast. I've enjoyed our visit. I'm going to suggest to Ollie to make a date with Eli to come fish with him."

"Eli'd love that."

Lucy, Anna, and James walked out to the carriage to say goodbye.

James helped Sarah in and said, "I can't wait for Beau James to get here."

"Thank you. I can't either," said Sarah, and she laughed knowing there was still much time left.

Daniel had asked Ollie to have the wagon hitched up Monday morning so he could deliver the benches to Caleb. The aroma of coffee came floating across the hall into their bedroom, so he knew Jetty was up, but she was so quiet he couldn't hear her. He was getting dressed when Sarah rolled over and rose up on her elbow.
"Is it time to get up?"

"I think so. It's a school day and I smell coffee."

"I think I'd rather have a cup of tea and a teacake this morning."

"Shall I get it and bring it to you?"

Then a thought hit him and he asked, "Sarah, do you feel all right?"

"I'm fine. Just lazy."

"I've got to deliver benches to Caleb this morning. I think I'll go by Dr. Wade's office and ask him to come out and check you this afternoon. Think of any questions you might have for him."

"Okay, but really I'm fine. Coffee just doesn't sound good this morning. You might tell Jetty I'll have a piece of toast and a small bowl of oat mush this morning."

By now, Daniel was dressed and ready to go to eat.

"I'm going on for my breakfast. You'd better come on soon if you're going to ring the school bell. I'll stop by and get the fire started in the school room before I go load the benches."

"Thank you. That'll be nice."

Daniel was half through with his breakfast when Sarah came to the kitchen.

"I guess I'm ready for my breakfast, Jetty. After I eat, I'll be on my way. I'm running a little late this morning."

Daniel had just taken his last bite, so he rose and kissed Sarah on the cheek.

"I'll see you and Mary at dinner. Hope you're feeling better by then."

"I will. I'm just sluggish this morning."

Ollie had the wagon waiting for Daniel. He hopped in and hurriedly drove to the school and started the fire in the stove. The room would be warm and cozy before Sarah got there. Then he went to the factory to load the benches. He was glad to see Latham already there.

"Latham, help me load some benches in the wagon. I need to take some in to Creel's store this morning."

"These benches are selling good."

"Yes, and I'm going to start pushing them even more, so I'll be needing to get more help to make them. If you know any hard working young men needing a job, tell them to come in to see me."

"I'll do that. I may know of a couple."

With the benches loaded in the wagon, Daniel headed to town. It was a cold morning riding in the wagon, and Daniel pulled his wool cap down over his ears.

Caleb saw Daniel drive up and stepped out to help him unload. They were talking and working when a man drove up in his wagon. He climbed down and came to talk to Caleb.

"Mr. Creel, I'm Henry Jessup. I've been in your store before. Perhaps you remember me."

"Yes, I remember you, Mr. Jessup. What can I do for you this morning?"

"I've got a little black gal sitting on the back of my wagon." Mr. Jessup pointed at the girl.

"My wife and I are moving, and I need to sell her. I'm taking her mama with us but don't have room for her, and we can't afford another mouth to feed right now. Do you know anyone who might want to buy her?"

Caleb thought, *I sure don't need her right now.*

He looked at Daniel and asked, "Do you and Sarah need any more help with the baby coming?"

Daniel thought for a moment and asked Mr. Jessup, "How old is she?"

"She's around fourteen years and in good health."

Daniel stepped back and spoke to the girl.

"What's your name?"

"I'm Remy, sir."

"If I give you a good home, food, and clothes, would you be interested in helping my wife with a new baby? The baby hasn't been born yet, but we'd expect you to do odd chores, too."

With sad eyes she looked at her mama and said, "Yes, sir, I can do that."

34

Daniel turned back to Mr. Jessup. "What's your price?"

They haggled a bit and Daniel told him, "I'll give fifty dollars and throw in one of these benches."

Mr. Jessup thought a minute. "I'll take it." He turned to the girl and said, "You're going with this man, so get your bundle and get in the back of his wagon."

Daniel stepped back to her mama and said, "My wife and I'll see she has a good home."

Sadly the woman smiled at Daniel and shook her head.

Mr. Jessup wrote out a bill of sale for Remy, and she started toward Daniel's wagon.

Daniel told her, "Just call me Mr. Daniel. It's cold out here. Go in the store where it's warmer. I've got a little business to finish up here and one more errand to run before we go home."

Remy gathered a little bundle of clothes from the wagon and walked slowly toward the store. As she entered, she turned and waved sadly to her mama.

Daniel and Caleb picked up the last two benches and went in the store.

"I'm always finding bargains at your store. I never know what I'll go home with."

Caleb laughed. "I knew you and Sarah would give her a good home. Goodness knows what could happen to a girl that age if you didn't take her."

"That's what I thought. I don't like buying a person, but it came to me that the same thing happened to my father years ago. That young girl, Dolly, is still with my family and helped raise me. She's turned out to be one of our family."

They finished stacking the benches.

"I've got an empty cabin just sitting there waiting on the right person. This isn't exactly what I had in mind, but we'll see how it turns out."

Caleb patted Daniel's shoulder.

"Trust me. I have a good feeling about this."

Daniel smiled and nodded his head toward Caleb.

"Come on, Remy. Let's go home."

Remy got her bundle, climbed into the back of the wagon, and Daniel headed toward Dr. Wade's office.

Daniel parked out front.

"I'll only be a minute. There's an old blanket there in the back of the wagon. Put it around you."

As he opened Dr. Wade's door, a bell clanged above his head. A nurse stepped out of another door in front of him.

"May I help you, Sir?"

"I'm Daniel Borden. I've met Dr. Wade and I need to talk to him a moment."

"Just a minute and I'll get him."

The nurse went into an adjacent room, and Dr. Wade soon came out.

"I'm Daniel Borden, Dr. Wade, Susan's uncle."

"Yes, I remember you, Mr. Borden. What can I do for you?"

Dr. Wade was a neat, nice looking middle-aged man with a heavy, black beard. He had a kind, pleasant smile and a reassuring manner. A watch chain was draped across his vest with a watch on one end and a fob on the other, both tucked into a small pocket.

"My wife and I are expecting our first child sometime in May. Would you have time to call on her at our home this afternoon?"

Dr. Wade had reviewed his schedule earlier and knew he had some free time that afternoon.

"Yes, I'll have time around four o'clock. Will that be all right?"

"That's good. She's doing well, but I guess I'm the one who needs reassurance that all's well. She may have some questions. If we could depend on you to come when the baby is due, we'd appreciate it. Our cook is a midwife, but being our first child, we'd especially feel better if you were there."

"I'll be glad to be of service to you and your wife. Noah and Susan were telling us about Noah proposing to Susan the night you and your wife were having the family in to announce about your baby. Noah felt bad about stepping on your good news, but he said you turned the awkward situation into a funny one. Noah likes you very much."

"We think the world of Susan. It's wonderful to see her so happy with Noah. We think Susan is smart and pretty, but we believe that Noah is worthy of her. He'll make her a good husband. We know you must be proud of him."

"Oh, we are. If only he could find something that he really wants to do. He has a good education. He didn't want to follow in my footsteps, which is all right with us. We do wish he could find some path to follow, especially since he's planning marriage."

"Things'll work out for them, I'm sure. I know you're busy, and I'd better go. It's been nice visiting with you. I'll tell Sarah to expect you about four."

Daniel climbed into the wagon, and he turned to Remy.

"I was longer than I had expected. I hope you were warm enough. I was asking Dr. Wade to come out to see my wife, Miss Sarah, this afternoon. She's doing well but this is our first baby, and I want the doctor to check her."

Remy's only reply was, "Yes, sir."

When they got home, Daniel pulled up to the empty cabin.

"This cabin will be your home. It's furnished and ready to be lived in. There's a wood pile and kindling out back to start the fireplace. We'll get you hot coals up at the big house to start it with. You see that cabin back there?"

Remy shook her head.

"That's Miss Sarah's school. She teaches until midday and then she and her assistant come to the big house for dinner. We have a cook named Jetty. You'll eat up at the big house with Jetty and her husband, Ollie. They're good people, and you'll like them. Put your bundle in the cabin, and I'll take you up to meet Jetty and Ollie. I think it's about time to eat."

Remy got her bundle and jump off the wagon. She laid it inside the cabin and closed the door. Without a word she came and hopped back in the wagon. Daniel drove the wagon up to the house.

Ollie was still working on paths. He looked up.

"I'll unhitch the wagon and take care of Midge, Mr. Daniel. Who have we here?"

"Ollie, this is Remy. She's coming to live in the other cabin and to help with odd chores. She'll help Miss Sarah watch the baby when it comes. After we eat, Ollie, would you help Remy get a fire started in her cabin?"

"Yes, sir, I'll take care of it. Well, lawdy, welcome Remy. You'll like it here."

Remy put on a weak smile and nodded her head. Daniel started toward the house.

"Let's go in, and I'll introduce you to Jetty. She might use your help setting the table or something."

Daniel did the introductions and left the two together while he walked down to the school to wait on Sarah and Mary. He would break the news to Sarah about what he had done while they were walking to the house. He didn't want Remy to overhear what he was saying.

It was almost time for school to be dismissed, and Daniel sat down on the edge of the front porch to wait. It wasn't long until the door opened, and the students came filing out. Eli and Rice stopped for a minute to talk to him.

Eli said, "I'll sit with you until Anna comes out. She stays to see if she can help Aunt Sarah with anything."

"Well that's nice of Anna."

"Yeah, I think someday she'd like to be a teacher like Aunt Sarah."

Rice was in a hurry to go because he had to eat and get to the law office. It was his afternoon to work. It was obvious that he did not have time to stop and visit.

Anna came out of the classroom. "Hello, Uncle Daniel, Aunt Sarah'll be out in a minute."

"Hello, Anna. Did you have a good lesson today?"

"Oh, yes. It was very good."

Then she and Eli walked on up the road toward their home. Daniel got up and stuck his head in the door.

"I thought I'd come walk you ladies to the house."

Sarah thought that was odd but just spoke and didn't ask why. She knew he would tell why he had come in his own good time.

"I think we're ready. We'll come back after dinner and finish up."

As they started up the road, Daniel said, "I went by Dr. Wades' office while I was in town this morning, and he'll be out to see you at four this afternoon. He's a very nice gentleman. We'd met before, but it's the first time we've ever just visited. I think you'll like him."

Mary asked, "Is there anything wrong?"

"No, Daniel thought I ought to be checked with this being our first child. It's more for his reassurance than mine. I'll be glad to visit with Dr. Wade myself, though."

"There *is* one other thing."

Sarah looked up and said, "I knew there was something else. What did you buy now, Daniel?" She laughed.

"Well, it was this way. While Caleb and I were unloading benches, this man drove up with this young black girl in the back of his wagon. He asked Caleb if he was interested in buying her. Caleb told him that he had no need for her now."

He looked at Sarah to get her reaction. It was consoling that he saw nothing negative in her face so he continued his explanation.

"Then Caleb turned to me, and I thought about our vacant cabin. The man said he and his wife were moving away and were taking the girl's mama with them. He said he was going to sell the girl because he didn't have room for her and couldn't feed another mouth. He didn't want that much so I bought her."

Daniel looked directly in Sarah's eyes.

"I didn't know what might happen to the girl, so I decided she could help you with the baby and do odd jobs."

Sarah reached and took his hand.

"I would probably have done the same thing. Where is she now?"

"She's helping Jetty-or probably watching Jetty. I don't know which. I didn't want her to hear me talking about her, so I walked down to tell you."

They were on the front porch now. Daniel opened the door for Sarah and Mary.

"Come on to the kitchen and meet her."

"Remy, this is Miss Sarah and her assistant, Miss Mary. Miss Mary is married to my nephew, John P. Crim."

Sarah knew Daniel had said *young* girl, but she hadn't realized she was quiet this young.

"Hello, Remy. Mr. Daniel's told me you've come to live here and help us. We're glad to have you."

Remy looked closely at Sarah.

"Thank you, ma'am. You're a very pretty lady."

Sarah smiled at Remy.

"Thank you and it's nice of you to say that."

Sarah looked at Jetty and asked, "Is dinner ready, Jetty?"

"Yes ma'am, me and Remy will get the food right on the table."

Sarah, Mary, and Daniel went in the dining room and took their seat while the food was being served.

"Jetty, did Mr. Daniel tell you that Dr. Wade would be coming to call on me this afternoon?"

"No, ma'am, he was busy introducing Remy, and then he went to meet you."

"Dr. Wade will be here at four. I'll be here, so it shouldn't interfere with what you need to do."

"I'd like to see him, Miss Sarah. Is it all right if I open the door for him when he comes?"

"That'll be fine, Jetty. Maybe you can even serve us tea."

"Would you ask him if there are any instructions for me? What to feed you or anything?"

"I will, Jetty. He'll be glad to know that you and Daniel are so concerned about me."

Jetty went back to the kitchen.

"I think it's wonderful that they're concerned about you. To be loved that much is so nice."

"I know, Mary, but you'd think I might break. I'm just with child and looking a little bigger all the time."

They all laughed.

"Yes, and Remy still told you how pretty you are. That should tell you something."

After they ate, Sarah went in the kitchen.

"Remy, I just thought-there are bed clothes in a draw in one of the chests in that cabin."

Sarah looked at Jetty.

"Would you mind helping Remy get settled in and be sure she has everything she needs? Then perhaps she can help you or Ollie with something."

"We'll be fine, Miss Sarah. Don't you worry about nothing."

Daniel came by and kissed Sarah on the cheek.

"I'm going back to the factory. I'll see you later."

Sarah and Mary went back to the school and worked for a couple of hours. Then Sarah went to the house so she would be there in case Dr. Wade arrived early.

The house was quiet. Jetty was at Remy's cabin helping her settled in. It wasn't long before Sarah heard Jetty back in the kitchen. She was getting fresh water on to boil for tea. She also was making a fresh pot of coffee.

There was a knock on the front door, and Jetty hurried to answer it.

"Hello, I'm Dr. Wade. I believe Mrs. Borden's expecting me."

"Yes, sir, please come in. She's in the parlor."

Jetty took the doctor's hat and hung it on the coat rack.

"You must be the lady who's the midwife. Mr. Borden was telling me about you."

This attention pleased Jetty.

"Yes, sir, I'm Jetty. I'll be here to assist you when the baby comes."

"That's very good, Jetty, and it will reassure Mrs. Borden."

Jetty led Dr. Wade into the parlor.

"Miss Sarah, Dr. Wade's here to see you."

Jetty went back to the kitchen.

"Do come in, Doctor. Thank you for coming to my home. Daniel told me to expect you."

The doctor had his black bag, but he didn't open it. He simply observed Sarah and asked several questions about how she was feeling.

"I believe, from what you've told me, we can expect the baby around the middle of May." Dr. Wade chuckled and remarked, "Of course, I don't have a crystal ball, and you've probably already surmised this for yourself."

"I have, Doctor, and I can tell you I'm doing wonderfully well. Your visit is more to reassure Daniel than me. Now, please sit down and let's have some tea."

"Thank you. Let me assure you that I haven't lost a father yet."

They both laughed at his casual remark. No doubt he had offered it many times before and had gotten the same reaction.

Sarah stepped to the kitchen and asked Jetty to bring tea. While Jetty was preparing the tea, Daniel came in the back door.

"I'm getting tea for Miss Sarah and Dr. Wade. Would you like a cup, Mr. Daniel?"

"Yes, I think I'll join them. Would you bring it in with theirs?"

When Daniel entered the parlor, Dr. Wade stood and shook his hand.

"What do you think about Sarah, Doctor?"

"I think she's doing fine, and there are no worries. She needs to continue what she's doing, and when time comes, Jetty and I will be here to assist her."

"That's good news."

Jetty came to serve the tea and brought a small plate of teacakes on a large, round tray.

"You'll check the baby when it gets here, won't you?"

"I surely will. I'm expecting it to be fine, too. Don't worry Mr. Borden. You and your wife are both healthy so I'm expecting a healthy baby."

"Do call us Daniel and Sarah. We'd be more comfortable with that."

"I do hear Noah say 'Daniel and Sarah,' but then, that's what he hears within this family. If it will make you feel more comfortable, then Daniel and Sarah it is."

"We think a lot of your son. In fact, would you please ask Noah to come out to see me? I have some ideas I'd like to talk to him about."

Dr. Wade wondered what Mr. Borden might want to discuss with his son but he didn't ask. That would be between Noah and Daniel.

"I'll tell him, and I'm sure he'll come soon for he'll be curious."

The doctor got up from his chair and requested his hat from the hall coat rack.

"I really should be going. Sarah was my last patient and my wife, Flora, will be holding supper for me if I don't get on my way."

Before the doctor could get his hat, Daniel asked, "Dr. Wade, how much do we owe you for your house call?"

"Daniel, I've noticed pieces of your furniture since I've been here, and I'm thinking about you applying my services toward some furniture."

"If that is the case, Dr. Wade, can you take another few minutes and look at the furniture better. Let me take you back to our bedroom, too."

"I'll take the time, and Flora will *have* to understand."

The three of them walked over the house, looking at and discussing various pieces of furniture.

"I now have an idea of our choices. I'm pleased I came to your home. I'll really be on my way now."

Sarah handed Dr. Wade his hat.

"Thank you so much again for coming. Have a nice evening."

George came by the next morning.

"Come on in, and let's have a cup of coffee."

"That sounds good. We wanted you to know that we've started moving into the big house. We've moved some everyday."

"I'll bring a couple of my men and help."

"No, that's not necessary. I've got plenty of men to help. The other thing is-Clay says he and Eliza are getting married soon. They don't want a formal announcement, as Clay says the family already knows they're going to get married."

"Yes, and it pleases us all. Eliza is a wonderful person. We think so highly of all the Stewarts."

George pushed back in his chair.

"They don't want a big wedding either. Clay said they've talked it over and would like to get married in the big room at the new house. They just want our families to attend. This suits me and Charity fine. I'm sure Susan's wedding will be larger and at the church. The town would expect it for the Wades. That suits us, too. We just want all the kids to be happy."

"George, let me mention something to you. We had Dr. Wade come out yesterday to check Sarah."

"Is there something wrong?"

"No, no, it's just me. I wanted to be sure everything is all right. The doctor assured us it is."

"Good! You scared me for a moment."

44

Daniel smiled and continued, "Anyway, Dr. Wade said Noah hasn't decided on a path for his life. I've been thinking I need a place to show off the furniture we're making. I'm going to talk to Tom Holder about building me a store in town and stock it with our furniture. What do you think so far?"

Jetty came in to fill their coffee cups.

"This sounds smart to me. I've heard you're selling your benches left and right."

"We've had very good luck with them. I've had people come out to the factory and talk to me about the furniture we've made. They've seen a piece at someone's house and want us to build them a similar one. After seeing my bedroom furniture, John and Mary had us build them some that's similar. I have them on a list for dining room furniture, too. We've built things for you and James, too."

George nodded his head 'yes.'

Daniel continued, "My men are working as hard as they can just trying to keep up. I'm looking for another skilled woodworker or two to hire soon."

Daniel couldn't help but show his excitement.

He continued, "I asked Dr. Wade to send Noah out to talk to me. I'm going to ask him if he'd be interested in working for me. I'd like for him and Susan to manage my furniture store in town. In the meantime, he can come out to work at the factory while Tom's building the store. Noah can learn about the furniture from start to finish."

Daniel sipped his coffee and continued.

"During this time, I'll ask Susan to start keeping records for me and to keep doing it at the store when it opens. Now, what do you think?"

George got up and patted Daniel on the back.

"I think this is terrific. I haven't said anything to anyone, but I've wondered what that young man was going to do. He's smart and very likeable. He has a good education. I hope he likes your idea."

George rubbed the whiskers on his chin.

45

"I'm not going to mention this to anyone, not even Charity. I just hope this happens for all our sake."

"I'll let you know after I talk to Noah."

When George left, Daniel went to the factory. About the middle of the morning, Daniel saw Noah entering the factory. He went to meet him and asked him into his office.

"My father told me you wanted to see me."

"Yes, your father was out yesterday to check on Sarah, and I told him I'd like to talk to you. I have a proposition for you. I'm thinking about having Tom Holder build a store building in town to show and sell our furniture. My factory is growing, and I feel this should be my next step. I'd very much like for you and Susan to manage the new store for me and help get it ready. Do you think you're interested?"

Noah's ears perked up.

"I'll have to talk to Susan, but I can say that I'm very interested."

"I'd like for you to start fairly soon in the factory and learn how the furniture is made. I might get you to go with me to make furniture deliveries to get to know some of our customers, too."

"I'll be anxious to talk to Susan and see what she thinks."

"Good. I'd like to talk to Susan, too. I'd want her to start keeping my records for me. She can do it at the store when it opens. She could work here in the office or even up at the house in my study until we get the store built."

"I think I'll ride out to Susan's while I'm this close and we'll talk. I may not get back to you before tomorrow, if that's all right."

"That'll be fine. I realize you'll both want to think this over. Let me show you through the factory quickly while you're here. You've met some of the men already."

Daniel showed Noah around the factory, introduced him to all of the workers, and they finished at the exit door.

Noah thanked him and left. Daniel wondered what his and Susan's answer would be.

Before Daniel knew it, the time had come to go to dinner.

He told Si, "I've got to run an errand into town this afternoon. I'll be back later."

As Daniel walked through the garden, Ollie was still working on paths.

"Ollie, would you saddle Bess for me after we eat? I've got some errands to run this afternoon."

"Yes, sir, I'll have her ready to go."

Daniel stopped on the back porch to wash his hands and headed in the house. Sarah and Mary were just coming in the front door. Remy was in the kitchen helping Jetty. Daniel walked on in the dining room.

"How was your morning, ladies?"

"There were no major calamities this morning. We got in a lot of good work."

Daniel had to tell them about building the store and Noah coming out to talk about a job. He had mentioned this all to Sarah a couple of weeks ago.

"Do you think he and Susan will take the offer?"

"Noah said he was interested, but he wanted to talk to Susan before he answered."

"Good for him. I think he should talk things over with Susan. That's a good sign."

"I do think I'll hear soon. I'm going to ride in and talk to Tom this afternoon. I don't know how long I'll be. It'd be a good time of the year for Tom to start a building."

Daniel finished his meal and excused himself.

"I want to try to catch Tom at his house. I'll see you later. Mary, Sarah will get you updated with what's going on, I'm sure."

Bess was tied to the back rail. Daniel mounted and headed up the road toward Tom's. When he arrived, Dorcus Holder opened the door.

"Good afternoon, Dorcus. Is Tom home?"

"Yes, come on in Daniel and I'll get him."

She led Daniel into the parlor and told him to have a seat. She disappeared for a moment and soon Tom came in the door.

Daniel stood and shook Tom's hand.

"I hope I'm not interrupting anything."

"No, not at all. We've just finished dinner and I'm not busy."

"Good, because I need to talk to you."

"Let's sit down where we'll be comfortable while we talk, Daniel."

Tom offered refreshments which Daniel refused.

"I've decided that I'd like for you to build a furniture store for me. I have some ideas and want to see what you think."

"Okay, let me hear your ideas."

"I want to buy a plot in town for it, so it can sit alone. I'd like it built all under one roof but almost in two sections. It'll display my less expensive furniture in one section and the more expensive in another area."

"Uhmmm, this has possibilities."

"I want it built out of my sandstone, and I want several windows in it for good light. I'd especially like a row of windows in the front. Would you suggest that we heat it with the Rumford fireplaces like in the factory? I like them, and they do a good job."

"Yes, I'd recommend them, and I feel they're safer, too. Your idea sounds very good, and I'd like to do the job for you. Do you have time right now to go to the courthouse and see what lots are available in town? We might have a look at some of them and choose one if you're ready."

It was obvious that Tom was intrigued with the idea.

"Oh, I'm ready and I'd like to get started as soon as we can."

Daniel was somewhat surprised that Tom was so eager to begin the project, too.

"You've caught me at a good time. I'm just finishing a job, and with spring coming very soon, it'll be a perfect time to start."

"I or my kin will have enough timber for the framing and shingles. Perhaps we can barter with Russell Hillman again in exchange for cured lumber."

Daniel still had plenty of timber on his property.

"I'll check that out in the next couple of days."

"You can come out, and we'll look on my land first for trees. James would like more of mine cleared because he wants to raise tobacco on some of it. You know he's my food store and meat market, so I have to think about his needs, too. I'll ask him to get with us when you come out. Between some of his land and mine, we should be able to find plenty of trees."

"You know, I like working with you. You have interesting projects."

They both laughed at what Tom said.

"Let me bring my horse around, and we'll go to town. I'll tell Dorcus and meet you out front."

Daniel was waiting at the front rail when Tom rode around, and they started for the courthouse. When they entered the courthouse, they went to look at the big map hanging on the wall showing the available lots in town. They found three lots that looked interesting.

The one Daniel chose to his best liking was on the south part of the main street. The lot was on the road going into town from his home. It would be convenient for furniture delivery and a quick trip for Daniel to visit. Tom liked the lay of the parcel for building. It was large with two nice oak trees spaced far enough apart to build between. He would not have to disturb them, and people could park in their shade to shop. These were all pluses in his opinion.

"Do we agree then? This is the lot for my furniture store."

"Yes, you can't go wrong with this one. It's a good location for your business."

Tom had made his decision.

"I'll do it then. Let me go and talk to John P. I want his input and to get him to tend to the business end for me. You get your part rolling, and John and I'll tend to the rest. I'll see you in a day or so to look at trees. While I'm in town, I'll go and talk to John and get him over to the courthouse."

They parted and each went his own way to attend to their respective business.

Daniel went to John's office and got him started on buying the lot. As he came out of John's office, he saw Noah across the street. He waved. Noah caught sight of him, and came toward him.

"I'm glad I ran into you. I was going to ride out to the factory to talk to you. Susan and I want you to know we'd like the jobs. We're very excited with the idea of working together."

"I'm so glad to hear this. I think you and Susan will be perfect in the store. Come out when it's convenient, and we'll talk salaries and getting you started."

They shook hands on the deal and Noah said, "We'll come out tomorrow."

While riding home, Daniel thought how well things were going in his life and gave a little prayer of thanks.

He decided to go tell George their decision just in case Susan hadn't told him. Daniel knew George would be happy and relieved to know.

Chapter Three

It was the middle of March, and spring was announcing itself with occasional light showers. The new downtown building was coming along nicely, but now the light rains had held up their work for a few days. They had finished building a privy out back since Daniel's store was alone on the lot.

Daniel wanted land to himself in case of a town fire. He would eventually have a large investment in his inventory and thought of its safety. The town ordinance stated there had to be a privy for every certain number of stores but Daniel's building didn't count since it was standing alone.

Tom had dug out and made a step-down near the center of the store building. It was built to separate the two different prices of furniture. A banister would eventually be along the step-down. The framing and roof were now complete.

Daniel was letting Susan help plan the inside of the building. The walls and ceiling were to be plastered, and Susan was going to have the walls painted a very light tan with white ceilings. The floors were to be stained a warm oak, and there would be a few lantern chains hanging from the ceiling. With both Susan's and Tom's ideas, Daniel was confident that it would be one of the most handsome buildings in town.

Daniel had managed to hire two more skilled furniture makers and two more apprentices for the factory. Nichols Findley was training one of the men to be a painter. Word was getting around about the very nice furniture the factory made, and they were extremely busy.

It was late afternoon, and Daniel and Sarah were sitting in the parlor just relaxing before supper. An unexpected knock came on the door and it was Clay.

"Come on in, Clay. Sarah and I are sitting in the parlor. We haven't seen you in awhile."

"I've really been busy with the horses. I wanted to come by and tell you that Eliza and I are getting married the last Sunday afternoon of this month. We want you and Sarah to be there. It's nothing formal. There'll just be our family and the Stewarts."

Sarah got up and hugged Clay.

"We're very proud for you and Eliza. She's a wonderful girl, and we know you'll be happy."

"Uncle Daniel, will you bring your guitar? I'll ask Uncle James to bring his banjo and maybe we can dance some after the ceremony. We're going to have the wedding at the new house in the big room."

"By all means we'll be there, and I'll be ready to play and dance a bit. I may have to dance with the new bride some though as my partner may not be up to much dancing."

He chuckled as he patted his stomach and pointed to Sarah. She was certainly showing. She was well with child now, and it wouldn't be long before it arrived.

"You still look very pretty, Aunt Sarah."

Clay twisted his hat in his hand as he was still timid about complimenting Sarah.

"I better go. I've got to call on John P., Uncle James, and then go by Hill's and Owen's. You're the first ones I've invited. I want to be sure everyone has it scheduled and can come. I'll see you later. Aunt Sarah, you take care. Hold off having the little one until I have my day," said Clay laughingly.

"I'll hold it, Clay. Nothing will mar your day."

Daniel walked Clay to his horse and said goodbye.

When he entered the parlor again, he told Sarah, "I'm glad to see this happening. Those two kids have been in love for a long time, and I believe it's a lasting love."

"Has Susan or Noah said when their wedding will be?"

"No, but I feel they knew that Clay and Eliza were getting ready to have their wedding and wanted to wait and let them have their time. Then I bet they announce their date. I've watched the two of them whispering and talking. They're making plans I'm sure. They look to be very happy with their jobs and are satisfied just to plan for awhile longer."

"Sarah, I'm thinking-what if I have an oak bedroom suite delivered over to Clay's house for their wedding present? I'm sure Mr. and Mrs. Drake have some extra, new mattresses stored. You know, they're making them to fit the bed frames my factory makes. I described and drew them a picture of a mattress like my father's. He ordered it from England, and it was the best. They're doing a terrific job making copies of it. They have a good business going, and it helps them and us, too."

"That sounds good. I think Clay and Eliza would be very proud to have nice bedroom furniture."

"The Drakes should give me a good discount on a mattress. I've sent them any number of customers. I'll go by and pick up the mattress and have Moseley or Latham help me deliver it."

"If anyone deserves it, they do." Then she added, "You know we'll have to do the same for Susan and Noah."

"We can do that and maybe an extra something since they both work for me."

Remy came to say supper was ready.

"I want to talk to Ollie a minute. Go ahead and sit down at the table, and I'll be right in."

Daniel went to the kitchen, and Ollie was just coming in the back door to eat.

"Ollie, would you hitch up the wagon in the morning and run an errand with me? I need to go get a mattress in town and deliver it out to Mr. Clay's house."

"Yes, sir, I'll be ready."

After they finished eating, Daniel got his guitar and sat in the parlor and played for Sarah.

"I thought I'd better practice a little before Clay's big day."

"As usual, your music sounds wonderful to me." Sarah suddenly winced. "I feel our little one kicking. Do you think it can hear or feel your music?"

"Now, that's an interesting thought, Sarah. I don't know, and I've never thought about it before. The baby's close by."

Daniel strummed a few chords again and laid his hand on Sarah's stomach.

"I can feel him kick."

"Is my playing that bad?"

Daniel laughed and strummed another chord.

"Did he kick?"

"Not that time. Oh well, it's probably a silly thought. You spoke of the baby as you know it's a male. What made you say that?"

"I don't know. Just a feeling, I guess. Sometimes when I think about it, I just think Beau. I don't know why. It really doesn't matter to me. I have so many brothers and only one sister. Maybe that's why I think in male terms."

Sarah laid her head on Daniel's shoulder and smiled pleasantly.

"I think we better get to bed. Beau and I are tired, and you have a busy day tomorrow."

It dawned a gorgeous morning, and Daniel arose embracing the new day. He was humming as he washed his face in the wash bowl.

"My, you sound in high spirits."

54

"I *am* happy because I know we're going to make a very nice young man and his lady happy today. That's the kind of a day I like to awake to."

"Oh, I wish I could see their faces when they discover the bedroom furniture. They will *have* to be pleased with it."

"I'm going to try to find George first. Maybe he can help us sneak the mattress into Clay's house. That is, if Clay doesn't see us drive up."

"If you go to George's house first, perhaps he'll think you're visiting there, but he's still living at George's."

Sarah wrinkled her brow as she knew that comment didn't quite make sense.

"I'm going to get a cup of coffee. Should I tell Jetty we'll be ready to eat soon? Maybe you'll be awake by then."

Daniel just grinned, and Sarah mischievously threw a pillow at him and he ducked.

"Yes. Tell her I'll have my same tea and a light breakfast this morning."

Daniel went to the kitchen.

"Good morning. Have you all eaten?"

"Yes, sir, we've eaten. Ollie wanted to get out and have the wagon hitched."

"Your man's an early bird."

Jetty laughed and replied, "He sure is. Then, we go to bed early so we're ready to get up."

"Either Ollie or me knocks on Remy's door every morning to get her going. You know how young folk is."

"Miss Sarah wants her tea and usual light breakfast this morning. She should be here in a few minutes."

"It'll be ready."

Daniel went to the table to sip his coffee. Jetty served his food, and he finished eating before Sarah, so he went on his way. He had things to do.

Ollie was waiting, and it didn't take long to get to the Drake's house. The sun was up bright when Daniel knocked on their door. Mr. Drake opened the door and saw that it was Daniel.

"You're out visiting early this morning."

"Yes sir. I need to buy one of your better mattresses that'll fit my oak bed frames. I hope you've got one."

"We do. We try to stay ahead of you in case we get a customer. I know your business is going well as is ours. I'll make you a good price, Daniel, because, without you, we wouldn't have the business we have now."

"You came highly recommended to me by both Tom Holder and Caleb Creel. When I asked for a mattress maker, they both recommended that I talk to you and your wife. I guess we're both lucky that we know the same good men."

By now they were in the storeroom where the mattresses were kept.

"We are that. Here's the mattress," said the businessman as he pointed toward a mattress.

"That's exactly the one I'm looking for. Let me get my man, we'll load it, and I'll settle up."

They loaded the mattress into the wagon, and Daniel paid Mr. Drake.

"I'm sure I'll need another before too long. Have you heard that I'm building a new store here in town to show my furniture?"

"Yes, I've noticed the building. I told Trudy that we better get some help in here because we won't be able to keep up with you when you open it."

He chuckled as he made that remark.

"I'd like to display your mattresses on a couple of my beds when we open. I think you'll be busier so get ready."

"That's good news for us."

"I'd better get going. This is a gift for one of my nephews, and I want to deliver it. Thank you, Mr. Drake, and stop by the new store and visit. Just see what's going on."

"I'll do that, Daniel, and thank you."

56

Daniel and Ollie headed to George's house with the mattress. When they got there, Daniel hopped out of the wagon and knocked on the door. Charity answered.

"Hello Daniel, what are you doing here this morning?"

"Where're George and Clay working?"

"They rode out to one of the back pastures this morning. One of the mares was delivering her colt. They couldn't stand not being there so they took off."

"Good. I didn't want to see them anyway. I'm delivering Clay's and Eliza's wedding present this morning, and I'd like to sneak it into their house. Will that be okay?"

"Certainly. Do you need me to go with you?"

"I have help, but there'll be about three loads. This is the first."

"Goodness sakes, Daniel, what is it?"

"It's bedroom furniture. I have the mattress now, and I'll bring the rest soon as I can get here with it."

"What a great surprise. Hurry and unload it. You don't want to be caught. I can't wait to see it myself. You can bet I'll be there when you bring the other loads."

Daniel hurried and pulled the wagon up in front of Clay's house. He and Ollie struggled up the stairs with the mattress, but they made it. With it unloaded, they headed back to the factory.

"I'll get Moseley and Latham to help me with the furniture. They're big strapping men and can lift more than we can, Ollie."

Ollie laughed, "Yes, sir, Mr. Daniel, they *are* strapping."

Daniel let Ollie out at the back of the big house and drove to the factory. He pointed out the furniture that was to be loaded on the wagon. It was the bed frame with a beautiful, tall, oak, four-poster head and foot board. There was a large armoire and a double, waist-high matching chest. Moseley and Latham had it loaded in only a few minutes. They didn't need Daniel's help.

"Hop on the wagon, and go with me to deliver this. You men are so good it won't take long."

By the time they got back to Clay's house, Charity was waiting on them. When she saw what they were unloading she was beside herself with excitement.

"I'll be gobsmacked. Clay and Eliza are going to be thrilled to death when they see this. I went up and saw that mattress, too. That'll be the next thing George has to buy for us. I'd better get busy making bedcovers, hadn't I? I know now that'll be part of our wedding present. I'll get Dora to help me."

Charity jabbered on while they were unloading.

Daniel could tell she was excited for the kids. She was grinning and talking as fast as she could, hardly pausing long enough to take a breath. He would have to tell Sarah about this at dinner. He wished she could've been there to hear and see the goings on. It was comical.

"Let's get out of here before we're spotted. Charity, don't say anything-just let Clay and Eliza find it, but do tell us their reactions when they find it."

Charity followed them to the door hollering, "Thank you, thank you."

When Daniel got back to the factory, he checked to make sure everyone had what they needed to do their jobs. The men were all busy. Noah was watching Si do some craving on a chest and handing him things as if he were assisting surgery. Daniel smiled as Noah looked very intense taking it all in.

Daniel glanced at his pocket watch. It wouldn't be long before Sarah dismissed her classes. He had time to go and walk the ladies to the house for dinner, so he slipped out the factory door and headed for the school. He wanted to tell Sarah about his morning.

Just as Daniel got to the school turnaround, the students came bounding out the door. They were all speaking to him as they passed by. When he got to the door, Anna and Eli were just coming out.

"I think Aunt Sarah is ready to go to dinner, Uncle Daniel."

"Good, I'm here to walk her to the house."

Sarah could hear her husband's voice and looked up. She smiled.

"What brings you here today?"

"I just wanted to share my joy with you. After all, it's part yours. Are you and Mary ready to go?"

"Yes, we'll be right with you."

The ladies gathered up their things, and the three of them started up the road.

"I wish you could have been there to see Charity this morning. You'd have thought the furniture was for her. First Ollie and I delivered the mattress. When we got back with the bedroom furniture, Charity was so excited she was like a young girl. Now we're waiting on Clay and Eliza to find it."

"Wouldn't you like to see their faces when they do?"

"I'm sure we'll be hearing from them shortly after they see it. Poor George, Charity already wanted one of the mattresses. I bet she'll have one soon."

Daniel laughed.

"We *Borden men* can't resist catering to our women, you know."

He reached and took Sarah's hand and gave it a little squeeze.

Mary was listening to their conversation.

"We'll never be able to come close to your gift."

"Well, you're a cousin, and I think an uncle and aunt should do a little more than a cousin. May I suggest a lovely oak *"Borden Factory"* kitchen table? Perhaps James and Lucy would get them four chairs to go with it. Mind you, that's just a suggestion."

Mary giggled.

"I like the suggestion. I'll talk to John, and we'll see if James is interested. Will the *Borden Factory* deliver it for us?"

"Since you have a special in with the owner, I think we can work something out."

Sarah snickered as she said, "Daniel, you're becoming the consummate salesman."

"*I thought* it was a good suggestion."

"It *is* a good suggestion, and I'm glad you made it. I think John will be, too."

Before supper that same day, a knock came on Daniel's door. He went to the door and answered it, and there stood Clay and Eliza.

"Come in. What are you two young people up to?"

"Is Aunt Sarah here?"

"Yes, we're sitting in the parlor. Come join us."

Sarah managed to stand up. Clay immediately went to hug her and then stepped back for Eliza to take her turn. Then Eliza turned and hugged Daniel.

"We came to say *thank you*. What a marvelous wedding present! I lay down across the new mattress, and I've never laid on anything like it."

Eliza added, "All of it is beautiful. We're so excited about the whole thing."

"Good, Daniel and I were hoping you'd like it."

"Uncle Daniel, you can be very proud of your furniture. Your factory turns out the best."

"Thank you, Clay. We try. I *do* have good men who care about their work. I have ideas back in my mind so together, we're good."

Daniel had a smiling, smug look on his face.

Clay told Eliza, "We better go. I have to help papa with the horses."

He turned to the couple and said, "We just had to come and thank you both for the present. It's wonderful!"

Sarah and Daniel walked out on the front porch with them and watched how they held hands as they walked down the road. It reminded them very much of themselves.

"I hope they know the same joys in their marriage that we've had in ours. I wish everyone could be as happy as we are."

The next morning gave every promise of a lovely day. As usual, Sarah rang the school bell and went inside the classroom. It was such a nice day that she decided to leave the top half of the Dutch doors open along with one of the windows. When everyone had arrived and took their places, they said their morning prayer and sang a hymn. Then they settled down, concentrating on their studies.

Eli was writing his ABC's on a small board with a graphite pencil. This morning he had brought a small, cloth bag with a drawstring closing it at the top. Inside the bag was a small wooden box that had a sliding lid. Eli had other treasures in his bag which included a small folding pocket knife, sling shot, and a few small, special, select rocks.

Everyone was working quietly. Even Aunt Sarah and Miss Mary were working at their big table. Eli thought he would take this opportunity to check his fishing bait which was in the wooden box. He slipped his bag up beside himself and slowly slid the lid on the box open slightly to take a peep.

While he was peeping, his Aunt Sarah looked up and questioned, "Eli, are you working?"

"Yes ma'am."

Sarah knew that she had caught him, but rather than embarrass him further, she said no more.

Eli hurriedly put the little box back in the bag and continued his work. Unfortunately, he didn't close the lid all the way nor did he pull the drawstring on the bag.

Everything was fine until one of the lively, brown grasshoppers hopped out and plopped up on the desk where Emily Stewart was involved in her penmanship lesson. Much to her surprise, the grasshopper landed right in the middle of the wet ink on her parchment paper.

61

First Emily yelled, then she squealed, and then she jumped up from her bench. The young girl placed both hands across her chest, so as to protect herself from the attack that she knew was coming.

The remaining grasshoppers were poised and ready to get out of that sack. They began to jump on the children, desks, the walls, and it seemed they were everywhere. All the girls began to scream and were trying to get away from them, and the boys started trying to stomp them with no luck. Even Sarah began swatting at the grasshoppers.

Eli sat there startled in amazement. This was a giveaway to Sarah as to whom the culprit was.

"Eli, did you bring these grasshoppers into the classroom?"

Eli's eyes grew large and he reluctantly said, "Yes ma'am."

"Girls, hurry and go out on the porch for a few minutes, and give the boys time to help Eli collect all of his little friends. Boys, when you get them back in the box, get them out of here. Set your bag and box on the porch, Eli. Do you understand?"

"Yes ma'am."

"Eli, when all of them have been caught, I'd like to speak to you on the porch. Then you can apologize to the class for the interruption."

The porch absolutely buzzed with conversation and excitement. Secretly the girls felt it was a fun break from what they considered as the boring task of penmanship.

After they began to settle down, they realized that the grasshoppers weren't dangerous. They were just such a startling surprise.

Soon the boys called out, "All's clear. We've finished capturing all of the grasshoppers, and you can return to the classroom."

When they got back into classroom, Sarah said, "Okay, Eli, it's time for you to step out on the porch."

Once the two of them were out on the porch, Sarah asked, "What are you doing with all those grasshoppers in that bag?"

"Ollie asked me to meet him at Uncle Daniel's factory this afternoon to go fishing. I'm going to fish with him off the dock."

"Eli, you shouldn't bring insects or animals into our classroom."

"I'm sorry, Aunt Sarah."

"Perhaps you'd better go apologize to the class for interrupting their studies."

Eli, who almost never got in trouble, stood in front of the class, somewhat embarrassed, and said, "I'm sorry for interrupting your studies, and it won't happen again."

"Class, I think Eli has learned a lesson. We don't bring insects or animals into the classroom."

Sarah then asked Anna to step out on the porch with her. Eli couldn't imagine what Aunt Sarah wanted with Anna. She had nothing to do with the grasshoppers.

"Anna, quickly go to your house and tell your mama that you and Eli are going to have dinner today at my house. Then Eli can go to the factory to fish with Ollie and Uncle Daniel after we eat."

"Oh, Aunt Sarah, that'll be fun."

"Would you like to fish?"

"No, ma'am, maybe I'll just watch for awhile."

"Well, go now and tell your mama, but don't say a word to Eli yet."

Sarah returned to the classroom and never said a word or even looked at Eli. She was very aware that Eli was wiggling in his seat. He kept slipping looks toward the door. Sarah knew he was in misery and wondering what was happening. She thought, *He probably thinks his papa is coming to kill him.* Sarah had a small, mischievous smile on her face.

Anna was gone about twenty minutes. When she came back into the classroom, Sarah could tell she had run part of the way. There were little sweat beads across her forehead. Sarah smiled at her, and Anna nodded her head, "Yes."

Sarah and Mary split the students into two groups, and they began to work on reading. Sarah was amazed at how smoothly her older students were reading now. This made her so proud because this would be Joel's, Allen's, and Rice's last term at her school. The boys had all improved so much in all their studies and would be ready to face whatever life presented to them.

When class was dismissed, Anna carried the joke on Eli a bit longer.

Anna told Eli, "Aunt Sarah wants us to wait behind today."

"What does she want with me?"

"She wants you to wait."

When Sarah and Mary were ready to go, Anna began to laugh, "We're eating dinner with Aunt Sarah today. Then we'll go to the factory with Uncle Daniel and Ollie after we eat. Do you know how to spell relief, Eli? Remember—R E L I E F!"

Anna, Sarah, and Mary had a very good laugh at Eli's expense.

The day of Clay and Eliza's wedding had arrived. The morning had started out cloudy with a short spring shower, but before midday, the sun shone through as if on command. The ride home in the open carriage from church was glorious. Some of the spring wild flowers were blooming in the woods and along the roads.

When they arrived at the house, Daniel and Sarah freshened up to get ready for the wedding. Sarah prepared them a plate of ham, bread, and dried fruit to snack on. They knew there would be plenty of food after the ceremony.

After they finished eating, Daniel took his guitar off its stand and checked to make sure it was in tune. He then slipped it in the bag that Sarah had made for traveling. He set it by the front door so he wouldn't forget it.

It was time to go, and Sarah was putting on her hat at the mirror.

She looked at Daniel, "I know I look frightfully awkward and tacky."

"Sarah, to me you're so beautiful, perhaps a little larger, but that won't be for much longer."

Daniel leaned and kissed her on the cheek.

"I have the carriage hitched and at the front railing. I thought that would be more convenient for you."

Daniel opened the door and hurried to help Sarah into the carriage.

They seemed to be the first ones to arrive at George's house with the exception of the Stewarts. Charity and Dora were upstairs with Eliza. The others began to arrive shortly, including Preacher Kent.

It was soon time to start the ceremony. Clay was nervous, as custom almost seemed to demand it. Eliza looked lovely when she came down the stairs to stand beside him. Susan and Noah stood behind them in witness. Both mothers dabbed at their eyes while the couple was saying their vows. Then the long awaited kiss and congratulations.

The dining room table was loaded with delicious food. Daniel ate a bite, and then he got his guitar and began to strum soft, romantic music, while the others finished. It established a lovely mood.

As the group began to finish with their food, James took up his banjo, and together the brothers stepped up the tempo of the music. The furniture in the big family room had been placed next to the wall, and the center of the room was clear for dancing.

Clay and Eliza started the dance, and then George and Charity joined them. After a few dances, George got his fiddle. The rest of the evening was filled with dancing, eating, and visiting. It was bedtime when the party began to breakup. It had been a wonderful, small family wedding.

As the days passed, Sarah found she was walking with less grace and much slower up and down the road to the school. She knew every day that her time was drawing nearer. This morning, however, she felt a new surge of energy as she made her habitual trip to the school.

The last term of the year was drawing to an end, and Sarah felt a tinge of melancholy when she thought about losing three of her young men to make their way in the world. She imagined it must be the same feeling that a mother bird had when one of her fledglings left the security of their nest.

Sarah, as usual, rang the bell as she walked by. She opened the tops of Dutch doors to let in the fresh, clean air. Mary soon arrived, removed her hat, and hung it on a peg. She began to make plans for the day.

The students came in a few at a time as always. They took their places on the center benches and followed the same morning rituals that had begun every school morning.

Sarah had assigned each student to write a little essay on what they had learned this term and what their hopes for the summer were. Each student, beginning with the youngest, was coming forward and reading their stories to the class. Nancy Borden had just started her story, when a strange look came over Sarah's face.

She whispered to Mary, "Send Joel to tell Daniel to bring the carriage for me. Also, send Eli to tell Ollie to get it hitched up for Daniel. Then send Rice for Dr. Wade. I need to go home."

Mary was scurrying around and told the boys to hurry as fast as they could to get the message out. Mary made the decision to dismiss the class for the day.

"I'll see you here in the morning as usual," she told the class.

Then she placed a chair on the porch for Sarah to sit while she was waiting for Daniel. Sarah had not waited long until Daniel came with Midge trotting as fast as she could.

He jumped out of the carriage and scooped Sarah up in his arms and placed her in the carriage. Mary pulled the school door closed and hopped in the back seat of the carriage. Away they went to the main house.

Ollie had gone to tell Jetty to get things ready because Miss Sarah was coming, and the baby was on its way. Jetty went to prepare the bedroom for the delivery. Daniel carried Sarah back to the bedroom. Mary stayed with Sarah. Jetty had Remy preparing things in the kitchen for the day.

It wasn't long before Lucy came. Anna and Eli had told her the baby was coming. Lucy began to help Remy in the kitchen. Mary came to the kitchen.

"Lucy, I'll trade places with you. You go be with Sarah and Jetty. You're more experienced with having a baby."

Lucy smiled, "I'll go, but I'm nervous, too, Mary."

Rice quickly made it into town and rode straight to Dr. Wade's office. Dr. Wade grabbed his things and went to get his carriage at the livery. Next, Rice went to tell John P. what was happening.

When he got to the law office, John looked up.

"It's early. What are you doing here?"

"Aunt Sarah's having her baby, and I came to tell Dr. Wade."

John stood up as the thought excited him.

"I only have one appointment for the day. I think I'll keep that appointment and then close my doors. I'd like to be with Daniel. You take the rest of the day off and come in tomorrow. Is that all right?"

"I can do that," said Rice eagerly. "I'll see you tomorrow afternoon."

The Stewart girls had gotten home and passed the word to Eliza, who in turn told Clay and George.

George went to tell Charity, "Eliza's sisters just came from school. Sarah is having the baby, and I'm going to go be with Daniel for awhile. Do you want me to hitch the carriage so you can go with me?"

"Yes, I'll be ready by the time you are."

The family was gathering. Lucy had gone to help Jetty with Sarah while Charity helped in the kitchen. Daniel was pacing up and down the hall as if that was helping. When Dr. Wade knocked, Daniel hurried to answer the door.

"Come in, Doctor. Sarah's back in our bedroom. Jetty and Lucy are with her."

Dr. Wade went right to the room. He checked Sarah and turned to Lucy.

"You can go out and tell Daniel and the others everything is going as it should be. It may be well into the afternoon when nature takes its course. Sarah's fine."

Lucy found Daniel and George in the parlor and relayed the doctor's words. Then she continued on to the kitchen to tell Mary, Charity, and Remy.

"Remy, would you go find Ollie and tell him what the doctor said? I know he's wondering, too."

Daniel looked at George.

"Let's go out on the porch. I think I can pace better out there."

Then Daniel laughed and eased some of his tension.

"I'm sorry, but I can't sit like nothing is happening."

James came to join his brothers.

"I got my men working and couldn't stand not knowing what's happening."

Daniel caught him up on what the doctor said.

"She's in good hands with both Dr. Wade and Jetty in there. Lucy is running in and out checking that they have everything that's needed."

The morning continued on, and Remy came to the porch to say food was on the table in the dining room.

"Miss Charity said we're going to serve buffet. You can fill your plates when you feel like eating."

Charity and Mary fixed a large tray of food and sent Remy to the bedroom with it. When Remy came out, she went back to the kitchen.

"Jetty said Miss Sarah is doing a good job."

"I'll go report that to Daniel."

The men were eating on the porch. Mary found them there and made her report. While she was talking, John rode up.

"How're things going?"

He walked over and shook hands with Daniel, and then with George and James. Daniel repeated Mary's report.

"There's plenty of food in the dining room if you haven't eaten," Mary told her husband.

"I'll fix you a plate and bring it if you'd like to sit here and visit."

Mary went to fix John's food and returned with it in a few minutes. Daniel had finished eating and sat for a minute and then walked to the porch rail, then to the door, but he never open it. He repeated this routine over and over, like he had a path.

The other men were talking, and Daniel was listening. He would smile or nod, but he wasn't joining in the conversation. They would cut their eyes at Daniel occasionally, as George and James well remembered the feeling.

About the middle of the afternoon, Lucy came to the porch. She hugged Daniel.

"Beau James Borden has made his debut. You can come see him and Sarah. They're doing fine."

Thankful relief flooded over Daniel, and his face literally beamed. James and George stood and shook Daniel's hand vigorously.

"Give Sarah our love, and tell her how proud we are to have a new nephew."

Daniel stuck his head into the bedroom. Dr. Wade saw him and immediately came to shake his hand. After the congratulations from the doctor and Jetty, he went straight to the bed and kissed Sarah on the cheek.

"Lucy told me we have a son. I can't tell you how proud I am and how much I love you."

By now Jetty had the baby wrapped in a soft, woolen blanket. She brought him and placed him in Daniel's arms. Daniel looked down at the tiny, red, wrinkled face and thought, *This is the most precious little face I've ever seen.*

Beau had a head full of dark hair. He already had his father's dimple when he puckered his lips, and his blue eyes were darker than his mother's.

"Bring our son to me."

Sarah was now propped up on pillows. Daniel carried the little bundle and laid him in Sarah's waiting arms.

She smiled, "Here, sit close to us."

She patted a spot for Daniel. Sarah pulled the blanket back.

"Look, he's all there."

She caressed Beau's little hand. Daniel reached and took his other little hand in his, and the baby curled his tiny fingers around one of Daniel's.

"Look at those miniature fingernails."

Sarah lifted the tiniest finger and looked at the nail.

"Amazing, isn't it?"

Daniel kissed Sarah again and turned to Jetty.

"Could you dress him so I can take him into the parlor for my brothers to see? I know they're anxious."

Jetty came to the bed and lifted the baby out of Sarah's arms.

"Jetty, look in the top of my chest. Some of the baby's clothes are there along with a few diapers."

When he was dressed, Jetty handed him to Daniel.

"He's ready for the world."

She smiled up at Daniel as he walked down the hall. The brothers were now sitting in the parlor. James saw them first and got up to see the baby.

70

"He's got that Borden look. He may end up with his mother's eyes, but he favors his father."

George added, "I'm old enough to remember. He's just his father made over when *he* was born. It does bring back memories."

The baby looked like he was twisting his face up to cry.

"I'd better quickly take him through the kitchen, so everyone can see him and get him back to his mother. I'm not much on this crying yet."

James laughed.

"It won't take long to learn. Wait until the wee morning hours."

When Daniel got back to the bedroom, Beau was a-sleep. Jetty had moved the cradle near Sarah's side of the bed, and it was all made up. Daniel looked at Sarah.

"Shall I put him in his cradle?"

"I'd like to hold him again for awhile."

Daniel complied.

"I'll let you both rest some now. I'll see you again in a little while."

Dr. Wade checked Sarah one more time.

"I think mother and baby are doing well, so with Jetty's good care, I think I'll get home. Sarah, I'm very proud of you. You'll be a wonderful mother."

"Thank you for coming, Dr. Wade. I do appreciate your being here."

"I'll check back with you in a few days. If you need me sooner, do send for me."

The doctor went to say goodbye to everyone in the parlor. Daniel walked Dr. Wade to the door, and he gave the new father a departing, congratulatory pat on his back.

"You've started a fine family, Daniel. You should be very proud."

"Thank you, sir. Also, thanks for coming so quickly. You and Mrs. Wade must come and choose your furniture whenever you like."

"I think I'll wait and shop when your new store opens. I hear whispers that I'll have a new daughter-in-law around that same time. Then she can help us shop."

"That would be wonderful."

Everyone else scattered to go and tend to supper for their families.

Jetty told Remy, "Come sit in the bedroom and keep an eye out for anything that Miss Sarah might want. I need to be in the kitchen seeing about our supper."

Daniel went to the kitchen to check on Jetty.

"I'm holding up fine, Mr. Daniel. It's been an exciting day. That baby is already something else. Can you imagine just how dear he'll be to all of us in a very short time?"

"I know, Jetty. He not only curled his little hand around my finger, he curled it around my heart."

The next few days, Daniel was in and out of the factory. More of his time was spent at the house with Sarah and the baby than with working. He did go into town one day to check on the new store. When he walked into the building, it was a big surprise. Susan and Tom Holder were doing a great job with the decorating. Even the empty building was very pleasant looking.

"Uncle Daniel, how's Aunt Sarah and Beau?"

"They're doing really well. I can tell that Beau is already growing. I do know he's losing that brand new baby look."

"I've wanted to talk to you. Noah and I are thinking about having our wedding the second Saturday in June. That is on the eighth day of the month. My family is having a party for us after the ceremony.

You'll be there at the party with your guitar, won't you?"

Susan continued excitedly,

"Tom says he should be through with the building and the outside work by the Saturday after our wedding. What if Noah and I planned a big opening for the store on that third Saturday in June? Aunt Sarah should feel like coming to it for awhile that day."

Susan elatedly jumped from one subject to another.

"We could have advertising handbills printed and post them over town in store windows. We could even hire a couple of kids to hand them out to people on the streets. Can your men have enough pieces of furniture ready by then to make a good showing in the store?"
Daniel thought all she was saying made sense.

"Slow down a minute and let me think. Having the furniture won't be a problem. We have quite a bit made for the store and covered in the storage room. Susan, you may want to check on a source for mirrors and order us some, too."

"Uncle Daniel, I've already taken care of that. They should be coming in soon. I hope you don't mind, but you were so busy. I kept forgetting to mention it. I really felt like some of the chests and dressing tables needed them."

"Susan, that's why I hired you and Noah. You have good judgment, and you're keeping my books, so you know what I can afford maybe better than I know at this point. You have my complete trust, and I wouldn't say that to very many people."

Those words of confidence made Susan feel very proud. Then she remembered a message for Daniel.

"Oh yes, Mr. Drake came in the other day, and we talked about mattresses for some of our displays. He told me you had asked him to have mattresses ready. I think between the two of us we're going to make this place a big success."

"Okay, Saturday, the middle of June, sounds great to me. Ask Tom and Dorcus to be here as he deserves credit for the building. Sarah and I'll plan on being here as much as we can. Then we'll especially invite other family members. Perhaps the Drakes can come that day. Of course, you and Noah will be up front to greet everyone, too. Both of you have worked hard getting ready for the day. Noah will want his folks here part of the day, too, I'm sure."

"Let's have some candy for the kids and perhaps teacakes and cider for everyone."

"Candy-that makes me think-let's have some peppermint because that's Sarah's favorite. Susan, you've really given this some thought. This'll be a big deal for the town and good advertising. Whatever you decide on, you have my okay. I better get back home now. I don't want to be gone too long. I do think I'll go by Creel's store and pick Sarah up a bit of peppermint."

The thought of the peppermint made him smile as he walked out the door.

When Daniel got home, he couldn't wait to go to the bedroom and tell Sarah about Susan's plan for opening day at the store.

"I have a small surprise for you."

Her husband handed her the little bundle of candy. Sarah untied the string.

"It's peppermint candy. What made you think of that?"

"Susan and I were talking about a celebration the day we open the store. She's going to have candy for the kids. When she mentioned candy, I thought of you and peppermint. I remembered one of the sweetest kisses I've ever had tasted of peppermint."

Sarah laughingly said, "I won't have to hide this from you like I did on the trail. Creel's store is fairly handy, and you can always stop in for more."

"A bit of news I picked up in Creels' store is they are expecting their first child in about six months. They are so excited. Just think-their child and Beau will be friends growing up. Oh, Susan and Noah are getting married the second Saturday in June. That's June the eighth. Do you think you can make it to the wedding by then? George and Charity are having a party after the ceremony."

"I should be able to attend by then. I'm really feeling wonderful. I don't think I should dance, though, but I really do miss dancing with you. However, you seemed to do all right with Eliza and Susan."

"Their dancing doesn't hold a candle to you, but I'll tell you who might one of these days, though. Did you notice that I danced with Anna at Clay's wedding? She has the beat down already."

"Ah, thinking of Anna and having the beat, I know we've had a lot of expenses building the house and store; however, there is one thing I'd really like to have."

"Sarah, things haven't been all that expensive for us. I did a lot of bartering for the house, and we used our own sandstone for the store building. Tom and I have bartered a lot for his work, too. What is the one thing you'd really like? You never ask for much for yourself."

"Do you remember when we had Sunday dinner with James and Lucy not all that long ago?"

"Yes, I remember. It was a good meal and a nice afternoon."

"Well, Anna showed me a picture of an upright piano she'd cut out of a newspaper. I would love to have a piano at the school."

"Sarah, you don't play an instrument."

"I know but I've heard that Miss Purdy teaches piano lessons. I'd like to take from her and give Anna lessons, too. The piano would be a wonderful addition for the school. Could we possibly afford one, Daniel?"

"Susan is becoming quite the entrepreneur. She corresponds with factories and finds good prices on lots of things. If it's for the school we might get a discount. Let me put her to searching and see what she can find for us. I'll ride to the store come morning and talk to her. I might ask her to talk to Miss Purdy, too. If she teaches lessons she might be a good source of information."

"It sounds as though Susan is going to be well worth her salary."

"Oh, she is. Susan had Noah carry a little table and chair to the office at the store, and she's setting up her bookkeeping there. I'm having a nice desk built for her office. She's making a terrific manager already. Noah has been working at the factory and hasn't really gotten to show what he can do at the store. I do believe together I couldn't have found better managers. Noah is learning all about each piece of furniture and how it's made. He's already making good suggestions about a few pieces we could make. This is exactly why I wanted him to work at the factory for awhile."

Little Beau whimpered, and Daniel went to the cradle and picked him up.

"I believe our son is hungry."

He placed him in Sarah's arms.

"Are you sure he doesn't need changing?"

Daniel looked shocked.

"I've never changed a diaper in my life, and I don't know how."

"Jetty has Remy changing diapers already. Perhaps she should teach you. Remy catches on to things very quickly. When she tends to Beau she absolutely coo's to him. I've heard her singing little songs when she rocks him."

When morning came, Daniel went to the factory and made sure things were going smoothly. He spoke to Si and Rich about the opening of the store.

"Perhaps you'll want to mention it to the men. They might like to bring their families to the store that Saturday and show their families how we'll display what they build. We're planning on having candy and cookies, too."

"It sounds like a fun day at the store. I'm sure some of them will come."

"Speaking of the store, I've got to run in and talk to Susan. I'm on a mission. I'll be back in a while."

76

With that, he left the factory and headed for town. When he arrived, Susan was already at the store.

"Good morning, Susan. I've come to ask a favor of you."

"What can I do for you?"

"It's more for Sarah than me. Sarah told me that she'd like a piano for the school."

"That's interesting. Who plays one?"

"No one who's at the school plays now, but Sarah would like for her and Anna to learn. It seems that Miss Purdy teaches piano. Could you find out about some piano makers and contact them? You might check with Miss Purdy. She may know something about finding a good piano. I know you're busy, but I'd sure appreciate this."

"For you and Aunt Sarah, I'll start on this right away."

"I'll tell Sarah, and she'll be very pleased."

After Daniel left the store, Susan decided the best place to start researching for a piano would be at Miss Purdy's. She tied on her bonnet and walked to Miss Purdy's house. As Susan entered the gate of the picket fence, she was struck with the beauty of Miss Purdy's small flower garden.

She proceeded to knock on the front door. A very neat, well built, lady answered the door. The piano teacher was not nearly as old as Susan had imagined. Susan surmised by her speech and manner that she was a well educated woman.

"Hello, I'm Susan Borden. I believe you know my aunt and uncle, Sarah and Daniel Borden."

"Yes, Miss Borden, I do. Please come in. What can I do for you?"

"My Aunt Sarah is interested in a piano, and we've heard that you have one and also teach lessons."

"Yes, that's correct. I'll be glad to show you mine."

"I've come on Sarah's behalf. I don't know if you've heard, but she has very recently had a baby. Anyway, Aunt Sarah would like to have a piano for her school."

"I hadn't heard about the baby but I'm very familiar with Mrs. Borden's school."

Her mind raced back to the incident of the privy and the tavern. She could not keep from secretly smiling.

"No one at the school plays the instrument, but Aunt Sarah would like to take lessons, and she has another young niece who would very much like to learn to play."

Miss Purdy thought that was very interesting. She took Susan into the parlor and showed her the piano.

"Come out to the kitchen, and I'll make us a cup of tea. We can discuss some possibilities."

Susan was impressed at how neat and attractively decorated Miss Purdy's house was. She thought, *This is a well organized woman.*

The two women sat at the kitchen table and had tea. Miss Purdy told Susan that she ordered and bought her piano out of Philadelphia.

"I have the maker's name and address on an invoice. Let me get it."

Miss Purdy left the room for a few minutes and came back with the invoice, a piece of paper, and a graphite pencil for Susan to make notes.

"You saw my piano. It's called an upright. I've been very pleased with its service and its sound. I'll play a short tune before you leave so you can tell Mrs. Borden about it. She intends to place hers in the school?"

"That's what I understand," Susan remarked.

"I'd like to call on Mrs. Borden and discuss some possibilities with her. Do you think she would feel like receiving a guest in a few days?"

"I think this would please her very much. I'll tell Sarah to be expecting you soon."

"If you mention that the piano is for a school when you write the maker, you might well receive a nice discount on it. They would surely see the potential of other sales from that one."

"Thank you so much for your time and help. I would love to hear you play, and then I'll be on my way."

Susan loved the sound of the instrument and couldn't wait to tell Daniel and Sarah what she had found out. She would stop by their house on her way home.

In fact, she decided to go to John P.'s office, and they might go to Daniel's house for dinner. She knew Mary ate there every school day, and Mary was keeping the school open these last few days while Sarah was indisposed.

Susan went straight to John's office from Miss Purdy's. She stuck her head in John's door, and he looked up.

"Are you busy?"

"Not too busy to see you. What are you up to?"

"I've come to see if you'd like to take me for a free dinner?"

"*Free* sounds interesting. Now where would we be going for this free dinner?"

"We'll go out to Sarah's and Uncle Daniel's home. Daniel gave me a chore to do this morning, and I've got some good news and can hardly wait to tell him and Sarah all about it. I know Mary eats dinner with them every school day and thought perhaps you'd like to take me. We're not expected, so should we chance that Jetty can handle it?"

John smiled.

"Let's chance it. It'd be a nice change for all of us. My carriage is at the livery so let's go get it and go early. We can visit and see the baby. Won't Mary be surprised when she sees me there this time of the day?"

"I'll go to the livery with you, and we can be on our way. This'll give Jetty some time to stretch her dinner or whatever she needs to do."

When John and Susan arrived and knocked on Daniel's front door, Jetty answered the door.

"Good morning, Jetty."

Jetty greeted them with a happy smile.

"How do you feel about two extra people for dinner?"

79

"I feel very good about it, if it's you and Mr. John. Won't Miss Sarah and Mr. Daniel be happy when I tell them you're here?"

"Is Daniel here now?"

"Yes ma'am, since that baby came, he runs in and out of here several times a day. He surely has a path worn from that factory to the back door."

Jetty rolled her dark eyes and laughed.

"Let's go back to their bedroom. They'll be surprised."

Sarah and Daniel would definitely be surprised. Sarah was dressed, and they were sitting in the two rockers while Beau slept. Jetty knocked lightly at the door even though it was open and stuck her head in.

"Look who I've got."

She stepped aside while Susan and John entered the room. Daniel jumped up to greet them.

"This is a wonderful surprise. Susan, I just saw you earlier at the store."

"We know you weren't expecting company but I have good news, and John was my ride out. We thought we'd surprise Mary, too, when she comes for dinner."

Sarah got up and moved to stand next to Daniel.

"I couldn't have had a better surprise. Come in and see Beau. He's asleep but perhaps he'll wake up while you're here."

After they oohed and aahed over Beau, Sarah suggested they sit in the parlor. She went to the kitchen first.

"Remy would you sit in the bedroom with Beau? He's asleep right now."

As they were taking their seats in the parlor, Daniel looked at Susan.

"Tell us your news."

"I went to talk to Miss Purdy after you came by this morning. She welcomed me, and we had a very productive and pleasant visit. She ordered her piano from a maker in Philadelphia and had his price and address on her invoice. I'll write him this afternoon and see what I can do."

"That *is* good news. I told Sarah you'd be the one who could make this work."

"Miss Purdy played the instrument for me while I was there. She's very good, and I liked the sound. Sarah, she wants to call on you in the next day or two. She said putting your piano in the school might have possibilities for her, too, and she wants to discuss it with you. Be expecting her to call soon."

"Susan, this is exciting. Thank you so much for your help. Daniel has been telling me how good you are at your job."

"Noah and I are both enjoying our new work. Getting to work together is going to be an added bonus for us. We appreciate Uncle Daniel and you giving us this opportunity."

"Talking about Noah, it's a shame for you to be here for dinner, and him not even know it."

Daniel turned to John and said, "John, let's walk down to the factory, and tell Noah to come have dinner with us. I'll tell Jetty to set another plate on the table as we go though the kitchen."

Daniel heard Beau awake as he went down the hall.

He hollered back, "Sarah, Beau's awake. He may want his mama."

Sarah went to the bedroom, and Remy was rocking him. The baby was fretting, and Sarah told Remy she would take him.

"He may be hungry since he's been sleeping."

"Yes ma'am. I know he's dry and clean."

Sarah took him and placed him in his big basket with the handle. She took basket and all to the parlor.

She picked the baby up saying to Susan, "I think I need to feed him. He's growing so fast he has to eat regularly,"

They talked while Beau ate. When he seemed satisfied, Susan asked if she could hold him. Daniel, John, and Noah came in the parlor while Susan was holding Beau. Noah went to have a closer look at the baby.

81

"Susan, you look like a natural for this job."

She looked up and smiled.

"Perhaps one day, Noah, perhaps."

"I was surprised when Daniel and John came to say you were here for dinner."

"Daniel came in the store this morning and sent me on a quest for Sarah. I had good news and wanted to share it with them, so John drove me out. Sarah wants a piano for her school, and I'm tending to ordering it."

"Sarah, I didn't know you played."

Sarah laughed, "I don't yet, Noah. I'm hoping I'm not too old to learn."

"I think it's remarkable that you have the interest. I know you're a busy lady and now taking on a new endeavor is admirable. I know Daniel plays the guitar beautifully. It'll be wonderful for you to play, too. I've never seen or heard a piano. I'll want to hear you play someday."

"We'll see how I do. Maybe you'll want to hear me play if I'm lucky."

Everyone laughed.

"I'm planning on Sarah teaching me as she learns," Daniel stated.

Sarah looked up in surprise.

"Now that's a thought that never crossed my mind."

Remy announced that dinner was ready. Sarah placed Beau back in the basket and covered him with a light blanket. He continued to sleep throughout the meal.

After the others went back to their work, Mary stayed for awhile to give Sarah a report on the school.

"Sarah, you wouldn't believe how Anna has stepped up and helped me since you've been gone. She's going to be a natural teacher and loves it."

"I saw this in Anna back when we were on the road moving out here. She's matured so much since then. I'm going to encourage her to go for some higher education when she leaves our school."

"Wouldn't it be something if one day she came to teach in your school?"

"Mary, I've never expressed it, but that is my dream. Lucy would love that, too."

Late the next morning, a knock came on the door. Remy hurried to answer it.

"Hello, I'm Priscilla Purdy. I'm here to see Mrs. Borden. I think she's expecting me."

"Yes, ma'am, come in and sit down. I'll get Miss Sarah."

Remy led Miss Purdy into the parlor and hurried to get Sarah. Sarah quickly checked her hair in the mirror and straightened her skirt. As she entered the room Miss Purdy stood and extended her hand.

Sarah shook it and said, "Please, let's sit. Would you like some tea?"

"That would be nice."

"I'll have Jetty bring some."

Sarah hurried back to the parlor.

"My niece, Susan, told me to be expecting you. I thank you for coming. Susan said you were so nice the other day to help her with information about the piano."

"Susan is a very nice and pretty young lady. I enjoyed her visit. She tells me you are thinking about putting a piano in your school."

"That's right. I think Susan wrote the maker the very day she spoke with you. We're hoping to hear something from him soon."

"When I was dealing with him, he was very reliable."

Jetty appeared with a tray of tea and teacakes. She served Miss Purdy first and then Sarah.

"Jetty, just set the tray on the little table. Since you have a pot of tea we can help ourselves if we'd like more."

Jetty did as told and went back to the kitchen.

"Susan told me that you would like to take lessons, and that you had another niece who would like to take, also."

"Yes, that's correct. Would you be interested in teaching us? Anna is a girl about twelve years—almost thirteen."

"I'd be very interested. In fact, I was thinking that if your instrument is going to be at the school, I would perhaps like to come there to work with you."

"That would be excellent as the regular school term is ending for the summer very soon. We only teach in the mornings. Classes are dismissed at midday during the terms."

"I was wondering if perhaps any of the other students might be interested in playing. If so, I might just teach them at the school. This would work out very nicely for me if it would work for you."

"Miss Purdy, this sounds very good to me."

"Please, call me Priscilla."

"Only if you'll call me *Sarah*."

"That's settled then, Sarah."

"Priscilla, will you stay and have dinner with us? I'd like for you to meet my niece, Mary Crim. She assists me at the school. She comes to have dinner with us every school day. Daniel will be joining us, too. I want to tell him of our arrangements. He'll be pleased."

"I'd very much like to stay. I'd like to get to know you better."

"Let me tell Jetty to set another plate."

"Would you point me to your privy? With two cups of tea, I feel I need relief before dinner."

Priscilla slightly bushed and smiled. Sarah noticed that she was a very attractive lady.

"Just follow me to the kitchen, and I'll point the way."

When the ladies settled back in the parlor again, they began to visit and become better acquainted.

"Do you have family in town, Priscilla?"

"No, I'm afraid I'm alone. I was an only child, and my parents both passed away. There was a typhoid epidemic in our town, and they both came down with it. They didn't make it. I was grown and in fact was engaged to be married. My young man became sick, too, and I lost him. By the grace of GOD, I was spared for some reason."

Priscilla took her handkerchief from her sleeve and dabbed at her eyes.

"I'm sorry, it has been awhile but the memories still brings tears. So much sadness for me was in my hometown and I just picked up and moved here."

"You're a brave young lady. I'm glad you told me your story."

"I'm not so young anymore." She laughed. "I'm what they call an *Old Maid*."

"You're not that old. You still have a lot of life ahead of you."

Remy brought the baby to Sarah in his basket.

"Excuse me, Miss Sarah. I think Beau is hungry."

"Leave him with me, Remy. I don't think Miss Purdy will mind if I feed him."

Priscilla leaned forward. "He is a precious baby. What's his name?"

"We call him Beau."

"Beau Borden, I love that name. You're so lucky, Sarah."

"I know I am, and I'm so thankful. As I was saying, you still have a life to live."

"I loved Austin so deeply. I've felt I'd never meet another man that would be right for me. It is lonely but, without love, I'd never marry."

"Don't worry. I'm going to keep you busy when I get my piano," Sarah laughed.

"My thought was it would do me good to get out more. That's why I suggested teaching in the school. I'll see more people and that'll do me good."

Mary stuck her head in the door.

"I smell food."

She stepped inside.

"I see we have company today."

Sarah did the introductions. Then they heard Daniel in the kitchen.

"Let's go to the dining room. Since Daniel is here, dinner will be served soon."

After their pleasant meal, Mary invited Priscilla to go look at the school.

"I have my carriage out front. I'll drive us. I'll say goodbye for now, Sarah and Daniel. This has been such a wonderful morning and meal. Please, tell Jetty how I enjoyed everything."

"Priscilla, please come back and visit. I'll certainly let you know when my piano comes."

Priscilla took Sarah's hand and squeezed it.

"I can't tell you how excited I am about this whole project. Daniel, it has been so nice getting to know you and Beau."

When Mary and Priscilla were walking to the carriage, Sarah turned to Daniel and remarked, "I really like Priscilla. I think I've just made a new friend."

"That's good. Isn't it funny what brings new friends into our lives?"

Chapter Four

The regular school term had ended. The girls at the school asked Mary to have the three-day-a-week cooking and sewing classes again this summer. It pleased Mary and Sarah that the girls had enjoyed it so much last summer that they wanted to have it again this summer.

Mary had taught that morning and, as usual, walked up to Sarah's for dinner. Daniel had come from the factory and the three of them had finished eating but were still visiting around the table. A knock came on the front door, and Daniel went to answer it.

When he opened the door, there stood Aaron Holder. Daniel could tell immediately that Aaron was distraught.

"Mr. Borden, my papa asked me to come for you. He needs you. It's my mama. Something's happened to her. Dr. Wade's with her, but papa says he'd like for you to come."

"Certainly Aaron, let me get my horse saddled and I'll be right there."

"I'll start back, sir, and tell him you're on your way."

Daniel closed the door.

"That was Aaron Holder at the door. Something's wrong with Dorcus and he said Tom wants me to come. Dr.

Wade is already there, but I'll go as quickly as I can. I don't know how long I'll be. It must be serious."

Mary got up and said to Daniel, "I'll go tell Ollie to saddle Bess. Then I'll have him to go to the factory and tell Si or Rich that you probably won't be back this afternoon. They'll wonder where you are or what might be wrong."

"Thank you, Mary."

When Daniel got to the Holder's house, he let himself in. Aaron was in the parlor with Amy and Rachel. Aaron saw Daniel when he came in.

"I'll go tell papa you're here. Have a seat, Mr. Borden."

Tom came into the parlor. Daniel could tell by looking that Tom was under a great strain. Tom took Daniel's hand.

"Let's walk outside. I need some fresh air."

When the two men got out the door, Tom broke down, and tears rolled down his cheeks.

"It doesn't look good at all."

"What happened, Tom?"

"We had dinner. Dorcus ate all right and then she got up from the table, took two steps and fell out on the floor. She wouldn't come to. I sent Aaron for Dr. Wade right away. She still hasn't come to. He said he's sure it's her heart. It's giving out and there's nothing he can do."

Tom wiped his eyes.

"I'm trying to be brave for the kids, but I don't think from the looks of her that she has long. I don't know what to say to them."

"I'll stay with them. You go on and stay by Dorcus in case she does wake up."

"Thanks, Daniel, thank you for coming."

Daniel wished with all is heart that Sarah could be here. She'd be much better with the kids than he. The two men went back into the house. Daniel went to the parlor and started a conversation with the kids in an attempt to keep their minds off of their mother.

"Aaron, Sarah has mentioned to me that you have two more terms at her school."

"Yes sir, I hope we get a few new boys this fall because all my friends finished this term."

"Do you know what you're interested in when you finish?"

"We've talked about me going off to school. I'd like to become a doctor."

"Well, that's a noble occupation. I'm sure you'll make a good one. Have you talked to Dr. Wade about it?"

"No sir. Not yet."

"I think you should as he'd be a good adviser. I'll get you together with him before long if you'd like. I know him well as my niece, Susan, is going to marry his son very soon."

"That would be good, Mr. Borden."

"Okay, I'll see that it happens."

Daniel turned his attention to the girls.

"Did Miss Mary tell you that Miss Sarah is going to get a piano for the school?"

The girl's eyes got big, so Daniel continued to tell them.

"Miss Purdy is going to start teaching piano lessons in the afternoons at the school after the piano comes."

Both of the girls said they would like to learn to play.

Amy, the oldest, said, "I'll talk to papa. Maybe he'll let us take lessons."

"That'd be fun. I'll tell Miss Sarah you're interested."

Dr. Wade came to the parlor.

"Daniel, could you come back for a moment?"

Daniel rose and followed Dr. Wade.

"She's gone, and Tom's taking it very hard. Perhaps you can give him some solace."

Tom was sitting in a chair with his head in his hands. Daniel went in and put his arm around his shoulders and tried to soothe him. After a few minutes, Dr. Wade motioned to Daniel for him to step out in the hall.

"I think we're going to have to let Tom cry it out. This has been a terrible shock for him. I'll have Mr. Quincy come pick up her body. He tends to the dead here in our town. He'll have a coffin but we'll need her nicer clothes for her."

"I'll go tell Mattie out in the kitchen and let her know what's happened. Perhaps she can pick out the things for Dorcus."

"That's good, Daniel. I hope Tom will feel like telling the children in a bit."

"I'll try to remind Tom of the kids and that he needs to talk to them."

"You're a great help and a good friend. I'll go for Mr. Quincy."

Daniel went to tell Mattie what needed to be done.

"Mattie, Mrs. Holder's passed."

Mattie was stunned.

"You need to hold up now and help me. Mr. Holder is taking this very hard. When I get Mr. Holder out of the bedroom, can you go in and pick out clothes for Mrs. Holder? You know some of her nicest things."

"Yes sir, I'll do my best."

"Mr. Quincy is coming for her body. Give him her things. Okay? Can you do that?"

"I will, Mr. Daniel."

"I know it's hard but I've got to go help Mr. Tom get through this and help his kids. I'm going to take them home with me for the night. When everything is done, can you close the house up and make sure it's all right?"

"Yes, sir, don't worry, Mr. Daniel."

Daniel turned and went back to the bedroom. Tom was still sitting there staring at nothing.

"Tom, we need to talk to the kids. Are you up to it? They're in the parlor, and I'm sure they're wondering."

Daniel took Tom's arm and physically pulled him up.

"Tom, for your kids, try to get a grip. They're depending on you."

When they got to the parlor, Tom sat down on the settee and held his arms out for the children to come to him.

Daniel could see they knew it wasn't good. Tom held back his tears, and looked deep into their eyes, and told them about their mother.

The children sat in silence for a moment, and then Aaron got up and went to his room. Rachel, who was not quite eight years old, climbed in her papa's lap and began to sob. Silent tears ran down Amy's cheeks, and she quietly shook. She was more than twelve years old and understood very well what her father had said.

Daniel wanted to cry himself but knew he had to be strong. He gave them all a few minutes of quiet.

"Tom, I'm going to hitch up your carriage. You and the kids are going home with me for the night. No arguments-just get ready."

Daniel told the girls to get their things and asked Amy to help Rachel. He stopped by Aaron's bedroom and told him to get ready.

"All of you are going home with me. It's best for you tonight, Aaron-all of you."

Aaron put up no resistance and neither did Tom.

When Daniel pulled up to his house, Ollie had seen him coming and hurried to help with everyone's things. Sarah looked at their faces when they walked in and knew the worse had happened. She got them settled in the parlor and went to tell Jetty and Remy what they needed to do.

"Jetty, the beds will need to be made and let's have a buffet supper. I don't think there will be any big appetites tonight."

Sarah went to the bedroom and got little Beau. If anyone could spread any cheer, it would be Beau. Maybe he would draw their attention away from their sorrow. Sarah was right.

The kids gathered around the baby, and Sarah let them take turns holding him. Beau didn't seem to mind at all. She was right-Beau was helping a lot.

Jetty and Remy put a good but light meal on the table. It was mostly things that could be eaten with the fingers.

Everyone got a plate of food and then they went to sit in the parlor. Sarah noticed everyone managed to eat some. Jetty had prepared the right things.

When bedtime came, Daniel showed Tom to the bedroom where he would sleep.

"We'll get the kids settled in so don't worry about them. You just try to get some rest. If you need me in the night, knock on our door. We'll talk whenever you need to."

Daniel took Aaron to the bedroom where he'd sleep while Sarah got the girls settled in.

"Girls, if you can't sleep or you need me, come to my bedroom. I'll come in and visit with you if you like, but sleep and rest if you can."

Daniel stayed and talked to Aaron awhile.

"Aaron you're almost a man now. This is a bad time for you and your family. We don't always understand why things happen, especially when they first happen. Things will be all right for all of you. It'll take time, but you'll see- it'll turn out all right. You'll always love your mother as she loved all of you so much. She'd want you to go on with your plans, and she'd be so proud of you if you make a doctor."

Daniel could tell Aaron was thinking now. He hoped to give him other things to have on his mind other than what had just happened. There was nothing that could be done for Dorcus now.

"Always give your mother's memory respect, and no matter how old you get, always remember the love you've had for her. Go on with your plans. That's what she'd want you to do. While you're off at school, Sarah and I'll keep an eye on your father and sisters."

"Thank you, Mr. Borden. You've given me things to think about."

Daniel patted him on the back.

"If you can't sleep and need to talk, come get me during the night. I'll get up with you, and we'll talk and have some milk or something."

Daniel shut the door as he left. He glanced at Tom's closed bedroom door and thought the best thing for Tom was to be alone with his thoughts for awhile.

Beau was asleep in his cradle, and Sarah was propped up on some pillows. Daniel sat on the edge of the bed to take his boots off.

"Oh, how I wished for you this afternoon. I've never handled anything like this before. You know the kids better than I do. I felt at a lost."

"I'm sure you did fine. I'm glad you thought to bring them home with you."

"I couldn't leave them there. Dr. Wade was sending Mr. Quincy to get Dorcus' body, and I wanted them out of there. I didn't want the family to see them take Dorcus out of the house. I left Mattie to shut up the house and to choose some nice clothes for the burial. I'm hoping she did all right. Tom is taking it very hard, but then I'd expect that."

"I'm sorry I wasn't there for you."

"I know you would've been if you could've been. I'm just glad you're beside me and little Beau now. He was a comfort tonight. I know I'm about the luckiest man on earth to have the two of you."

His thoughts turned to so many things to be done.

"I'm thinking I'll ask Jetty to go with me tomorrow and help Mattie straighten up Tom's house. His bed linens will need changing and a few other things taken care of. He doesn't have any family here. I guess we're as near to family as it gets."

"You'll have to help Tom make arrangements for Dorcus' memorial."

"Yes, the next few days will be the roughest ones. I'll offer for them to stay with us a while if that's okay."

"It's fine. Under other circumstances, I'd enjoy having them."

"Daniel, I noticed tonight while the kids were playing with Beau that his eyes are getting lighter. They're still blue but they were dark when he was born and now they look lighter."

"I'll look closer at them tomorrow. I know babies are amazing."

They all had a fitful sleep that night. Even Beau woke Sarah up a couple of times.

Tom and the children stayed with Daniel and Sarah until after the funeral.

"I've decided it's time for us to go home and get on with our lives. The house will be empty but we'll get used to it."

After Tom and the children left, Daniel rode in to check on his store. As he walked through the front door, Susan approached him, smiling.

"I have good news. We heard from the piano maker from Philadelphia. I'll get their letter from the office."

She retrieved the letter and handed it to Daniel.

"Hey, he's willing to give us a twenty percent discount for the piano being kept and played in the school. You did well, Susan."

"Shall I get the payment in the mail to him?"

"Yes, along with a note asking him to ship it as soon as possible. Sarah'll be like a child waiting on a gift."

Susan turned her attention to the Holders.

"How are Tom and the children holding up?"

"They're doing a little better every day. They're back home now. It'll take a while, but they'll get in a routine. Aaron has two more terms at Sarah's school, and then he says he's off to study to become a doctor. I'd like for Aaron to talk to Dr. Wade. That'll give them something to look forward to. They need that in their lives now-something to look forward to," his voice trailed off as he talked.

"Daniel, I think we can start moving some of the furniture to the store now. Construction is still on schedule. Tom's workmen know he's going through a rough time. He's lucky to have a good crew. Oh, by the way, that load of mirrors came in this morning. I'm unpacking them, but the men'll have to hang them."

"Okay, two of my men'll be here this afternoon to help. Will you be here to show them what to do? It's time for Noah to come to the store to help you manage. He'll know how to hang mirrors."

"Don't forget that my wedding is next Saturday. I know you've had so much going on that time has gotten by you."

Time *had* gotten away from Daniel.

"Are you ready? Can I help do anything for you? Knowing you, I'm sure you have everything under control."

Susan laughed.

"You're right. Everything's almost ready. Did Dr. Wade tell you that he and his wife still own the first home the two had when they came to Burkesville? He's been having it remodeled from top to bottom for us. It's to be our wedding present. After it's completed, it'll be a lovely home, and I'm so excited."

"No, he hasn't. I've been with Dr. Wade lately more than I have you, but he hasn't mentioned it. When we've been together, a lot has been happening, and we haven't talked pleasantries. Where is this house?"

"It's on High Street. We'll be able to walk to the store from home."

"That's a nice present."

Daniel looked at his pocket watch.

"Say, I'd better be on my way. If you need time off to work on your wedding, take it. That's important, and we want it to go smoothly."

As soon as Daniel left the store, he went straight to Dr. Wade's office. The nurse came out to greet him.

"Does Dr. Wade have a moment to talk to me?"

The nurse went to ask, and Dr. Wade immediately came out to the small waiting room.

"Daniel, what can I do for you?"

"Susan was just telling me about the house you're giving them. What a very nice wedding present."

"I thought it would do them more good than it will me and Flora."

"I want to deliver some bedroom furniture to their house before the wedding without them knowing. Susan said you were having the house remodeled. Is it ready for furniture?"

"Yes, the inside work is done. Feel free to move in whatever you want."

Dr. Wade gave him the address so Daniel and his men could find it.

"Thanks. I'll see you at the wedding."

Daniel went by John's office to tell him about the house. He suggested that furniture would be a nice wedding present.

"If you and James want to give furniture for a present, make up your mind and let me know. We're delivering the bedroom furniture tomorrow, and we can deliver for you, too."

"I'll go talk to James and Lucy about it before I go home. Also, I'll go tell Hill and Owen, and I'll let you know before dark today."

On his way back to the factory, Daniel stopped to tell Sarah about the piano. Then, walking to the factory, he made arrangements to deliver the bedroom furniture to Noah and Susan's house. Moseley and Latham seemed to be the chosen ones when it came to deliveries. They were pleasant, strong, young men and didn't seem to mind.

True to his word, John talked to James, Hill, and Owen. John decided to get the table and James bought the six chairs for the engaged couple's kitchen. Additionally, Hill and Owen chose two nice rockers for the parlor or bedroom. The group agreed that Daniel would deliver the furniture for them.

Tom came to the factory early the following morning. "I need to talk to you."

"Okay, come in the office where we'll have some privacy."

Daniel couldn't imagine what his friend had on his mind.

"With so much happening, it almost slipped my mind that this is the Saturday that Susan and Noah are to be married."

"That's right."

Tom shifted uncomfortably in his chair and continued his thoughts. It was hard for him to talk of his previous plans.

"Of course, Dorcus and I had planned to go to the wedding, but now I don't know what to do. Susan has especially become a good friend since we've been working together on the store."

"I suggest that, if you feel like it, dress the kids up, and take them to the wedding with you. It might do all of you good to do something together."

"You've got a point there. We could just go to the ceremony, and Susan will understand if we skip the party."

"I know she will. She'll be glad you made it to the ceremony."

"Thanks for the advice. Dorcus and I hadn't chosen a gift. What are you giving them?"

"Bedroom furniture."

"I should've known it'd be furniture. What can you suggest for me to give?"

"Susan had a new shipment of mirrors come in this morning. She and Noah will need one over their double

97

chest. Chose one, and we'll settle up later because I don't know what they'll sell for. It'll be in your pocketbook range, though."

Daniel grinned at Tom as he said that.

"Can you deliver it?"

"Yes, I'll deliver it today and even hang it. In fact, we're delivering a load of furniture to their house now. Why don't you hop in the wagon and go with us? If we can find Susan out of the store, we'll go by and snatch a mirror."

"That sounds pleasant, and I'm for anything that's even remotely *pleasant*."

The wagon was loaded with the first load. Latham went with Tom and Daniel to unload, and the three got the first load moved.

"Let's go by the store and see if Susan's there."

When the trio arrived, the store was locked.

"Good. I've got a key and this means she's not here. Latham, you know her when you see her, so keep watch out a front window. If you see her coming, let us know."

"I've never been in on a theft before-not even with an owner," Tom said laughingly.

"Which mirror do you want?" Daniel pointed at them.

Susan had them all leaning against the wall.

"You said it goes over a double chest, so that means a big mirror. I think she'll like this one. After working with her and choosing paints and accessories, I think I have a feel for what she likes."

"Let's move the mirrors back together so she won't notice the vacant spot. Okay, let's get out of here before we're caught," Daniel added.

It was heavy, so both carried it. Getting it to the front of the store, Latham took Daniel's end of the mirror while he locked the door. The mirror was laid on one of the old blankets in the back of the wagon.

"Let's take it back to their house and not haul it around more than necessary. We have another load and the mattress. Tom, do you want to stick with us?"

"I may as well. You're pretty fun fellows to run with. I'll even help hang the mirror and straighten the furniture."

Daniel grinned, because that was not a job Tom would normally enjoy.

The trio got the mirror in the house and headed back to the factory for the rest of the furniture. With it loaded, they started back to Noah's house.

When that was unloaded, Daniel suggested, "Let's put the bed together before we get the mattress."

Next, the group went to the Drakes'. The mattress was paid for and loaded. This was the last thing to unload, so now they discussed where to place the furniture.

"You helped decorate the store and knew what mirror she'd like, so you may as well plan their bedroom. I'm glad we brought you with us."

Daniel smiled at Tom. Tom stood back and looked at the furniture for a few minutes.

"Okay, the bed on this wall facing the fireplace and windows. Put the armoire here and the double chest on this wall. Then center the mirror over it. Noah and Susan will like this. Daniel, this is beautiful furniture."

"Ironically, Noah saw it while it was being built. He knows every inch of it and loves it. He just didn't know it was going to be his. Tom, there's a graphite pencil in this tool box. If you have a scrap of paper, leave a note in the corner of the mirror saying, *from the Holder's*. Then they'll know you were in on doing all of this."

"That's a good idea. Gee, I'm glad I came with you fellows."

Daniel mentioned, "Tom, if you want more fun, you can bring your big wagon and help my men move furniture to the store this afternoon."

With their fun deeds done, they headed back to the factory. After dinner, Daniel rode back to the store. Susan saw him walk in, and immediately she headed toward him.

"Uncle Daniel, I've something to tell you. I went for the final fitting of my wedding dress this morning, and I locked the store up tight. I'm sure of that. Later today I was looking at our new mirrors and one's missing."

"How could that be, Susan? Maybe you miss counted them."

"No, I know one's missing. I've double-checked both back doors, and they're still locked. The windows have not been tampered with. I know the front door was locked, because I doubled-checked when I left."

"Are you sure you're not mistaken? Surely all of them are here."

Daniel was slyly trying to cover up their 'theft.'

"No, it was my favorite mirror, and it's not here anymore."

Susan was getting impatient with Daniel.

"Well, let's not worry about it. You can request another on your next order. Don't fret. I hope the store doesn't have ghosts," Daniel laughed.

Susan looked disgusted with his remark. The very idea that he would make fun at a time like this. Daniel sensed her frustration and quickly changed the subject.

"Noah and the other workmen will be bringing in loads of furniture anytime now. I rode ahead to be sure you'd be here."

"I'll be ready for them."

"I need to get back to the factory, so I'll leave everything in your good hands. I'll check back tomorrow to see how things are going. There is one thing I want to tell you."

Susan's attitude changed instantly and she listened.

"I don't want you to try to lift or push any of the heavy furniture in this store. We'll get a man to help if you need more than Noah. It's for your own health, Susan, and I insist on it."

"Okay, I promise so don't worry."

Daniel nodded his head once to emphasize that he meant it. Then he quickly left before she could bring up the subject of the missing mirror again.

Daniel had borrowed George's and James' wagons to use along with his own. As the wagons were being loaded, Daniel looked up and saw Tom with his large wagon coming. Tom pulled his wagon in line to be loaded.

"I was jesting with you about hauling. You didn't have to come."

"Well, I didn't want to miss out on any more fun."

Daniel picked up on *fun*.

"Talking about fun, Susan missed the mirror and told me it was gone. I tried to convince her that she must be mistaken, but Susan said that it was her favorite mirror, and she knew she wasn't mistaken."

"See, I told you that was *her* mirror. Do I know women, or do I know women?"

Daniel chuckled, "I'm glad you do, because I made a joke and told her I hoped the store didn't have a ghost. You know, she half got mad at me."

Tom couldn't help but laugh.

A stream of wagons was going to and coming from town. Moseley and Latham went to pick up a couple of mattresses from the Drakes.

Noah rode his horse to the store to help Susan receive the furniture. He went into the store and looked around.

"Susan, where's the bedroom furniture that was delivered here this morning?"

"No furniture was delivered here this morning," said Susan.

His statement puzzled her immensely.

"Daniel, Latham, and Tom Holder—hey, wait a minute! What was Tom doing helping with the furniture? The three left with two wagon loads of bedroom furniture. I thought

101

they were bringing it here. It was my favorite bedroom set. I watched Si carving it and made suggestions. I think I better pick you up tomorrow and go by to check our house. Something rotten is going on here."

"You're right. My favorite mirror went missing from the store this morning. Oddly enough, I hadn't told a soul that it was my favorite mirror. How would they know to take it? Something really *is* funny. I'll tell you what-don't let on. We'll go check our house in the morning."

There were two extra large back doors in the store building. Each door had been placed to bring in the different priced furniture. Susan had made signs for each door stating *Less Expensive* and *Expensive.* Both signs showed when the doors were propped open. Susan and Tom had designed the doors for efficiency.

Noah saw the wagons coming and went to unlock both back doors.

Susan told the men, "Just put the furniture inside and later we'll worry about making displays and placing it for its best effect."

Susan was pleased that there was enough furniture to make a very good showing. The large building had her worried that it might look almost empty. Of course, some of the furniture such as an assembled bed and some of the dining room tables were large. Finally the wagons quit coming, and the big move was completed. Tom, Daniel, Susan, and Noah were standing surveying all the furniture.

"Now my work really begins. Trying to decide what displays to put where and it won't be easy."

Tom volunteered, "Susan, I'm between jobs, so I wouldn't mind coming in and helping you and Noah. I can judge the size of items, and I also have a pretty good eye for placing them. I guess that comes with designing and building all these years."

"Tom, we'd love to have your help. Do you work cheap?" Noah asked.

Tom looked at Daniel.

"A few good meals for a family of four might do it."

"Well, I think I know where those good meals can be found. There's a place less than two miles out of town and on the Cumberland River. The cook's name is Jetty, and she's a good one. Just tell me when you want to come, and I'll make your reservations."

Tom looked back at Susan and said, "I'll be reporting for work in the morning."

Daniel was glad to hear Tom was interested in helping. He had worried about his friend hanging around home between jobs and feeling sorry for himself.

Early the next morning, Noah and Susan went by their house. When they walked in, their mouths flew open! The two lovely rockers were sitting in front of their parlor fireplace. The charming oak table with six chairs was in the kitchen. In the bedroom was Noah's favorite bedroom set. Susan's very favorite mirror was over the beautiful double chest that Noah had helped build. The bed was complete with soft linens and spread with a gorgeous colorful bedcover. On the floor at the foot of the bed was a beautiful, round, wool rug.

"They've surely been busy," said Susan as tears of joy began to form in her eyes. "The bed linens are mama's work and the platted rug is Dora Stewart's."

Susan saw the note in the corner of the mirror. She pulled it and read the note, *from Tom and his children.*

"It was Tom with Daniel's help that took the mirror." Susan laughed, "That Daniel didn't want to tell a falsehood. He tried to blame it on a ghost."

The Saturday afternoon of the wedding found everyone primped and dressed in their finest. The bride's dress was beautiful. Susan had designed her bridal wardrobe and had it made by the best seamstress in town. The church was lovely with the flowers and ferns placed throughout, and people were beginning to gather.

103

Tom Holder had his three children dressed in their best. The widower looked more rested, and he had a genuine smile on his face. The haggard lines on his face were slowly fading. It was obvious that things were getting better for the whole family.

Sarah and Daniel had Beau in his basket, and he was getting a lot of attention. Sarah was radiant and looked like the beautiful Sarah they all knew and loved. Daniel beamed with Sarah beside him, and his darling little son was at peace, not withstanding all the adoration coming his way.

George and Charity were a handsome couple, and Rice, standing straight and tall, was becoming a good-looking young man. Clay and Eliza were to be the couple's witnesses.

Dr. and Mrs. Wade were standing at the door of the church and were greeting and welcoming everyone. The Borden's were to sit together. Tom Holder and his children blended in with the Bordens. It seemed Tom was becoming one of the Borden's family members by osmosis.

Preacher Kent conducted the ceremony, and everything went off without a hitch. After the ceremony, the preacher made an announcement inviting everyone to the party to be held at George Borden's house. Directions to the house were given.

After Noah kissed Susan, they walked down the church aisle with Susan's arm tucked tightly over Noah's. When the couple got to the church steps, the race was on. Susan lifted her skirts, and with her hand in Noah's, they fled to his carriage.

It was now decorated with flowers and bright colored ribbons flowing from the back. They had hurried so Susan could get to her father's house and change into a party dress that was more suitable for dancing. She wanted for her and Noah to be standing at the front door to greet guests as they arrived.

Susan took a deep breath and smiled as she looked up at Noah. They had made it. The flowers were still in her hair

104

and she was glowing. Noah's blond hair was a little tousled, and Susan tried to fix it with her fingers. James and Lucy were the first ones to the door.

James said, "Eli wanted me to catch you. You were too fast, and try as I might, we couldn't. Daniel's close behind me, though. We'll be in the big room playing music when the guests arrived."

"That'll be wonderful. I'm glad you and Daniel thought of it."

Daniel helped Sarah down from the carriage and passed her Beau in the basket.

"I'll get my guitar and be right behind you."

George, Charity, and Rice arrived next followed by Clay and Eliza with the Stewarts. The Wades were not far behind the Stewarts. As planned, the Holders skipped the party. The big procession of guests was driving slower.

Charity checked the dining room table which was now groaning with food. Jetty, Ollie, and Remy had come to George's to help Alma with the food and serve the guests.

Music flowed from the big room. Moseley had brought his hammered dulcimer. The party turned out to be a great success, but Beau slept through most of it.

Susan and Noah broke away from the party just before dusk. They would spend their wedding night in their new home. After the newlyweds left, the other guests began to say goodbye.

George whispered to Daniel, "You and Sarah go and get Beau settled in before dark. I'll get Clay to drive Ollie, Jetty, and Remy to their homes."

"That's thoughtful. I'll get Sarah and Beau and we'll leave."

When the food was all put away and the kitchen clean, George slipped some money to Ollie, Jetty, and Remy.

"Thank you for your wonderful help. Charity and I appreciate it so much. Clay'll drive you home."

The three thanked George and were proud of the extra money they had earned.

"If you ever need us again, Mr. George, let us know."

After everyone had left, George looked at Charity.

"Do you realize our nest will soon be empty? We can be thankful that Clay and Susan are near."

"George, what do you think is in Rice's future when he finishes school?"

"We'll just pray and trust that it will be something good, Charity. That's all we can do."

Susan and Noah arrived at their new home and went inside. A second large, new table and eight chairs were setting in their dining room. There was also an elegant cabinet with leaded-glass doors in the corner. A note was on top of the table that read:

May this table always be set with delicious meals and surrounded by happy people. With Love—
Papa, Mama, Rice, Clay, and Eliza.

They both were taken aback. It was such a wonderful surprise.

Chapter Five

Susan and Noah had a very busy week being in their new home and trying to get the store ready for the opening celebration, too. They both loved their job and wouldn't have it any other way. Tom was there at the store beside them helping and giving suggestions. Latham and Moseley had worked all week helping to arrange the new store furniture.

Both of their mothers got together at the newlywed's home and made sure they had all the small necessaries a house needed to run smoothly. They had also supplied food for several days. Flora advised Noah to hire a cook, and Noah felt it was very good advise with Susan working.

The *Grand Opening* handbills had been printed and posted in most of the stores in town. Susan had hired her brother, Rice, and Aaron Holder to hand out the handbills to people on the street on Friday afternoon and also Saturday morning.

About an hour before the celebration was to start, Dr. and Mrs. Wade came to the store door. Noah and Susan went to greet them.

"May we come in early? We'd like to choose our furniture before it's sold. Daniel has bartered a couple of pieces of the furniture of my choice for my services. Then we would like to purchase a few additional pieces."

Flora looked at Susan and Noah and remarked, "We'd like your opinions and advise."

The Wade's toured the whole store. They ended up back in front of an exquisite walnut four-poster bed and mattress.

"I want this bed and Flora wants the armoire that matches it. I'll buy the mattress and the dressing table. How did we do, Susan?"

"You did very well, in my opinion."

"Good. I feel your uncle is greatly over paying me for my services."

"He wouldn't think so. Just having you there when Beau was born was worth the world to him. You gave both Sarah and Daniel confidence and comfort."

Noah spoke up.

"You *did* make a good choice. This set is not only beautiful but it's very well built. I can vouch for that. We'll deliver it to you Monday morning. I'll write you up an invoice. Come back to the office and we can settle up."

Susan made sold tags to put on the pieces the Wades had chosen.

When Daniel went home to eat dinner and to get Sarah and Beau, he stuck his guitar in the carriage. They arrived at the store shortly after Dr. and Mrs. Wade had made their furniture choices. Daniel and Sarah walked into the store along with Remy and Beau, and they saw the Wades coming out of the office.

They walked back to greet them.

"Have you found the furniture you want?"

"Yes, and we bought a few more pieces, too. We were just settling up with Noah. He said it would be delivered on Monday morning. I bought one of your excellent mattresses. Flora and I have been hearing nothing but how wonderful this mattress is to sleep on. I had to buy one."

"Good, I'll tell the Drakes. They make the mattresses for me, and they are the best mattress makers anywhere around. Dr. Wade, I have one more favor to ask of you."

"Just ask it, Daniel. As I was telling Susan, I'm afraid you've over paid me for my services as it stands. Sarah handled that birth herself. I just did some minor things. I want you to understand this is a compliment, when I say your wife is no dainty little wallflower. She's in excellent health. She fools one in her presence. She's small but much physically stronger than she looks. She's a giant in her mental determination, too. It would take a lot to knock her down and keep her down."

"Dr. Wade, you've just described Sarah better than I probably could. Her beauty first attracted me but her depth and strength made me love her even more. Now, let me get back to that favor I'd like to ask."

Daniel gathered his thoughts again.

"My very good friend, Tom Holder, has a son named Aaron."

Dr. Wade interrupted Daniel by saying, "Yes, I briefly met Aaron when his mother died."

Daniel continued, "He lacks the fall and spring terms finishing at Sarah's school. He's a very smart young man and well mannered. He would like to go to a school of higher learning and become a doctor after he graduates. I've told him you would be a good mentor for him. I would appreciate it if you'd talk to him about his plans."

"I would be more than glad to do that. I saw Tom walk into the store a few minutes ago. I think he's talking to Susan. I'll ask him if Aaron will be here today. If Aaron will, could I talk with him in your office just to get familiar with the young man? Then I'll invite him to my office to look around and get better acquainted," Dr. Wade remarked.

"That'll be great, and I thank you so very much."

Daniel saw George and James come in the store with their families. He and Sarah went to greet them while Dr.

Wade went to find Tom Holder to ask if his son was coming to the store.

Aaron walked in the door just as his father was talking to Dr. Wade. Tom introduced Aaron again to Dr. Wade, and Daniel noticed the doctor and the young man go back to the store's office.

Tom walked toward Daniel.

"Thanks for setting Aaron up with Dr. Wade. It was better coming from you than from me especially for Aaron and probably even for Dr. Wade. To know that someone other than his father has faith in a young man goes a long way."

Tom and George both came with their fiddles, James brought his banjo, and Moseley was there with his hammered dulcimer. Daniel got his guitar, and they decided to stand out under the wooden awning in front of the store, and a little before two o'clock, they began to play.

People started arriving. Susan, Noah, and Sarah were at the front door greeting and welcoming people to the store. Remy went to watch Beau while he slept in the office. It looked as though there would be a large crowd. Susan had fresh bouquets setting all over the store. Everything looked very nice.

People were walking through the building discussing the different pieces of furniture. Si, Rich, and their wives were set up to take orders, and they were selling furniture, too. Latham and Amos were loading pieces of furniture that sold to people who wanted to take them home. Anna was placing tags on the pieces that were sold and to be delivered later.

Mary Crim and Priscilla Purdy were serving cider and fruit punch. Owen, Hill, and their wives and children attended. They were impressed with the store and Owen's wife, Laura, bought a pretty mirror.

Tom saw Si and Rich there and made a point to speak to them.

"I've wanted to see both of you. Tell Joel and Allen I meant it when I said I'd hire them and train them to be good builders. If they're interested, tell them to meet me at the factory Monday morning and we'll talk."

"Thank you, Mr. Holder. They'll be there Monday morning. They'll be two excited boys."

After Tom walked off, Rich looked at Si and said, "Maybe that Miss Purdy episode wasn't such a fiasco after all. Something good may come out of it."

They both laughed.

Several weeks had passed. Early one morning, Susan went to the post office at Creel's General Store, and there was a letter waiting for her. It was from a freight company saying that the piano would be delivered to the school that very day. Susan was so excited she could hardly keep from running. She had to remember that she was a married lady now, and a certain amount of decorum was expected with that position. When she stepped in the store, she let out a "Whoopee" and was dancing around.

Noah looked up, "What on earth has come over you?"

"There's a letter from a freight company that the piano will be delivered to the school sometime today. Hurry, you need to ride out and tell Sarah. She'll want to be there and have the school unlocked."

Noah laid the papers aside that he was working on.

"I'm on my way."

He hurried out the door and headed to the livery stable to get his horse. He kept his horse at a good pace and was at Daniel's house shortly. He tied the horse to the front rail and hurried to the door. His knock on the door was so rapid that it must have sounded alarming.

Jetty and Sarah both came to the door. They were surprised when they saw it was Noah.

Before they could ask, Noah spat out the words, "Your piano is being delivered to the school today."

Sarah was so excited she grabbed him around his neck and kissed his cheek. Then she thought what she had done and was embarrassed and so was he.

She gathered herself, "Thank you so much for coming to tell me. Do come in and have a glass of cider before you start back to town."

Noah's face was still a little flushed from Sarah's display, but he managed to say that would be nice.

Sarah and Jetty stepped back to let him in.

"Come back to the kitchen, and we'll sit while you drink your cider. Jetty, would you tell Ollie to go tell Mr. Daniel about the piano. He'll want to know."

Sarah poured two glasses of cider, and she sat down at the table with Noah.

"How's Susan this morning?"

"She's excited like you. She was hollering and dancing around when she opened the freight company's letter. She knows you and Daniel have been waiting for this piano. I'm sure we'll have to drive out to see it Sunday afternoon."

"Do come and plan on dinner with us. Perhaps we'll make it a small party. I'll ask Priscilla Purdy and Tom Holder and his children. I'm sure Priscilla will play the new instrument for us."

"Count on us. Susan'll be excited about coming when I tell her. I better get back to the store or she'll wonder where I am."

"Come for dinner as soon as you can after church."

When Jetty came back to the kitchen, Sarah told her, "Jetty, I just did a no-no."

"What did you do, Miss Sarah, besides kiss Mr. Noah?"

"Oh, that was nothing. Anyway, I just got caught up. Not thinking, I just invited him and Miss Susan for Sunday dinner. Not only that but I told him I'd ask other people, and we'd have a small party to hear the new piano."

"There's nothing wrong with that, Miss Sarah."

"Sunday is the day you and Ollie have off."

"No matter, why can't we have Saturday off this week instead? I can fix supper for Ansell and Effie. I'll ask them to spend the night. That'd be fun and a change. They can sleep up in our loft. I'll ask Remy to eat with us, too."

"You don't mind, Jetty?"

"Mind? I'm already planning it."

Sarah patted her on the shoulder.

"You're a saint. You just wait. I'll do something nice for you."

Daniel came in the back door.

"I figured you and Beau would already be at the school waiting on the new piano. I'll get him and come to sit with you while we wait."

As they walked out the door, Jetty thought, *They're just two kids waiting on a gift.*

Sarah had the big basket and Daniel was carrying Beau on one arm. Still they managed to hold hands as they walked down the road.

"Sarah, look at Beau's eyes out here in the sun. They just keep getting a lighter blue. They look iridescent. When you look into them there is no end. When he's older, the young ladies will get lost in his eyes."

Sarah came to have a closer look.

"You're right. They're dazzling."

The summer school was closed today, so Sarah had to unlock the school door. She opened them and the windows to let in a breeze. She started trying to decide where to put the piano. With Daniel's suggestion, she thought to have it set on the back wall beside the door.

While they waited, Sarah and Daniel had time to talk.

"Sarah, you haven't mentioned Mittens much lately. She's fine I know because I see her at the barn, and she visits at the factory occasionally."

"I've been so busy with Beau. I'll admit I'll haven't thought of her as much as I once did. I still care about her, but it seems she has taken up with Ollie and Jetty now. I watch her playing in the garden right under Ollie's feet. He never steps on her. He reaches down and pets her or picks her up. Jetty feeds her now, and she follows them to their cabin. I guess it's different when you have a child. They take up your thoughts and time."

"I know. I find I don't play my guitar as much anymore, either. I guess that's why I'm looking forward to you learning to play the piano. We can walk down here in the evenings and perhaps play together. We may even have to get Beau a tambourine so he can join in."

Sarah laughed.

"Wouldn't he be cute shaking it all around when he walks? I can hear those bells jingling now."

The two sat there with the image of Beau dancing with a tambourine and doubled up laughing.

It was almost midday, and the morning had passed quickly. Daniel could hear voices coming up the school walk. It was Jetty and Remy. Remy was carrying a big basket, and Jetty had a jug in her hand. Daniel stepped out on the porch.

"What do you have here?"

"We thought we'd bring a picnic for you and Miss Sarah. We figured you'd be getting hungry and thirsty by now."

Daniel took the basket from Remy.

"Well, you figured right. Thank you."

He set the basket on the table and Jetty came and began to set the food out.

"I'll take Mr. Beau, Miss Sarah, so you can eat and enjoy it. Jetty's fixed you a good picnic."

"You and Jetty are among the nicest people I know. We don't know how much longer we'll have to wait. We might have starved, but I'm not leaving until they bring that piano."

"Is there any cleaning you need us to do while we're waiting?"

"No. Get some chairs and sit on the porch and rest. Enjoy the good breeze."

114

That's what they did, and they took Beau with them. A little butterfly came and lit right on the top of Beau's head. Remy was shooing it, but it insisted on flying around his head.

"It must be his clean smelling hair attracting that butterfly. Look, he sees it."

Beau let out a little gurgle of a laugh.

Jetty shouted back to the parents, "Miss Sarah, did you and Mr. Daniel hear that laugh?"

"We did, Jetty. He smiles a lot but that's the biggest laugh I think he's ever had."

"That was a precious moment, Miss Sarah."

"It certainly was, ladies, and you heard and saw it."

When the picnic was finished, Jetty gathered things up and put them back in the basket.

"Would you like for us to take Mr. Beau with us?"

"No, we're enjoying him, and surely it won't be much longer."

"Well then, we'll be going back to the house."

"You were thoughtful, and we do appreciate it. The food was very good."

Another hour passed, and Daniel went to stand on the porch.

"There's a large wagon coming down the road from town. It could be going to the sawmill, but it could be coming here."

In a few minutes he called out, "It's coming here. It turned on our road. This is it, Sarah!"

She jumped up and came out on the porch, leaving Beau asleep in his basket.

"He misses some of the best parts sleeping his life away."

Daniel chuckled, "He could care less that his mama is getting a new piano."

"Do you think he'll ever play an instrument?"

"I'll have him playing a guitar or maybe a mandolin by the time he's six. Will you teach him piano?"

"I will or Miss Purdy will."

By that time the wagon was in the turnaround. Daniel stepped out in the yard and motioned for the driver to pull close to the porch.

When he got the back of the wagon even with the steps, Daniel hollered, "Whoa."

Two strapping, tanned men jumped off the wagon and came to the back.

"Do you need my help?" Daniel asked.

"No sir, we've got three long heavy boards. Just move back and watch us."

Daniel and Sarah both did as instructed. The men had the piano and its crate off the wagon before they could turn around. They put two heavy straps under it and lifted.

"Where do you want it, sir?"

"On that back wall on the left side of the door."

The men put it there with no strain.

"Is this all right?"

"That's fine."

Daniel handed each man a nice coin. The men pulled the straps out, said thank you, and were gone.

"I need a hammer. Guess I'll have to go to the barn."

"There's a claw hammer right at the top of the stairs. Mary and I use a hammer occasionally."

"Good for you. I'll have this thing uncrated and shoved back nearer the wall in a minute."

Daniel got the hammer and went to work. He popped the crate off quickly. He pushed one end of the piano toward the wall and then moved the other end.

"How's that?" he said as he reached for a bench. "Now sit down, Miss Sarah, and let's hear a tune."

Sarah laughed, "You must be joking."

"No, sit down and just touch the keys one at a time and let's hear it."

Sarah did as told.

"Oh, I wish I could play. Here you sit down."

She scooted over, and Daniel sat down beside her.

116

"I used to watch my mother. I believe she put her hands like this."

He placed both his hands on the keyboard. He ran his fingers much like he was playing chords on a guitar. A nice sound came out.

"Daniel, you should be taking the lessons from Miss Purdy."

"Oh no, it's your piano. You're going to teach me."

"Let's play with it awhile longer, and then we can go to the house."

Daniel listened as he hit the keys. In a minute he played a bit of *Rock-A-Bye-Baby.* Sarah was so excited.

"I'm going to teach you? Daniel you'd be playing it in a few hours."

"Not correctly though. You learn first, and then you can show me the proper way. I can pick out tunes by ear, Sarah. I can't read music and probably never will. You can show me how to place my fingers. If I hear you play something and know where to place my fingers, I can play it back to you. Understand?"

"I understand enough to hope and pray that Beau inherits your musical talent."

"I'm nothing special. George and James both play like I do. In fact, that's the way mother plays. Sarah, your father and your brother, Benjamin, play the fiddle. Do they read music?"

"I don't know. I've never thought about it. I've never seen them with any written notes. They just play."

"I'm curious why you've never learned to play?"

Sarah tilted her head in thought.

"I don't suppose we ever had an instrument that I was interested in. I love to hear other people play. I was always so busy outside with the horses, especially after father bought Glory for me."

Sarah looked outside.

"I liked being outdoors. Perhaps I didn't give you a true look at the real me before we married. The first time we met I was all dressed up for Polly and Joshua's wedding. I was almost instantly interested in you when I saw you. Then when I came to visit Polly, I'd be in frilly, pretty dresses. You never saw me in my brother's breeches riding a horse. You didn't see the real me until we married, and I came to live at your home."

Daniel took her hand.

"I'll admit I was attracted to your beauty the first time I saw you. I sensed something deeper within you though before I ever mentioned marriage. I knew you were strong, but as I told you on our trip when we were moving, you have always surprised me. When you wanted to learn to shoot, I was surprised but at the same time very pleased. You digging in the soil and learning about the plants with Toby pleased me. Sarah, I'll admit I've loved you more everyday of our lives, and it will never end."

Sarah leaned and kissed Daniel.

"My love for you has grown tremendously as well."

"At the store opening, Dr. Wade talked to me about you. He told me how strong you are and that your looks are not all that there is. He described you to me, and told me things I already knew about you, but he learned it in a very short time when you gave birth to Beau. It took me awhile to learn it, but you're a very remarkable woman—."

Beau fretted, and Daniel stopped in mid sentence to look and listen, then continued, "And a wonderful mother. We should get back to the house. We don't want Jetty and Remy bringing us our supper, too."

Daniel bent down to get Beau out of his basket. Sarah wrapped a little blanket around his shoulders.

"I'll close up the school and be ready to go. Thank you so much for the piano. I'll need to let Priscilla and Anna know it's here."

"I'll go to the store in the morning and ask Susan to call on Priscilla to tell her the piano's here and to invite her to Sunday dinner. Why don't you and Beau walk over and tell Anna tomorrow? It'll thrill her so. Let's come and play with the piano again tomorrow. I want to get the sound of the notes in my head a little better."

"I'm pleased because I think you'll be playing it very soon," Sarah told him.

"We'll see. I think you'll do much better than you are expecting. Music runs in your family, too, and as smart as you are, you'll be reading music before you know it."

It was Sunday morning, and Sarah heard Jetty singing in the kitchen.

"My, you're happy this morning."

"Yes, we had such a good supper last night, and we all sat out on our porch afterwards. It was such a pleasant evening. Ollie's feeding Ansell and Effie breakfast this morning, and then he's going to church with them. It was such a good family visit."

"I'm glad I didn't ruin your time off, Jetty. Could you manage if I ask Mr. James' family to join us for dinner today? I thought perhaps the adults could eat in the dining room while you serve the young people in the kitchen. Am I asking too much at this late time?"

"Lawdy, Miss Sarah, Mr. James furnished me with enough food for a banquet today. I have part of our dinner cooking already. I started it early this morning. You ask them. Would it be all right if Ollie and I slip down and sit on the porch at the school this afternoon? We'd like to hear Miss Purdy play that new piano of yours. Then I'll make and serve a cool fruit punch with teacakes down at the school later. I'll keep the punch cool in the well."

"That would be wonderful. I'd like for Remy to come along to watch Mr. Beau. You can all watch him and listen to the music."

"See, it'll be a good day for all of us. I'm cooking a good breakfast for you and Mr. Daniel this morning since dinner'll be a little late today."

"I'll take Mr. Daniel a cup of coffee this morning. He's always bringing one to the bedroom for me."

Jetty hurried and fixed a little tray for Mr. Daniel.

Daniel was dressing when Sarah walked into the room with the tray.

"That coffee smells good. It was nice of you to think of me."

"I *should* think of the man who buys me a piano and always brings me coffee or tea."

Sarah walked to her husband and kissed him on the cheek. Then she took a peep at Beau lying in his cradle sound asleep.

"I'll start getting dressed and hope the baby remains a-sleep. I'll dress him for church after we eat breakfast."

Daniel sat down in a rocker to enjoy his cup of coffee.

"This is the best cup of coffee I think I've ever had."

"I drank tea this morning. What seems to be the difference in it and our usual coffee?"

"Take a sip of it and see what you think."

"It *is* very good. I would have had it if I had known. Let's ask Jetty what she's done to it."

When Sarah was almost ready, Daniel stood, "I'll take my tray back to the kitchen, and ask Remy to come in and sit with Beau while we eat."

"Good. I'll be there in one second."

Remy came in the bedroom and Sarah turned toward her.

"He's still asleep, and I didn't want to wake him."

Remy just smiled and looked at Beau in the cradle. When Sarah walked into the kitchen, Daniel was asking Jetty about the coffee.

"You know Ansell and Effie came out yesterday. When we were talking on the porch, Ansell was telling about this man coming through the blacksmith shop. Ansell heard him telling another man about the way they make coffee in one of those foreign countries. Ansell over heard him say to pour the boiling water through the ground beans and a patch of cloth. The stranger told the man it made coffee so much better, so I tried it this morning."

"It does make a wonderful difference, so much better than just boiling the beans in the water. I hope we have plenty of patches of cloth."

"We do, Mr. Daniel, and I can wash 'em and use 'em more than once."

"I'll try a cup of coffee with my breakfast this morning instead of my usual tea. I tasted Daniel's, and it was exceptionally good."

While they were having breakfast, Jetty came to see if they needed anything else.

"Nothing more; breakfast was very good. I really liked the coffee. Let's have it today with our dinner. I'd like the others to taste it. Jetty, you're known for our bread that's like Dolly's. Now you'll be known for your coffee."

Jetty gave out a good laugh and rolled her eyes.

"I'm glad I'm known for something good."

When Sarah, Beau, and Daniel returned from church, they could smell dinner cooking all the way out in the yard. Ollie had already returned from his church and was waiting to take their wagon to the barn.

As Sarah walked through the back door, she asked, "What is that cooking? It smells especially good."

"It's a great big pot roast in our biggest iron pot with a lid on it. I have it simmering in a little water and its own juices. I put carrots, sliced white potatoes, and some sliced onions in the pot to simmer with it. I put some of your dried herbs in, too."

"That's what smells so good. Those onions and herbs really add to the pot."

"I'm boiling some green pole beans in a pot with a bit of salt pork."

Jetty stopped to stir the beans.

121

"I think it's that beef and onions you smell, though. Mr. James told Ollie that he bartered with Mr. Hill for this beef. That pot roast is as big as a great big paper hornet's nest."

Jetty held up her hands to show how big.

"There's no bone in it either. It's all beef. Mr. James told Ollie to come get it at the spring house when we needed it. That's what I started cooking very early this morning."

"I'm glad I asked Mr. James to join us since he's furnished the dinner. They'll be here soon. They weren't far behind us."

Just as Sarah said this, a knock came on the door.

"I'll get it Jetty. Go on with your work."

It was James, Lucy, Anna, and Eli at the door.

"Goodness, gracious, that food does smell good."

"Doesn't it? Jetty tells me it's that pot roast, onions, and herbs cooking together. Aren't you glad I invited you to come?"

They all agreed, and Sarah led them into the parlor.

"Have a seat. Everyone should be here before long."

"You bet I'm glad you asked us, and so is Lucy."

James smiled.

"I went to get my banjo before we came. I thought Daniel and I might try playing some with Miss Purdy. It would be interesting to add a piano into the mix and see how it sounds."

"Aunt Sarah, I can't wait to hear your piano. I was so excited when you came to tell us about it. Mama and papa have talked it over and said you can give me the piano lessons since I can take them at the school. I'm so excited."

"I'm excited too, Anna. That's why I wanted you to be here the first time Miss Purdy plays it."

Eli spoke up, "Papa said it might work out if Anna learns to play the piano and I learn the banjo. Then we can play together."

"Well, that would be fun. That's why I'll take lessons. I hope Daniel and I can play together."

122

Sarah looked over at James.

"I hope Tom thinks to bring his fiddle. I didn't mention it to him."

"He'll probably think of it. He loves to play. I wonder where Daniel is?" James questioned.

"I imagine he's out talking to Ollie. Go tell him he has company. He better wash up as more company'll be here at any time."

James got up to go look for Daniel. He stopped in the kitchen to tell Jetty how good the food smelled. As he stepped out the back door, he could see Ollie and Daniel standing in the garden talking.

Daniel saw James and remarked, "I didn't know you were here."

"Sarah says to wash up. The rest of your company should be here soon."

Tom and his children were coming in the front door as Daniel and James were going in the back. They met in the entry hall. When Eli and Anna heard, Aaron, Amy, and Rachel, they went to meet them.

Amy said to Anna, "I didn't realize you were going to be here."

"Yes, Aunt Sarah wanted me to hear Miss Purdy play her piano. I'm very excited as I'm going to take lessons."

"My papa says that if Rachel and I want to take lessons, we can. I think it'd be fun."

Aaron went in the parlor with the adults. Eli asked Rachel Holder if she'd like to go out on the front porch and swing. They could see Susan and Noah coming up the road. Eli jumped up to go tell Aunt Sarah they were coming.

"Aunt Sarah, there's a lady with Susan and Noah."

"I'm sure it's Miss Purdy. I'll go tell Jetty everyone's arriving. Would you invite them in when they get here, Eli?"

"Yes ma'am, I will."

Eli opened the front door.

"Aunt Sarah says come on in."

123

Susan stepped in the door, and as she did, Sarah came through the dining room.

"Do come on in. We're sitting in the parlor."

The men all rose as Susan and Miss Purdy entered the room. Aaron stepped back behind one of the settees. Daniel went to get a couple of chairs out of his study. When Aaron saw Daniel trying to carry two chairs, he quickly went to help. Daniel sat down on one chair and Aaron on the other.

"Did you have a good visit with Dr. Wade at the store opening?"

"Yes sir, I did. I've gone to see him in his office a couple of times since then. He's a very nice man. His office is very interesting, too. We've gone over some of his charts, and I've looked at a lot of his medical tools. He also has some books he's lending me to read."

"Do you still think you'll want to be a doctor?"

"More than ever. We've scheduled for me to start going into the office three afternoons a week to observe his work on some patients. If someone comes in who needs stitches, I might watch that. It's according to the patient and the injury what I'll get to watch. I think after I do that for awhile, I'll have a definite answer if that's what I'd like to do with the rest of my life."

"That makes a lot of sense. I'm glad you're getting this chance, Aaron."

"It's thanks to you and Dr. Wade, Mr. Borden. I do appreciate what you've done for me."

"I have every confidence you'll make the right decision, whatever it is."

The others were talking and laughing when Remy came in to announce that dinner was ready and on the tables.

Sarah told everyone, "We've put the young people at the kitchen table and the others in the dining. Note--I didn't call anyone older people."

Everyone laughed at Sarah's little joke.

When the adults gathered in the dining room, Sarah said, "Daniel, if you'll sit there at the head of the table, then

James can sit on your right and Lucy on your left. Susan, please sit next to James and Tom next to Susan. Noah you take the chair next to Lucy and then, Priscilla, if you'll sit next to Noah, please."

Everyone seemed comfortable with this arrangement. Sarah observed she was right. This made for a good conversation pattern. She hadn't wanted to put Tom and Priscilla sitting next to each other. She didn't want it to appear as though she was match-making. Dorcus had been gone such a short time.

Jetty had sliced the very large pot roast before she brought it to the table. It was setting in front of Daniel.

He stood to ask the blessing and then said, "The roast platter is heavy. I won't try to pass it. Sarah, if you'll pass your plate up the line, I'll serve you a slice. Then Tom your plate, please, and so on."

Everyone was saying how delicious the food was. The bread and the meat were especially being raved about. When everyone had their fill, Jetty cleared their empty plates. Then she brought out a tray of small bowls filled with strawberry cobbler with toasted nuts on top. The *ah's* sounded around the table as everyone was served.

She brought in cups and poured everyone a cup of coffee. She had cream and honey for the coffee. Everyone wanted to know the secret of Jetty's coffee when they tasted it. Sarah called Jetty in to tell them the story.

Sarah could hear the young people talking and laughing in the kitchen. She could tell they were enjoying their meal, too. When everyone had finished eating, Sarah suggested they all walk to the school and enjoy some music. Everyone stuck their head in the kitchen and complimented Jetty on the meal. Her face lit up with the recognition.

Sarah slipped back to the bedroom and asked Remy to bring Beau down to the school later. The group would walk on ahead. Everyone had gathered in the entry hall. Daniel hurried to get his guitar. Tom and James went to their carriages and got their instruments.

125

The children and the ladies stepped out on the porch. In their excitement, the children decided to start on to the school. Sarah noticed that Aaron and Anna were walking next to each other and were having a nice conversation.

When everyone got to the school, Daniel unlocked the doors and propped them open. He opened a few windows, also. Priscilla walked over to the new piano and ran her hand caressingly over the keys. The bench Daniel and Sarah had been sitting on was still in place.

Priscilla turned to Sarah and said, "May I play?"

"That is what we're all breathlessly waiting on. Please do!"

She spread and smoothed her skirt and petticoats beneath her as she took her seat on the bench. She held her hands over the keys and bent and flexed her fingers a couple of times as to loosen them. Everyone made sure that Sarah and Daniel were up close to see and hear her strike the first notes. She started with the old tune, *Evening Star Waltz*.

Sarah smiled and squeezed Daniel's arm. He was watching Priscilla's fingers fly across the key board. It intrigued him, the sound of the piano and the ease with which she played it. Next she played *Irish Washerwoman,* followed by *Pop Goes the Weasel*. She played a polka and another waltz.

She stopped playing and said, "Gentleman, have I played anything that you could join me in?"

Tom spoke up, "Let's try *Irish Washerwoman.* I recognize it. Daniel and James can listen to any of them and play with you. It may take me a little longer. I'm not quite as accomplished as they are."

Sarah stepped back while the three men all got their instruments, and Priscilla gave them a note to be sure all were tuned.

"On the count of three, gentlemen. One, two, three—"

They all started to play. Sarah was amazed at what the piano added to the stringed ensemble.

When they finished the song, everyone clapped, even the children.

"That sounded so good. It is unbelievable for your first time to play together."

Priscilla turned and smiled at Tom.

"You did very well. You *have* to know *Pop Goes the Weasel.* Let's give that a try. One, two, three—"

Tom played that with even more self-assurance.

"You know, I'm beginning to like this piano."

Everyone laughed.

Jetty and Ollie came in with large jugs of cool cider, fruit punch, and a plate piled up high with tea cakes. That was an instant hit. When everyone was through eating, Daniel suggested that James take his guitar and they play *Evening Star Waltz* again.

"I'm going to dance with my wife this time. We haven't danced since before she was expecting Beau. You're all good friends and family and if Sarah is up to it I'm asking for this dance."

Sarah tried to look coy.

"I accept, kind sir."

Everyone backed up and gave room for them to dance. Priscilla gave the count and the waltz began. Daniel and Sarah danced beautifully together. While they were dancing, Daniel whispered in Sarah's ear.

"I'm going to ask Anna to do the jig with me."

He twirled Sarah around the floor, and she was back to her graceful self once more. When they finished, everyone clapped.

Daniel turned and said, "The Irish jig, again, please," and he walked and bowed to Anna. "May, I have this dance, pretty lady?"

Anna glowed as she gave Daniel her hand. Once more Priscilla gave the count. Daniel didn't have to guide Anna. She was a natural on the dance floor. She was not as good as Sarah but she was getting closer. Aaron Holder was taking this all in. Daniel bowed and thanked Anna. She was floating when she walked off the floor.

Priscilla played two more songs alone, and everyone decided they should be going.

People started to pick up the jugs and Ollie said, "I brought it all down in the small cart, so I can get it back."

Daniel said, "Let me pull Beau home in the cart and see what he thinks. I hadn't thought of that before. He's going to be too large for that basket soon."

The ladies picked up the jugs, glasses, and the leftover plate of cookies to carry to the house. James took his banjo and Daniel's guitar. Sarah closed and locked the school. Everyone waited for her to walk back to the house.

As they were going up the road, Aaron walked with Anna again.

Eli loudly teased Aaron by saying, "Aaron's got a girlfriend."

It embarrassed Aaron and he answered, "Ah, she's too young for me."

That somewhat embarrassed Anna. She looked down, and then turned to talk to Amy. She never gave Aaron another look. Sarah noticed the whole episode and thought, *Young love can be so difficult.*

Before she said goodbye, Priscilla asked Sarah, "When shall we start our piano lessons?"

"I'm free tomorrow afternoon if you are. Shall I ask Anna to come to?"

"That will be fine. I'll speak to Mr. Holder about his daughters. I can well teach four in an afternoon. Now you all will have to plan your own practice time."

"We'll work something out."

"Susan, if you and Noah will wait a moment, I need to speak to Mr. Holder."

Priscilla walked over to Tom saying, "Sarah and Anna are going to start their music lessons about one tomorrow afternoon. I should be through with them by half passed two. If your girls would like to come, I would love to teach them. I think lessons for the four of them will be on Monday and Thursday afternoons. They'll have to work out their practice times."

"I think my girls would like to give it a try. I'll have them here tomorrow. If they are any good and like it, I'll buy them a piano to practice on at home. I realize it takes a lot of practice to become good."

"You're right Mr. Holder. I'll expect the girls tomorrow then. It's been nice getting to play with you this afternoon. You're a much better musician than you take credit for."

"Well, thank you, Miss Purdy, and I enjoyed hearing you play the piano very much."

Priscilla smiled, nodded and walked away.

The next afternoon, Sarah and Anna took their first piano lesson. Sarah was first and Anna stood and watched. Priscilla showed the key called the *middle C* and how to place your hands on the keyboard. Then she demonstrated how to hold your hands and run your fingers on the keys to play the *C* scale. Then Priscilla had Sarah cross her right thumb under her hand and continue on down the scale. She explained this was called *playing a scale*.

She also explained an octave. Sarah repeated the move until she was doing it smoothly. Next she did the same move but with her left hand. Priscilla told her that when she practiced, she must do this move over and over. She continued showing her the different scales. Practice all of them a lot.

Priscilla had brought some printed pages of parchment paper and continued explaining how to read the notes on a sheet of music. She taught her student first to read the right hand notes and then the left. Before Sarah finished her lesson, Priscilla had her playing a very short and very simple tune. This was always encouraging to a new student.

When it was Anna's turn at the piano, she repeated the same procedure while Sarah watched.

"I consider you both had a very good first lesson. Practice what you have learned as often as you can before our next lesson on Thursday. If you can do this smoothly and easily, we will proceed then with our next step on Thursday. Do you have any questions?"

"I do have a key to the school door for each of you. I won't have to worry about being here for everyone's lessons, and Anna can get in to practice when she has the time."

Anna felt very grownup knowing her Aunt Sarah trusted her with her own key.

"Anna and I'll be on our way now, so your next music students won't be distracted by us. We'll see you on Thursday at one o'clock."

As they walked up the road, Sarah could tell that Anna was very excited about their first lesson.

"Aunt Sarah, remember I have summer classes on Thursday. May I bring my lunch and just stay at the school for my lesson?"

"No, Anna, you'll come to our house with Mary on Thursdays and have dinner with us. Then we'll come back together for our lesson."

This pleased Anna very much.

"Anna, yesterday I couldn't help but hear Eli teasing Aaron Holder about you. I also heard what Aaron said. Secretly I think he really likes you. He was just embarrassed with being teased. My advice to you is more or less to ignore him until he tries to get back in your good graces."

Anna looked up and smiled, "You think he really likes me?"

"I'm pretty sure he does. I can tell by the way he looks at you. He was certainly watching you dance with your Uncle Daniel yesterday. I could almost see his brain turning and wondering if he'd ever be able to keep up with you on the dance floor."

Anna laughed and said, "I'm going to practice more with Uncle Daniel and you then, and that will surely give Mr. Aaron Holder something to think about."

Before Sarah got to the house, she saw Tom Holder drive up to the school with his two daughters. They would take their lessons next. Tom let them out and drove up the road toward the factory. Sarah knew he was going to visit with Daniel and the other men while the girls took their lessons.

Sarah could hardly wait for Daniel to come from the factory that afternoon.

As soon as he walked in the door Sarah asked, "Could we go back to the school, and let me show you what I learned today?"

Daniel kissed her on the cheek.

"Let me see Beau for a few minutes and then we can go."

"Let's take Remy and Beau with us. You can be the lucky one to carry the heavy little chunk down the road."

Daniel laughed, "Let me go get them, and we'll go."

While they were walking down the road, Daniel and Beau were cooing to each other. Beau jabbered at his papa, and Daniel answered. Beau would laugh like he understood everything Daniel was saying.

"He thinks I'm funny."

"Well, you are," Sarah replied.

She opened the school and spread a quilt out on the floor for Remy and Beau. She had carried a wooden rattle for him to shake and a few other little things to entertain the baby.

"Daniel, come and sit on the stool beside me. I'll show you what I learned today, and then you can practice with your fingers."

Sarah demonstrated, and then she watched Daniel move his fingers along the keys. He caught on very quickly. After he had run the scale several times, she took the little sheet of parchment Priscilla had made for her and placed it on the music holder. Sarah played the little song for Daniel. And he could tell Sarah was very proud. He kissed her on the cheek.

"That was very good. I'm so proud of you. Now, Sarah, I'm going to cheat, and this is why. I've heard the tune and watched you play it, and I don't need to read the music. It's stuck in my head now."

Daniel proceeded to play the tune with no problem. Sarah looked at him in amazement.

"Don't let it discourage you. As you practice and learn more, you'll get to where you don't need the music either. Let's practice some more."

Daniel didn't say a word, but he felt like he was catching on to this instrument, and it was simple. He wasn't about to discourage Sarah by letting her know he thought this. He knew he had a special gift with music.

When he was young, he thought everyone played like he and some of his brothers did. He thought the part of his family who didn't play, just didn't want to. As he got older, he began to realize not everyone heard the musical notes like he did.

Sarah loved music, and he knew she had the rhythm and timing by just dancing with her. It would be easier for her to learn than most people.

He felt Anna had this talent, if not more. Anna had never been interested in playing until she saw the picture of that piano. It would be interesting if she not only learned to read music, but if she was sensitive to the sound of each note, and they stuck in her brain as she heard them. Reading the notes and also having the talent to just feel which note to play would be truly wonderful.

Beau began to fret. He had been such a good boy. Sarah knew they needed to go. They gathered their things, and Daniel scooped up Beau. Sarah closed and locked the school, and they started to the house.

Walking up the road, Daniel started thinking he would slip back to the school tomorrow after Mary had closed it for the day. He wanted to just sit and see what he could do with the piano now that he knew where to place his fingers and work them. It would be his secret for awhile until Sarah began to get more confidence in her playing.

Sarah, Daniel, and Mary had dinner together as usual, and then Daniel went back to the factory. He looked at his watch waiting until almost three o'clock. This would be a good time to go to the school house and play the piano.

Being deceitful didn't come easy for him, but he decided to cut through the woods instead of walking on the road. He made it to the school unseen and unlocked it.

Then he raised the windows on the side away from the big house but left the doors closed. He sat down at the piano and stretched his fingers as he had seen Priscilla do. With his fingers on the keyboard, he ran the scales a few times to loosen up and remember the sound.

He played the little song Sarah had played for him the day before. Then he improvised some on it and embellished it. He thought that sounded pretty good. Then he tried *Rock-A-Bye-Baby* which was a simple tune. He was doing pretty well so far. He closed his eyes and remembered Priscilla's *Pop Goes the Weasel*. Then he started and was playing the little songs all over again.

The school door opened. He turned and there stood Anna.

"Uncle Daniel, I could hear music and thought perhaps it was Miss Priscilla playing. I didn't know you could play so well."

Daniel looked sheepish.

"I didn't know either. That's why I came down here alone. I wanted to try, but I didn't want to discourage Sarah by it coming so easily for me. Now you've caught me. Will you promise not to tell a soul for awhile until Sarah gets better?"

Anna thought before she answered, "I won't tell, but while you're here can we try together? I didn't say anything to Miss Purdy or Aunt Sarah yesterday, but I felt like I could take that tune we learned and play it right back without the music. I came to try that today. Would you play a tune while I listen and watch? I'll try to play that tune back to you."

"Okay, let's give it a try."

Daniel played *Pop Goes the Weasel* again. Anna played it back with only a mistake or two.

"Anna, I believe you have the gift. It's just never been developed."

Anna was puzzled.

"What gift, Uncle Daniel?"

"The gift of playing music by ear. You can play without ever seeing a note of music. Listening will be enough, and then you can play it if you learn how an instrument functions. I want you to learn to read music, too, while you have the chance. You pay attention to Miss Purdy and learn how to read music."

"I will. I want to learn everything about it I can."

"While you're here practicing, I don't think it will hurt for you to think of hymns or songs you know, and then try to play them. I'm sure there are more scales to learn and correct ways to use different fingers on the different keys. That's what I need to learn, too. I'll let your Aunt Sarah teach me that as she learns."

"I'm glad you were here and we got to talk. I understand things better now and what's going on in my head," said Anna.

"I better get going. You stay and practice as long as you like. Just get home before dark and close the windows and lock the door. Remember this is our secret for awhile."

"I have some other things I want to talk to you about. Aunt Sarah and I've talked but I'd like your help, too. That can wait, and we'll talk later."

"You've got it. I'll see you later."

Daniel slipped out and returned to the factory through the woods. Nobody was the wiser but him and Anna.

When Daniel came in from the factory later that afternoon, Sarah was sitting in the parlor with Rice.

"Hello, Uncle Daniel, I've come to say goodbye for a while. I'll be leaving for *William and Mary* on Wednesday. I wanted to thank Aunt Sarah for all she's done for me. I've learned so much at her school and John P. has taught me a lot about being a lawyer."

"Rice, we'll miss you around here, but then you'll be home every once in awhile, won't you?"

"Oh yes, you'll see me around. I'll study for two years and then John P. has asked me to take a permanent position in his office. This will always be home."

Rice stood and hugged his Uncle Daniel, and as Sarah stood, he hugged her.

"I better get going. Mama and Alma'll have supper ready soon. You two take care, and take very good care of Beau."

"Drop me a note, Rice, when you get settled, and let us know how it is up there."

"I'll do that, Aunt Sarah, and I'll see you soon."

He turned and walked out the door.

"What a fine young man. Lucy and George can be very proud of him."

"Sarah, you've touched his life in a very positive way. He'll never forget it."

Thursday afternoon had come, and Sarah and Anna had a good piano lesson again. Sarah could tell that it was coming easier for Anna than it was for her. Anna just seemed to have a natural touch or something. Perhaps Anna was practicing a little more than she was or perhaps it was the difference in their ages.

While they were walking up the road, Sarah saw Tom come and let his girls out and he continued on to the factory. She wondered how the Holder girls were doing. Tom had brought the girls out to the school a couple of times to practice.

He came to the house to get the keys when they wanted to practice. Daniel suggested they hide a key down there for Tom, so he could get into the school when they wanted. They decided that a hidden key would work a lot better.

Sarah noticed on Monday after their lesson that when Tom brought the girls he went in with them. Sarah took Beau out to sit and swing him on the front porch. It was so nice out. While they were swinging, Tom came out in about thirty minutes and went to the factory.

After that, Sarah got a little curious on lesson days. It seemed Tom was going in with the girls now and was staying a little longer each time. Sarah decided it was time to plan another meal for Tom's family.

She asked Susan and Noah to have them bring Priscilla. Sarah issued the invitations for the next Saturday afternoon after the store closed. Tom told her that his girls had other plans, so it would be just him and Aaron for the evening.

Sarah planned the supper and asked Jetty to roast two hens on the spit in the fireplace. She wanted baked apples with honey and cinnamon like Dolly had fixed. They decided steamed asparagus with melted butter over it would be good.

Jetty was busy in the kitchen all afternoon. She was singing while she cooked, so Sarah knew she was happy that they were having guests. Jetty certainly liked to show off her cooking.

Sarah checked the table to make sure it was set to her satisfaction. She decided that she and Daniel would sit at the heads of the table. But she had an odd number of people this time. She would put Aaron on her left and Susan between him and Noah. She would put Priscilla on her right and Tom beside Priscilla this time.

Everything was ready, and Daniel and Sarah were sitting in the parlor. Tom and Aaron arrived first and

Daniel asked them in. The talk moved to the piano lessons and music. All of sudden Aaron spoke up.

"Mr. Borden, I noticed how well you and Miss Sarah dance. Then you and Anna did that jig as well as anyone I've ever seen. I was wondering if you might have time to teach me?"

"Well, Aaron, Miss Sarah is one of the best lady dancers I know. She could teach you to lead much better than I could. I can help, but she's the one to teach you."

"Aaron, I'd be delighted to teach you to dance. Could you come out to the school on Saturday's or a few evenings? If your father could come, perhaps he and Daniel could play for us."

Tom mused, "Well, I can come. I just didn't know Aaron wanted to learn to dance. There must be a girl involved."

"Papa, I just thought I'd like to know when I go off to school."

"Oh, I see. I guess that *would* be a good thing to know."

"Why don't you two come out tomorrow afternoon, and we'll have our first lesson?"

Aaron answered right away, "We'll be here around two."

Tom laughed, "Maybe I'll take a lesson while we're at it. I could stand it."

There was a knock on the door. Noah, Susan, and Priscilla had arrived for supper. While they were sitting in the parlor, something was said about dancing lessons tomorrow afternoon at the school.

Priscilla asked out of the blue, "Do you need a pianist, if I'm not barging in?"

"That would be wonderful. We're meeting at two."

Nothing more was said about the lessons.

At supper Sarah told Aaron, "The school term starts two weeks from Monday. We have several new students who've already enrolled."

"Is there anyone new who's my age?"

137

"Let's see, I have Garrett Adler coming. He's fourteen. Then there's Payton Dunbar. He's twelve. There's a young lady, Mercy Estep, who's thirteen. The other two are younger. Silas Hayes is eight, and Jane Keaton is seven. Eli'll be glad of that."

Tom spoke up, "Garrett Adler? His father is the silversmith. I know them. Payton Dunbar's father is the tailor. I've dealt with him. They're all nice people."

Sarah noticed that Priscilla and Tom were finding more to talk about this time. Priscilla knew Tom's girls better now that she had given them piano lessons.

Priscilla asked Aaron about assisting Dr. Wade. He was enjoying telling her about some of the things that happened in the office without mentioning any names. He had her laughing at his tales.

The evening was very pleasant. This group of people was very congenial and seemed to like each other. That was plain to see.

As they were leaving, Priscilla said, "I'll see you at two tomorrow."

Sunday afternoon Sarah put on a good skirt and shoes for dancing. She really was looking forward to the afternoon. It would be good music, and Aaron was a cute young man. Sarah would enjoy helping him learn to dance.

She remembered back to the afternoon Anna and Daniel did the jig. Aaron watched Anna's every move. If he wanted to learn to dance for a girl, it must be for Anna. She was sure of that.

When Sarah and Daniel stepped out on the road, she could see Priscilla's small carriage already at the school. She had her key and was probably already playing the piano. Beau was napping when they left, so Remy was to put him in a special little cart Daniel had made for him and pull him down to the school when he woke.

Priscilla played, and she watched Daniel and Sarah dance to a couple of songs. They were in the midst of their dancing when Tom and Aaron arrived. Tom had brought his fiddle, and he tuned it to the notes Priscilla played on the piano for him.

Tom had a bit of news to tell.

"I heard the Creel's had a baby girl yesterday. Molly and the baby are doing fine."

"Do you know what they named her?" Priscilla asked.

"It was something common yet unusual for a name. Let me think." He hesitated and then said, "Sage-yes, that's it."

"That *is* unusual. I like it though."

Sarah turned her attention back to the music and suggested that she and Aaron start out with a waltz to warm up. She showed Aaron how to hold her and the posture he should take. They went over the steps slowly a few times for him to get accustomed to the dance pattern.

"Now with music, please."

The music makers all joined in, and Sarah and Aaron began to glide over the floor. In a minute he stepped on her toe.

"Oh, Oh, I'm sorry, Miss Sarah."

"Never mind Aaron, they've been stepped on before."

"Not by me, Aaron," Daniel teased. "I've never stepped on her toes."

"Okay, here we go again."

Sarah nodded her head. The music started again. They made it through without another incidence. She then went over the moves in a jig.

"Daniel, would you come demonstrate a few moves?"

Daniel came and showed Aaron the proper way to hold her for a jig. The music started and Daniel and Sarah were showing how it was done.

"It's your turn, Aaron."

He placed his hands on Sarah and took a deep breath. The music started, and Aaron almost tripped.

"Just relax Aaron. You're too rigid. Smile and have fun when doing a jig."

She turned to Daniel and said, "Come back, Daniel, and let him watch you again."

Aaron watched and then asked Sarah, "Do I ever have any hope of being even nearly as good as he is?"

"It'll take more practice," and then she added laughingly, "you may come close."

Tom laid down his fiddle.

"Okay, time for part of my lesson. Give us the jig."

As the music played, Tom was laughing.

When they finished, Tom said, "Okay, I wasn't too rigid. What do I need to do to improve?"

Sarah looked at Daniel and asked, "What do you think? I'm at a loss."

"Priscilla, you come try with him, and let us critique you."

Priscilla looked a little embarrassed.

"I'm not a great dancer, and the jig is not my best."

Daniel chuckle, "You'll look good dancing with Tom."

Daniel played a jig and Priscilla and Tom didn't do badly.

"You two looked pretty good together. Priscilla, perhaps you should try with Aaron, and let's see what happens."

Tom came back and picked up his fiddle. Aaron looked more relaxed with Priscilla. They twirled and danced around, and Priscilla was laughing. When the song was finished, Priscilla could hardly catch her breath.

"I haven't danced in so long, I'm out of shape."

"Here, Aaron, try with me again. You looked pretty good with Priscilla. Now relax and have fun with me."

Priscilla took her seat at the piano again. The jig started, and Aaron had improved. He was enjoying it now.

Tom looked at Priscilla.

"Miss Purdy, may I have this next waltz?"

Priscilla rose from the bench and went to the center of the floor and curtsied to Tom.

Daniel started a very nice waltz on his guitar, and Tom and Priscilla glided across the floor.

"Mr. Holder, you certainly don't need any lessons for the waltz. Thank you. That was a lovely dance. Now Aaron, let's see if you can do as well as you father."

Aaron took the proper stance and looked very nice twirling Miss Purdy around the floor.

"This tells me you Holder men are meant for waltzing," Priscilla smiled.

Aaron improved greatly by the end of the afternoon, and they all had so much fun.

"I have one more surprise. Daniel took his seat at the piano. Name a song you've played this afternoon, Priscilla."

She named a waltz, and Daniel began to play unbelievably well. When he finished he stood and took a bow.

"How and when did you learn to do that?"

"I have a confession, Sarah. I've slipped down here a few times and practiced. Anna helped me a couple of times. It's been mine and Anna's secret."

"Oh, Daniel, I'm so proud."

"You don't mind, Sarah? It has come so easy for me."

"I'll just have to work all that much harder to ever come close, but that's all right. I know you have the gift."

"Speaking of the gift, I'll tell the rest of the secret. Anna's found out she has the gift, too. We both made a promise. She wouldn't tell I could play the piano, and I wouldn't tell that she's been holding out on you ladies. I suggested she learn to read notes as well. Think what she'll have if she can read notes and also know it naturally by listening."

"Daniel, you're right, but Sarah and I'll want to turn her loose now to be free to use her God-given talent. Sarah doesn't have the gift, but she is doing beautifully well and

141

learning quickly. Sarah has the love," Miss Purdy commented.

Tom thanked them all when he and Aaron started to leave.

"I've had such a good time with you folks, and I can tell Aaron has, too. You're all good for us."

"Well, we'll have another party here at the school soon. Aaron I'll expect to be asked to dance again then."

Chapter Six

The fall term of school was in full swing now. The new students had learned the routine and knew each other. It was the middle of the morning and time for their recess. Eli and Rachel were enjoying having a few students their age this term.

They were playing shadow tag. Some of the older students were standing around talking. Garrett Alder was standing near Anna. It seemed he had taken a fancy to Anna ever since he saw her.

He reached in his pocket and pulled out a small box and handed it to Anna. She opened the box and inside was a small silver cross.

"This is beautiful."

"I'm glad you like it. It's a gift for you. I told my father that I wanted it for a special friend."

Anna handed it back to him.

"I'm your friend, Garrett, but I can't be your *special* friend."

"Why not, Anna?"

All she could think of to say was, "You're too old for me."

Garrett instantly said, "No way. I'm not too old for you."

Aaron had been listening to what was being said, and he knew Anna was at a loss.

He stepped forward and said, "It's because she's *my* special friend."

"She can't be because I've never even seen you talk to her."

"Well, you ask her and just see what she says."

Garrett turned to Anna, "Are you his special friend?"

Anna looked down at the ground and then she looked Garrett right in the eyes.

"Ah hmmm, yes, I am."

Aaron reached over and took Anna's hand.

"See, she is."

"I'm sorry, Anna, I hadn't realized it."

"Garrett, you might have a better look at Emma Stewart. She's a very pretty girl."

"Not as pretty as you."

Garrett walked off.

"He's right, Anna. Emma is not as pretty as you. She *is* nice though."

"I'm sorry, Aaron. I thank you for getting me out of a spot. Garrett's nice, but I didn't want to wear his cross."

"I'm glad you didn't want to wear it. Anna, I've wanted to tell you that I don't think you're too young for me. I just didn't want Eli teasing and embarrassing both of us that afternoon. Then you got mad at me, and I didn't know what to say after that."

"I wasn't mad. I just didn't want to bother you."

"Could we be friends again?"

"Aaron, I'll always be your friend."

"Well, I guess I'm asking for a little more than just a plain friend. You know I'm going off to school in about a year. We're both young and shouldn't be too serious, but it'd be nice to know that you'd be here to dance with me when I come home on holidays and breaks."

Anna thought for a minute.

"I'll be here. You know, I want to go off to school, too. Aunt Sarah says I'd be a natural teacher, so I want to get more education."

144

"Wouldn't it be something if you ended up here as a teacher and me as a doctor? Of course, if you find someone special while you're at school, I'd understand. Do you mind if I ask occasionally, so I'll know where I might stand?"

"You can ask, Aaron, as I'll be wondering about you, too."

It was time to go in. Aaron hadn't noticed that he had been holding Anna's hand all the time they'd been talking.

The piano lessons were continuing, and now Daniel could play anything that he could hum. Sarah had progressed into more difficult pieces and was readily reading music. She was playing a lot of the pieces by memory, as she had practiced them so much. However, Sarah could not hold a candle to Anna's playing.

Anna could read music quite well, and she had the gift of playing by ear. Anna would now sing along while playing and she had a beautiful voice. Sarah had a very pleasant voice, but it didn't have the strong, clear tones of Anna's.

Lucy and James were so thankful that Sarah had insisted on giving Anna piano lessons or they may never have discovered Anna's talents.

The Borden's along with the Holder's and Creel's had gone in together and bought a piano for their church. Anna was playing it every Sunday for the congregation. Sometimes Sarah would play a special hymn and let Anna sing a solo, and the pair soon became a welcome addition to the Sunday service.

It was the beginning of December and they were occasionally feeling the blast of cold winds. School was going smoothly this term. Priscilla Purdy had a few new piano students taking lessons at the school. Her

145

arrangement of teaching piano at the school was working out nicely for all of them.

Sarah spoke to Daniel about having another party. They both decided it was time to plan one for family and a few friends and to have it at the school. Sarah involved Mary with the plans. Of course, Mary was glad to help as the thought of a party excited her.

Also, Sarah discussed it with Jetty and Remy since they'd be in charge of making the food. Sarah and Mary started making out a guest list. They wrote simple invitations on parchment, and Daniel helped deliver them.

Mary decided they should decorate the school with greenery, a few colorful ribbons, and fruit.

"Let's make this party festive."

Sarah agreed, so the morning of the party both Daniel and John 'volunteered' to help decorate. However, they found it to be pleasant volunteering with a lot of laughs.

The evergreens they used brought a cheery aroma to the indoors. Hanging from a ribbon that was attached to a rafter, they positioned a discreet mistletoe ball in front of the piano. One would have to look up to notice it.

"This should create a little fun before the evening ends," Daniel observed.

Jetty and Remy had made a good assortment of food. All the benches and tables at the school had been pushed backed for dancing; however, people could still sit down to rest. Everything was ready, and Daniel's whole household was at the school to serve and welcome the guests.

Family members, along with the Stewarts, began to arrive first. Tom Holder and his children arrived next followed by Dr. and Mrs. Wade. Susan and Noah, with Priscilla Purdy, were the next group to arrive. The Creels and Si and Rich with their families came. The Creel's baby girl, Sage, was growing so fast. She was a very pretty baby.

After everyone had said "hello" and visited a short time, the music began.

Susan and Noah were the first out on the floor to dance. They were followed quickly by Clay and Eliza. Aaron Holder kept looking at Sarah. She looked straight at him and smiled.

Finally, when a waltz started, he came and asked Sarah to dance. She rose and they walked out onto the floor. The dance started and Aaron didn't make a bobble. Sarah was pleased and felt as though they looked pretty good.

"Shall we try a jig, Miss Sarah?"

"I'd love to, Aaron. The very first one they play."

"I'll stand by you so we'll be ready."

Daniel saw Sarah and Aaron still talking. He had seen them dance a waltz so he figured Aaron must be waiting on a jig.

"Priscilla, let's play the jig Aaron practiced the other day."

She shook her head in consent. Daniel wanted to cross his fingers for Aaron because he was hoping the boy would do a good job.

The music started. Sarah and Aaron took the floor. Their start was very good. Daniel was surprised. Aaron was actually smiling like he was having fun. Daniel couldn't tell what Sarah was saying, but he knew she must be saying words of encouragement.

The next jig, Clay went over and told Aaron, "I'll trade partners with you."

Aaron's eyes grew big, and Sarah gave him a slight push in the center of his back.

"Another jig, Priscilla," Daniel told her.

Priscilla smiled. Daniel and Tom both held their breath. Aaron gathered himself, smiled at Eliza, and away they went.

Tom exhaled, "My boy's growing up, Daniel, right before our eyes."

Daniel could tell Eliza was complimenting Aaron. *This is the confidence he needs*, Daniel was thinking. Tom and Daniel both cut their eyes at each other. They nodded and

147

grinned. Both were waiting to see if he had the courage now to ask Anna to dance.

Aaron walked Eliza back to Clay and thanked her. Then he walked right over to Anna and asked her to dance.

"I didn't know you could dance until now," Anna remarked to Aaron.

"I'm not very good, but I'm learning."

"I thought you looked very good, especially with Aunt Sarah."

Daniel said, "A waltz this time, Priscilla."

"Are you directing this dance, Daniel Borden?" Pricilla questioned.

"I'm only doing a young friend a favor. I think you can call your own songs from here on out, as I'm going to ask my wife to dance."

Priscilla just laughed.

After another three songs, Daniel came back to play and Tom laid his fiddle down. He went directly to Priscilla and asked her to dance.

Daniel said, "Hey, we lost two of our musicians when you two dance. I guess I'd better get Anna."

"Aaron, I'm going to take your partner away for a few dances as we need her to play the piano. You can go ask my partner to dance again if you like."

Both Anna and Aaron smiled.

"I'll see you in a few minutes," Aaron told Anna.

James was smiling when Daniel came back.

"I've never played music with Anna."

"Then you're about to have one of the thrills of your lifetime."

Lucy moved nearer to the piano so she could see James and Anna when they were playing.

Anna was good, and you could tell she was enjoying it. Aaron came to stand very near the piano while Anna was playing. He could see her fingers flying up and down the keyboard.

Tom and Priscilla were having a very good time dancing together. They were laughing and talking. Daniel was glad to see that. They looked good together on the dance floor.

When Priscilla started back to the piano, Anna got up from the bench, but was still standing at the piano to say something to Miss Purdy. She was waiting for Mr. Holder to finish what he was saying to her.

All of a sudden Aaron came close, and before Anna knew what had happened, he kissed her quickly right on the lips. Anna, along with other people, was taken by surprised. Anna turned not just red but maroon. Aaron grinned and pointed up to the mistletoe.

James laughed and looked at Aaron, "That was my daughter you kissed."

"I know, sir, but custom dictated that I must kiss her."

James reached over and pulled Anna from under the mistletoe and everybody laughed.

When the music started again, James danced with Lucy. Aaron was dancing with Anna again. As the song finished, George called out for a mixer. That meant to quickly change partners.

James grabbed Anna and left Aaron to dance with Lucy. Aaron didn't quite know about dancing with Anna's mother. Lucy soon put him at ease.

"You dance very well, Mr. Holder."

"Thank you, ma'am. I'll have to confess that Mr. Borden and Miss Sarah have worked with me."

"They've taught several in our family to dance. I think you danced with Clay's wife, Eliza."

"Yes, ma'am, they're both good dancers."

"Anna has mentioned you're planning to go off to school soon to study to become a doctor."

"Yes, that's my goal. I hope I can make the grades."

"From what I hear, you will. You know Anna wants to become a teacher like her Aunt Sarah, don't you?"

"Yes ma'am, she's told me. She'll be a very good one. Anna has a way with the younger ones."

The music ended, and Aaron returned Lucy to James and mannerly thanked her for the dance.

James told Lucy, "I think that young man is interested in our daughter."

"I think you're right. He has very good possibilities. He comes from a good family, and I think Anna is very interested in him right now. They're young, and Aaron has ambitions. He wants to become a doctor, and I understand Dr. Wade has taken a shine to him. You don't have to worry for awhile, James."

"I'm not worried. I know Anna has ambitions, too. I'm just watchful."

It was early March and the dogwood buds were swelling. Also, the redbud trees were showing the promise of a little color. Sarah suspected she was with child again. This time she told Daniel right away.

"When do you think we can expect it?"

"I think in October. That means school will be in session when the baby comes. We'll find Mary some help, and she can run the school. Perhaps by then Anna can assist her. It'd be good experience for Anna."

"Beau should be walking pretty well by then. That's when Remy will earn her keep. Are you sure enough this time that we can tell everyone now?"

"You may tell anyone you chose to tell. I'm sure this time."

Daniel got up and went right to the kitchen and told Jetty and Remy.

"We're having another baby this fall-sometime in October."

They both said, "Congratulations, Mr. Daniel. We can stand another Mr. Beau around this place. That is the sweetest child."

150

It was the middle of the week, and Sarah had just remarked to Mary that very morning how smoothly everything was going this year-no mice or grasshoppers.

"I don't know what we've done to have this good turn of events."

She had bragged too soon. It was recess time, and the whole class was outside getting fresh air and sunshine. The boys were full of energy and were running everywhere. As usual, the girls were clustered in a group talking and giggling. Nancy was teasing Rachel about her pigtail, and Eli came over to join in the teasing.

Suddenly, Garrett Adler looked up in the corner of the roof over the porch and spotted a wasp nest. What a surprise that was. He had not noticed it before, and he wondered why. There were several wasps flying up and around and landing on the nest. That nest had to come down!

Garrett called to some of the other boys to come over and see his find.

"Let's get some rocks and get that nest down from there." Garrett ordered, "You girls move out of the way, and let us get that nest down."

Emma Stewart urged him, "Leave it alone. You're going to get stung or one of us will."

Garrett, stubborn as usual, urged, "Get back because we're bringing it down."

The girls saw there was no reasoning with the boys who were all charged up to get the nest down, so they retreated out to the edge of the yard.

The boys searched around until each found at least one good rock to throw at the nest. They went to the porch and formed a semi-circle around the corner and peered up at it. They were sizing it up to see what was the best line of attack. Garrett decided he would fire his rock first so he stepped up and let it go.

It got close but didn't seem to disturb the wasps, so Aaron took his turn. His throw was better than Garrett's, and he hit it dead center. Wasps went everywhere. Boys went everywhere. Even the girls backed farther back lest they get stung. However, Aaron's rock did not knock the nest down. It only bruised it and made the wasps mad.

They called to the girls to keep their distant and to go to the back door.

Payton Dunbar was finding rocks for Aaron and Garrett. They were a little older and stronger and their aim was better. Sarah could hear rocks pelting the porch, and she stuck her head out the door.

"Look out, Miss Sarah-wasps!"

She immediately ducked back into the schoolroom to avoid getting stung. The boys decided it *must* come down now to save everyone, so they kept throwing. They repeatedly pelted the nest until it was on the porch, somehow avoiding the wasps' stingers. Satisfied that they had done their good deed for the day, they all went inside but the excitement hadn't died down.

"We got it down, Miss Sarah, so it'll be safe for you to go out later. Those wasps are mad right now."

Sarah shook her head.

"Thank you, boys, I'm glad it's down, but I'm amazed you weren't stung."

Studies continued on but Sarah noticed it was getting a little dark outside. She walked to the window to look.

"Class, I'm going to dismiss you early today. There's a dark cloud coming up, and I want you to make it home before this weather blows in. You may go, and I'll see you tomorrow."

Mary and Sarah were gathering some things to carry to the house with them in case the rain started, and they couldn't get back to the school. They could work at the dining table so that would be no problem. They barely made it to the house when the wind came up. Daniel had seen the cloud coming, and he, too, had come to the house early.

Jetty nearly had their meal ready when she heard Ollie come up on the back porch.

He opened the door, "It's getting dark out there. I'm expecting the rain to pour."

A bolt of lightning flashed, a few seconds passed, and then the boom of thunder. Remy had Beau and she came running to the kitchen.

"I don't like lightning, and I don't want to scare Mr. Beau."

Daniel heard what Remy said, and he went to get Beau. He didn't want Beau scared of a thunderstorm either. There was another bright flash and the boom came right away.

"That one struck nearby."

Then the flashes were closer together and the booms more deafening. Remy just sat down in the kitchen corner and hid her face. Daniel stepped to the kitchen door.

"Ollie, do you happen to know where the horses are? They were out in the pasture, but I saw Glory come up to the barn when the wind came up. I don't know if the others followed or not."

"Well, it's too bad to go out to see now."

The rain had begun to pour.

"I hope they had sense enough to get in the barn."

It took about forty minutes for the storm to blow through. By then, they had finished eating, and Remy had come out of the corner. Daniel was getting ready to go back to the factory.

When he got to the kitchen he asked, "Where's Ollie?"

"Soon as the storm let up, he went to check on the horses."

Daniel looked out the window, and he could see Ollie almost running toward the house. Daniel stepped out on the porch.

"Is there something wrong, Ollie?"

153

"Yes, sir, it's Bess. She's down. The lightning struck her. I checked, and I'm sure she's dead. She was at the back of the pasture and didn't make it to the barn."

Daniel felt like he'd just had a blow to his stomach. He was almost sick. He grabbed the railing and bent over it for a moment.

When he regained control, he asked, "You're sure she's dead?"

"I'm sure, Mr. Daniel. She's got burn marks down her neck and she's rigid. You stay here, Mr. Daniel. I'll go get help and take care of her. There's no need in you seeing her. Shall we bury her behind the pasture in the edge of the woods?"

"That'll be fine, Ollie. Pick an easy place to dig. It'll have to be a deep, big hole."

"Yes, sir. It's best you stay home for awhile."

Daniel turned and went back in the house. He entered the dining room where Mary and Sarah were working, and Sarah looked up.

"What in the world has happened? You look like you've seen a ghost."

"I feel sick. Ollie just came to tell me that the lightning got Bess. She's dead."

Sarah got up and went to him.

"Oh, I'm so sorry. Come, let's go to the parlor."

She put her arm around Daniel's waist and led him to a rocking chair. She knew rocking could be soothing.

"I'll get you a glass of water."

As Sarah went through the dining room, Mary whispered, "I'm going to take this stuff and finish it at home. Daniel needs you now."

Sarah got the water and went back to the parlor. Daniel was rocking and staring out in space. She handed him the water, and he took a few sips. She took a seat and thought she'd let him be quite for a few minutes and think this out.

Ollie got four shovels and started to the factory. He walked in the factory door and looked for Mr. Si.

154

"Ollie, what are you doing with four shovels?"

"I've come to ask for help. Mr. Daniel's horse, Bess, was struck by lightning in that storm that passed through. It killed her. She's lying out in the back of the pasture, and I need help burying her. Mr. Daniel's pretty shook up, and I don't want him helping."

"I'll get some of the strong, young men. That hole'll have to be pretty big and deep. You'll show them where she is and where to bury her, won't you?"

"Yes sir, I appreciate this."

Si came back with four young men.

"Ollie, you'd better get a couple of ropes to drag her to the grave."

"You're right, Mr. Si. I wasn't thinking."

After Daniel had sat for a few minutes, he looked up at Sarah.

"I know she was just a horse, but my father had given her to me when I turned sixteen. She was very special to me."

"I know she was."

"I don't want to carry on like she was human. I remember Tom losing Dorcus. That was terrible and this can't compare, but it does hurt."

"Daniel, you can love an animal. A relationship with them can be special, too. Bess was a friend even if she was a horse. She was a connection to your family back home, too. That makes it twice as hard to lose her."

"I guess I'll have to borrow Glory from you for awhile until I find another horse. I'm sure George will have one I can buy."

"Don't worry about that now. You can ride Glory. I don't think I'll be riding her for quite awhile."

When John P. came in from his office that afternoon, Mary told him about Bess.

"Daniel's taking it pretty hard."

"I think I'll go down and talk to George, and we'll see what we can come up with. I may stop by and tell James while I'm out."

"Good, I think his brothers need to know."

When John told George about Bess, George said, "That's too bad. Daniel's had that horse awhile. Our father got her for him. You know, I got a beauty of a horse about a month ago. She's a light, golden horse with a lighter mane and tail. She has a white blaze down her nose. She'd be a good horse for Daniel. The horse wasn't cheap, but I guess for Daniel I can afford it."

"Maybe we could all split up the price. I'm going by to talk to James."

"I think Susan and Noah will want to help, too. We'll all want to help. Just think what Daniel and Sarah have done for all of us."

"Can I have a look at the horse? I'd like to be able to describe what everybody's going in on."

"Sure, she's out in the barn now."

George pointed her out, when the two men got to the barn.

"Wow, she *is* a beauty. She's a little bigger than Bess was, but Daniel is bigger than he was when he was sixteen. She'll do Daniel real justice."

"She's a pleasure to ride. If she has to go, I'll be glad she'll be with Daniel. When should we take her to Daniel?"

"Let's give him a few days. He'll probably ride Glory for awhile. I think he might have trouble deciding to buy a horse right away."

John swatted at a pesky fly near his head and continued, "He'd come to you if he decided to buy one, anyway. If that happens, just give him the horse, and tell him she's from all of us. I hate to say this, but I think that horse needs a light tan saddle with some brass on it and maybe some on the tan bridle, too."

"You're designing what a horse should wear? Plus, wanting us all to chip in more money?"

"We can all afford it. I'll start shopping for the horse's outfit tomorrow," John laughed.

"Okay, go by and tell James and then tell Susan and Noah tomorrow. Let me know how much on the saddle and bridle, and we'll get all of this figured out and divided up."

John left and went right on to James' house and told James about Bess being killed. James instantly wanted to help with another horse. John told him about the horse George suggested for Daniel.

"She sounds good to me."

"I'm going to shop for a new saddle and bridle for her."

"Figure up what I'll owe and let me know."

When John drove by the furniture store the next day, he stopped and went in. He told Susan and Noah about Bess and asked them if they wanted to chip in. They were all for it.

John then went by Mr. Hines wagon yard. Mr. Hines not only dealt in wagons and carriages, but in tack for horses. John described the kind of saddle and bridle he was looking for.

"Let me show you what I have. I think it'll be what you're looking for."

He carried John back to his tack room. There was a rich, tan saddle with some brass inlay on the pommel. It had brass conchos on each side of the back housing with a matching concho at the top of the tie strap. John liked the idea that the saddle had a billet strap, too. The matching bridle had brass inlay on the brow band.

"This is what I was looking for. Make me a good deal, and I'll take it."

Mr. Hines hummed and hawed for a minute, and then he named a price. He wanted to sell it, but he wanted to squeeze every nickel he could get. John wanted to buy it, but he wanted to save every penny he could for the group.

"Shave the price a little more, and throw in that dark brown saddle blanket and it's sold."

Hines came back with a slightly lesser price than the first one he had set. Then he reached over on the shelf, and he laid the blanket on top of the saddle.

"That's the best I can do."

The standoff was over and John said, "You make a hard deal, but I'll take it."

Mr. Hines loaded it in John's carriage, and John left a happy man. He unlocked his office and carried in the bridle, saddle, and blanket. He decided to store them in a closet in his office for a few days.

The group made their plans. They'd all but Daniel and Sarah have Sunday dinner after church at George's house. Then they'd saddle up Daniel's new horse, and all would go to present the gifts to him. Clay and Eliza decided they wanted in on the gift, too.

When Sunday came, the whole Borden clan was at church. Daniel and Sarah didn't notice anything out of the ordinary.

After church, Daniel did hear Susan say to her mother, "We'll follow you home for dinner."

Daniel thought nothing about it, as Susan and Noah ate fairly regularly with Charity and George. They were almost like a parade going down the road after church, but that was usual, too.

John turned off at his house, as he came to his lane first. He wanted to give Daniel time to get home before he continued on down the road past Daniel's house to George's home.

By the time John turned around in his lane and returned to the main road, Daniel had turned down his road and pull to the back of his house. He helped Sarah and Beau out and then went on to his barn. John pulled back onto the road and proceeded to George's house.

Charity and Alma had a wonderful meal waiting for them. There was a touch of excitement knowing they had

158

all kept the secret, and they were pulling off their plans so cleverly.

James mentioned to Charity, "I feel sorry for Daniel and Sarah. They're missing out on your great meal."

This struck them all as being funny.

George asked, "Did you notice Daniel never mentioned a thing to any of us about Bess. I think he's still grieving about her."

"When he gets his gift, maybe that'll lift his spirits. Wait until you see the saddle and bridle on that horse. George, have you named her yet?"

"If I was keeping her, I'd named her, but now I'll let Daniel have the honor."

When the meal was finished, the ladies helped Charity clean the table while the men went out and saddled the horse.

John suggested, "Tie her behind your wagon, George, and you be our spokesman."

Everyone was ready. George with Charity, Clay, and Eliza led the way in his wagon. The others fell in line.

When they got to Daniel's house, they all parked and made noise. George had tied the horse to the front rail. Daniel and Sarah with Beau came out on the porch.

"What's going on? You all are sure noisy. I hope you didn't all come for dinner. It's Jetty's day off."

Daniel grinned.

"If you did, you're out of luck."

George motioned and said, "Come on out. We've got something to show you."

All three came down the steps.

"George, is that your beautiful horse?"

"She was at one time. Now she's yours."

"Mine?"

"We all heard about Bess. We hated it so badly that we decided we better do something about it. We came up with this nag knowing she could never replace your loss, but maybe she'd help."

159

The funniest look came on Daniel's face and tears formed in Sarah's eyes. Daniel came and began to hug everyone. Tears were streaming down his cheeks, too. Sarah tired to laugh.

"Gosh, Daniel, Glory and I are going to look really dowdy riding beside you."

Daniel wiped his tears on his sleeve.

"Sarah, you'd never look dowdy riding beside anyone."

John suggested, "Ride her down the road. Let's see how you look on her back."

Daniel climbed on her and tapped her. He urged her into a trot and went to the school turnaround and back.

"She's a beauty."

Mary asked, "What will you name her?"

Daniel answered, "Look at her-nothing but *Honey* will do. When I saw her standing there, my first thought was she was exactly the color of honey. Her mane and tail remind me of melted butter."

"Sarah, did you feed this man dinner?" James asked, and he laughed at his own joke.

"Undoubtedly not enough. You all come on in and have some cider or coffee."

Daniel said, "Sarah, give me Beau. We're going to ride down the road. You all go on in. We'll be back in a few minutes."

Clay quipped, "I think he likes that horse."

When Daniel and Beau returned, they came in the back door. They all turned their attention to him and the baby.

"Beau and I took Honey on to the barn. Ollie and Jetty were back. Ollie saw a man going out to the barn and didn't recognize me or the horse. He came to check me out and was shocked when he saw it was me and Beau on a new horse."

"Daniel, tell us how you were going to unsaddle Honey while you were holding Beau."

160

Daniel though for a minute and answered, "I guess I was going to put him in the wagon or toss him in the hay. I hadn't gotten that far. It was good that Ollie came."

Everyone had a good laugh.

"Honey's a great horse. I won't say she's better than Bess, but by the time I train her, she has hopes of being better. I know she's prettier, and I can already tell she's smart. I thank you all so much. I can't believe you got me a new saddle and bridle, too."

George spoke up, "Everyone thought that horse was so pretty that she deserved something better than that old saddle and bridle of yours. I've been training that horse and if you whistle, she'll come to you in the pasture."

George demonstrated and then he said, "That is, if she likes you as well as she does me."

George chuckled a bit.

"Oh, she'll like me. I've already turned on the old charm. I slipped her a few oats before I turned her out in the pasture. I'm glad to know about the whistle. Seriously, I guess you all can tell I'm very proud of her."

They all turned their attention from Daniel and the horse to Beau. They were all passing him around, and *he* turned on the old charm. He was jabbering to them. They'd laugh at him, and he'd laughed back. Beau's eyes were sparkling, and his dimple was showing at every turn. George shook his head.

"I said this when he was born. He's his papa made over except for those eyes. Those eyes are magic."

James stood and remarked, "I hate to break this little party up, but I need to get on home. I've got a few things to do before dark."

They all began to get up and make their way toward the door. Daniel followed George to the door.

"Hey, give me my son back. He wasn't a trade in on the horse."

"I didn't think you'd miss him, and I could use another boy at my house."

161

"I feel for you, but I can't help you. Hey!"

Daniel stepped out on the porch and hollered for everyone to hear.

"Did Sarah tell you we're having another baby in October?"

Lucy hollered back, "She never said a word. That's wonderful news for all of us. We'll have to all get together again soon and talk about this."

Everyone waved goodbye, and Daniel could see they were all discussing another baby.

After they were out of earshot, Sarah laughed and said, "What a way to announce we're having another baby."

"Well, you told me I could tell anyone I wanted to. There was so much going on that I forgot to tell them until just then. I wanted to share our happiness with all of them."

Daniel squeezed Beau.

"Can you imagine any more happiness than we already have?"

"I am so brimming over with happiness that it's hard to imagine there's more to come. I know I am one very lucky woman."

"You know, Beau will soon be a year old and really has out grown the cradle. I think I need to build him a small bed. I'll make it low so if he falls out of it, it won't hurt badly. We can put a rug for him to fall on just in case. I'd like to put it in our room. I can't stand to think about him being upstairs by himself."

"Should we move our bedroom up while the children are young?"

"That's a thought, but I don't really want to move up. Our bedroom is large and can hold us all until he's older."

They heard Jetty coming in the back door to fix supper.

162

Chapter Seven

Beau had just turned a year old and had been pulling up, but he had never turned loose and tried to walk. Sarah and Daniel were sitting in the parlor, and Beau was stacking wooden blocks on the floor.

The baby turned and crawled to one of the settees and pulled up. He looked up at Sarah, when, all of a sudden, he gave a little grin and turned loose. He was standing alone. Sarah tapped Daniel on the leg, but she didn't say anything. She nodded her head toward Beau for Daniel to look. She held her finger over her lips and signaled for quiet.

Beau stood there a minute and bounced up on his toes a time or two. He was wobbly but then he took two steps and plopped on his little butt. His tiny mouth screwed in a little circle, and he looked as though he would cry. Sarah got up.

"Don't cry. You've done so well. Here, let mama help you."

She picked him up and stood his little back against the settee for support. Then she knelt in front of him and held her arms out.

"Come to mama."

Beau gave a laugh, and he took three steps to Sarah. She hugged him to her chest and bragged on him.

Daniel said, "Let me try it with him."

He repeated what Sarah had done. This time Beau took four steps. Daniel picked Beau up, and they spun around. Beau thought that was funny.

"Once more, Beau, try again."

Daniel got in front of him, and he took five steps this time. He picked Beau up.

"We've got to go tell Remy and Jetty. Remy's work is just beginning. He'll be running by next week."

There were just a few days left in this school term. Aaron and Anna were very aware of it. Summer meant they wouldn't be seeing as much of each other anymore.

"Perhaps you can come see Amy some during the summer. You've always come to our house to see her. I'd be there, and the three of us can do things together," Aaron said.

"Maybe you could bring her out to see me, too. We'll work it out," Anna replied.

"This summer'll go quickly, and I'll be leaving the end of August for medical school."

"Aaron, don't worry, if it's meant to be for us, things will work out. If either of us finds someone else, let's promise to write to the other right away. I think we'll be all right if we always know where we stand in our hearts. I promise you, I'll write to tell you if I've changed my mind. Promise me you'll do the same."

"I promise, Anna. I'll never—"

Anna put her fingers over his lips.

"I don't want *that* promise. I'm only asking that you let me know if you have a change in your heart."

Summer did pass very quickly. Sarah and Daniel had one more dance at the school toward the end of summer.

Rice was home on vacation, and Aaron would soon leave for school. Out of all the students, Aaron Holder was the only one to graduate this school year.

Emma Stewart decided to come two more terms and so did Garrett Adler. Garrett's father thought he needed to refine his education more before deciding on his life's work.

It was early October, and Rice and Aaron both had left for school. Sarah's baby was due in a couple of weeks. Beau was growing so big and was running everywhere instead of walking.

Daniel's factory was still very busy trying to keep his store full of furniture. Tom had built another section on the back of the factory enlarging it considerably. Daniel had hired more men, and by now, some of the apprentices had become skilled furniture makers.

Susan and Noah were doing great with the store. They were shipping furniture to nearby states as well.

Anna still loved school, but it seemed lonesome with Aaron gone. They wrote long letters at least twice a week to each other. It was not the same as getting to talk and to see each other. Still their young hearts stayed true.

Sarah and Mary had come from school to eat lunch when Sarah told Mary, "Get Jetty. The baby's coming."

Daniel had just walked in the back door and Remy told him, "Mr. Daniel, Jetty just went to help Miss Sarah to the bedroom. The baby's coming. Miss Mary's watching Mister Beau while I'm watching the food."

Daniel hurried to the bedroom and told Sarah, "I'll go get Dr. Wade."

"Daniel, there isn't time. It's on its way, and I mean soon."

"I'm going to get Lucy then. Jetty may need help."

Daniel flew out the back door and through the woods. He never slowed down. James saw him running toward their house, and he hurried to meet him.

"The baby's on its way! Can Lucy come give Jetty a hand? There's no time to get a doctor."

"You get back home. I'll get Lucy there right away."

Daniel was out of breath when he got back to the house.

"Mary, I'll take Beau. You go stay with Sarah and Jetty until Lucy gets here."

Mary barely made it in the room, when Daniel heard the cry of a new born. He took Beau's little hand.

"Walk with papa up and down the hall."

Beau walked a few times up and down but that was no fun for him. Daniel picked him up and walked with him in his arms. That was no fun either.

"Beau, I really need you to be a good boy right now."

James and Lucy were coming through the hall and heard Daniel say this to Beau. Daniel looked up.

"The baby's already here. I heard it cry."

"I'll get in there and send Mary back to watch Beau."

"Thanks, Lucy."

James reached and took Beau.

"Come see your uncle for a minute. You're getting to be a big boy. I bet you're hungry."

"You're probably right. No one's had time to worry with food."

"Then I'm going to find this boy something to eat."

James went to the kitchen with Beau.

"Remy can you help me? This boy's hungry."

Mary came out to the hall.

"Sarah and the baby are fine. Jetty and Lucy are getting them cleaned up and then you can see them."

"What is it, Mary?"

"Forgive me, I was in there just as it came, and I'm still in awe. You have a beautiful little daughter."

Daniel sat down on a bench in the hall.

"I'm exhausted. This has all happened too quickly."

"You mean you didn't have most of the day to pace?"

"Well, when you put it that way. I guess this isn't so bad. I only had less than an hour to panic. What day of the month is this Mary?"

"It's Thursday, October the tenth, eighteen hundred and seven."

"I knew the year, but I have to remember these birthdays and enter them in the family bible, you know."

Lucy came walking out in the hall with a little bundle all wrapped in a blanket.

"Daniel, here's your healthy little daughter."

Daniel reached and took her. She seemed so tiny. He could see her little face, and something reminded him of Sarah and how she must have looked the day she was born, except Sarah had told him they said she was almost bald. This baby girl had a head full of very dark hair much like Beau's when he was born.

He couldn't tell about her eyes. Beau's had changed to a much lighter color as he grew. Now when you looked at Beau, you saw clear, light blue eyes and black hair that had a slight curl like his father's.

Jetty stuck her head out the door.

"Miss Sarah wants you to come in now and bring the baby."

Daniel took his new daughter and carried her to her mother. Sarah patted the bed and asked him to sit.

"I want to see her better as things moved so fast I haven't counted all her fingers and toes."

Daniel placed her in Sarah's waiting arms. Sarah pulled the blanket back.

"Ten toes on those tiny feet." She picked up a little hand and said, "Four fingers here and a thumb."

167

Daniel took the other tiny hand, and the baby curled it around his finger just as Beau had done when he was born.

"She's all here, Sarah, and beautiful. Is her name Kate Caroline as we had discussed? I like that very much. I think Carolina would like it, too. Kate Borden. That sounds strong, and I want her to be strong like her mother."

Daniel leaned over and kissed Sarah tenderly.

Jetty came back into the bedroom and busied herself making up the cradle for little Kate. Beau was now sleeping in his new, big-boy bed in the corner of their bedroom.

When Kate was about a week old, Priscilla Purdy came to call on Sarah. Jetty let her in and asked her to sit in the parlor to wait for Miss Sarah. When Sarah entered the room, Priscilla came to hug her.

"You're looking marvelous, Sarah. I've missed your piano lessons and visiting with you."

Jetty had the big basket, and Kate was sleeping peacefully in it. Jetty set the basket at Sarah's feet. Priscilla couldn't wait to see the baby. She knelt down and peered in at the little sleeping face.

"She's beautiful! I think she's too young to tell who she favors yet. Her hair is more the color of Daniel's; yet, I see what I imagine you looked like at this age."

"That's what Daniel keeps saying. We've been blessed with two healthy babies, and to me, that is what's important."

"You're absolutely right. Are you feeling well?"

"Oh yes, I feel my recovery will be more rapid than it was after giving birth to Beau. Kate came so quickly, and it was over before we were really ready. I had to laugh. I think Daniel almost felt left out of the process as he didn't get to pace much this time."

Priscilla grinned.

"That is priceless. How wonderful that it went so well."

Priscilla changed the tone and direction of her conversation.

"Sarah, I've wanted to talk to you because I've told you about my earlier life before I moved to Kentucky. I feel you're my friend now, and I can talk to you."

"You know that I'm your friend, Priscilla. What's troubling you?"

"It's not trouble-just confusion."

"I'm very attracted to Tom Holder, and I'm beginning to feel he's attracted to me."

"That's fantastic. I've felt I'd seen glimpses of this when I've been with you both. You and Tom are our dear friends, and this would please us very much to see you happy together."

"Oh, Tom has not said a word to me, and it could be purely wishful thinking on my part. There're just little things I've noticed. He stays through the whole piano lessons now when he brings the girls. He helps me to my carriage with my things and helps me in. He has squeezed my arm a few times. I'm noticing his attention even more since Aaron is off at school."

"Priscilla, why don't we ask you, Tom, and his girls for dinner this Saturday afternoon? Daniel can suggest that he pick you up since Susan and Noah won't be coming. Perhaps that would give him a little shove. Do you mind if I mention this to Daniel?"

"That would be splendid, as I've felt stuck as to how to move a possible relationship forward. I told you I never thought there would be another man in my life. I feel differently now, and I don't want to miss this opportunity if there is a chance for me. I don't want to push, but I don't want to miss out on something that might be."

"Why don't you come back to see me before lessons on Thursday, and Daniel will have talked to Tom by then."

"Thank you for understanding. I better go now but I'll see you Thursday."

When Daniel came in for dinner, Sarah told him about Priscilla's visit.

"I would like to give Tom a little shove and ask Priscilla and the Holders to supper on Saturday. Will you suggest that Tom pick her up?"

"Are you matchmaking?"

"I don't feel as though I am. I've noticed the way Tom looks at Priscilla and the way he holds her when they dance. Priscilla is clearly interested in him. I think they just need a little push."

"Oh, I've felt like Tom is definitely interested. I think he's hesitated out of a loyalty to Dorcus."

"It's been over a year now and that's long enough. Dorcus will never be back, and he can still cherish his memory of her. Priscilla would understand that as she cherishes a memory, too."

"I'll talk to Tom and issue the invitation for Saturday supper."

Daniel saw Tom the next morning at Creel's General Store. They stopped to talk in front of the store, and Daniel issued the invitation for supper on Saturday.

"Sarah would like to ask Priscilla to join us, since this is our first entertaining since Kate was born. We'd like to keep it a small supper. Could you and the girls possibly pick Priscilla up? You might stay until after dark, and we wouldn't want Priscilla out alone."

"That sounds nice, and we'd like for Priscilla to join us. You know, my girls are crazy about her. Will Sarah make the arrangements, and tell Priscilla we'll pick her up at three on Saturday afternoon?"

"Yes, I'm sure either Sarah or I'll see Priscilla before Saturday. Tom, you said your girls are crazy about Priscilla. I feel Aaron likes her, too. What do you think about her?"

170

"I've tried my best not to think about her. I'll admit she's very attractive to me. When we dance, I almost feel too comfortable with her in my arms."

"You know, it's been considerably over a year since you lost Dorcus. I think if you are interested in Priscilla, it's well within decorum to explore your interest. Life is short so don't miss out on a chance at happiness. You and Priscilla are still young."

"That's probably good advice. I'll think about it, and we'll see you Saturday."

After they spoke, Tom went on his way, and Daniel went into the store. He hadn't seen baby Sage in quite a while. She was toddling up and down the aisles with Molly chasing right in behind her.

"You've got the same problem we do trying to keep up with a young one. She's growing into a little beauty. I want Sarah to see her. You must bring her to visit us."

After a short visit at the store, Daniel headed for home.

When he arrived, he told Sarah about his conversation with Tom.

"You've got me out matchmaking now. Yes, Tom's more than interested in Priscilla. He and the girls will pick her up at three on Saturday afternoon. Something will come of this, Sarah. I just feel it. Tom just needed a little push. I also saw Molly and Sage Creel in the store. That little girl is very pretty."

The next day Priscilla called on Sarah.

"I've been anxious to know if Daniel has invited Tom."

"Oh yes, the arrangements have been made for supper on Saturday. Tom and the girls will pick you up at three. Daniel said Tom just needed a little push as he's very interested in you."

Priscilla's cheeks turned pink.

"Sarah, I feel almost like a school girl again. I don't know how I can thank you enough."

"This is wonderful. I like to see two of our friends happy-that's enough thanks."

Saturday afternoon arrived, and Jetty had fixed a wonderful meal. Sarah had decided to put Amy and Rachel on one side of the table and Tom and Priscilla across from them. When a knock came on the door, Sarah answered it. It's was the dinner guests.

Sarah had thought that Priscilla was a very attractive lady, and this afternoon she glowed. She was dressed in a light blue, soft wool dress. Sarah had realized Priscilla had blue eyes but this blue dress bought them out. She was wearing her light brown hair loose and around her shoulders this evening.

If Tom Holder wasn't attracted to this woman, it would be hard to find another he would be attracted to. When Sarah hugged Priscilla she got a subtle whiff of lavender. This would be very attractive to most any man.

Sarah suggested to the girls that Beau and Kate were upstairs with Remy.

"Beau is playing on the landing and Kate may be a-sleep. Go up and Remy will help you find games or other things which might interest you."

Tom said, "The baby will interest them more than anything."

Priscilla nodded her head in agreement with Tom.

Tom and Priscilla sat on one settee, and Daniel and Sarah across on the other. As they talked, both noticed that Tom found excuses to lay his hand on Priscilla's arm. On occasion Priscilla returned the gesture.

Jetty announced the meal was ready, and the girls came down and joined them at the table. The conversation was very pleasant. Priscilla and the girls were telling little stories of their piano lessons, and Tom joined in when possible. They already looked like a family. To keep the dialog moving, Daniel and Sarah told little tales of their children's antics.

Daniel asked Tom what he was hearing from Aaron.

"Tell us about Aaron and school. We're both very interested in his progress and how he likes it."

"He's doing very well. I think he even surprises himself with some of his good grades. He attributes it all to Sarah and Dr. Wade. They're his heroes. I think he misses a certain young lady back here, though. Amy hears more than I do, and he inquires about Anna frequently. I think he wants almost constant reassurance that Garrett Adler isn't moving in while he's absent."

Sarah spoke up, "Tell Aaron to relax. I know our niece quite well, and Garrett Adler is not her type. I think with Aaron away, Anna is only interested in her studies."

Amy looked at her papa.

"I'm going to write Aaron, and tell him just what Miss Sarah said. I've tried to tell him before. Anna and I talk regularly, and I know her feelings. I think it's hard for Aaron to believe she's only interested in him."

Priscilla joined the conversation.

"I can tell you from what I've observed that Aaron and Anna have a relationship much as you and Daniel. They are meant for each other, and with care, it will be everlasting."

"I didn't realize you were such an expert on relationships, Priscilla."

Priscilla wasn't sure how Tom had meant his remark. She got a little defensive.

"I suppose it's from the lack of my own relationships that has made me such an acute observer."

Fearing he had offended Priscilla, Tom said, "I wasn't teasing you, Priscilla. It's just that lately I've been, I guess you could say, fascinated that such a pretty, young lady as yourself has never married."

"Remind me someday when we have time, Tom, to tell you my story. Perhaps then you'll understand."

Tom saw an opening.

"Speaking of having time, the girls and I would like to issue an invitation for dinner tomorrow after church at our house. Priscilla, we'd like to pick you up in the morning and have you attend our church with us."

Tom looked at Sarah and then Daniel.

"I know you haven't been coming to church the last couple of Sunday's with your new baby. Why don't you bring Remy and the children, and come to my house about two tomorrow afternoon?"

Priscilla said, "This sounds very nice, and I accept. What time should I expect you and the girls in the morning?"

"We'll be there a little before ten. We're looking forward to it, aren't we girls?"

Both girls smiled and Amy said, "It'll be nice to have company for dinner again."

"We'll be looking forward to it, too, as you know Jetty and Ollie usually have Sundays off," Sarah remarked.

With the meal finished, Tom and Priscilla stepped to the kitchen and complimented Jetty on her cooking. That always made it worth her time to give the food her extra touches.

Sarah had to excuse herself a couple of times to feed Kate and make sure the children were okay. She knew the others understood the children were her first priority. She always hurried back and joined right back in the conversation. The guests had settled down to visit in the parlor.

"Next time you come, perhaps Ollie will go fishing and catch us a mess of fish for dinner. Jetty can fry some of the best fish you've every put in your mouth."

"That sounds good. Daniel, maybe next time Sarah will feel like going fishing, and Priscilla will know not to dress so pretty if we give her forewarning. I'd like to catch our

174

own fish, and I bet the girls would love it. Perhaps Ollie would clean them for us."

"It's been so long since I've fished, but as a girl I loved it. I would like to wear something a bit more suitable for fishing as Tom suggested."

"You've fished before, Priscilla?"

"I used to love to fish."

Priscilla seemed to address the next statement to Tom more than anyone.

"I do bait my own hook, be it with worms, crickets, or liver just in case you're interested."

She smiled and turned to Daniel.

"I guess you fish with bait. I've done a bit of fly fishing but that was so long ago. I'd have to practice that again to do any good fly fishing."

Tom looked a little sheepish.

"You keep amazing me Priscilla. You seem so proper I've never featured you standing in the middle of a stream with a fly rod in your hand."

Daniel laughed.

"Now I know why Sarah and Priscilla hit it off so well. You should see Sarah shoot. She can beat most men. I've never seen her fly fish, but I started giving her swimming lessons last spring."

Then Daniel thought and asked, "Tom, you remember when Sarah fell in the river a couple of years ago, and I had to jump in and rescue her? Well, after that she overcame her fears and jumped back in the river and has learned to handle the water."

"Sarah, that's great. I guess if you live by a river you should know how to swim."

"Now if there was something I've always secretly wanted to do, it's learning to swim. I've never had the opportunity. Sarah, may I ask what you wore to swim in?"

"I altered a pair of Daniel's old breeches and took the sleeves out of a fitted waist. They worked wonderfully well."

The girls were listening and joined in.

"Now, Papa, that's something we'd like to do."

"James, Lucy, Anna, and Eli went swimming with us. Daniel and James taught us all. Daniel and James are excellent swimmers. We felt safe with them as teachers."

"If things work out, perhaps we'll come out and give it a try in the river, if Daniel and Sarah will go with us."

Tom looked directly at Priscilla with his remarks.

"You have an invitation as we'd like to do it again. Sarah can use the practice."

Sarah and Priscilla glanced at each other. The thought ran through both their minds what Tom had meant by *if things work out*. It was getting to where they could almost tell what the other was thinking at certain times.

The guests left before dark. They'd had a wonderful evening.

Daniel remarked to Sarah when they were alone, "Wouldn't you love to be at church in the morning when Tom Holder walks in with Priscilla Purdy on his arm? Some chins may hit the floor. Now that we've gotten to know Priscilla better, I'm sure she is a few years younger than Tom."

"Who in the world would've thought about those two finding each other? I think she's some younger but not a scandalous difference."

"No, I'd say Tom is in his late thirties or maybe forty. Priscilla is about thirty or thirty one. That's not bad at all."

"What do you think Tom meant when we were talking about swimming and he said, 'if things work out'?"

"I'm not sure. I do know I gave him a little push to see Priscilla, and he's jumped in neck deep. You don't take a girl or woman to church on your arm unless you're stating that you're serious."

"I wondered if he was thinking about teaching Priscilla to swim if they weren't married. I might have been reading too much into his words, but I thought he meant if they were married by then they'd come swimming."

"You may be right, Sarah. I think they'll be married by then. The one sure sign is him asking her to church and her accepting."

Sarah went to get the children. They needed to give them some attention now. She also wanted to tell Remy they were going to Mr. Holder's house tomorrow afternoon and wanted her to go help with the children.

They played until bedtime, and Beau's antics made them laugh. He was saying a few words, and he kept calling the baby *Cat* instead of *Kate*.

Sunday afternoon Sarah let Daniel dress Beau, and she dressed Kate to go to the Holders.

"Dressing two takes longer than just dressing one's self, doesn't it?" Sarah mused.

"I'd never thought of it until we had Kate, as I wasn't dressing Beau then, you were. Getting Beau to stand still to put his clothes on is an experience. At what age can they dress themselves?"

"You can't really depend on them to get everything on right until sometime after six years, I think. Something will be backwards or shoes on the wrong feet. Little things you have to watch for."

"Then we've just started."

"I'm afraid so, but that is just one of the hazards of becoming parents. There're so many good things that I find it all quiet worthwhile."

"I do too, Sarah, and I wouldn't trade a minute of it. Are we ready? The carriage is hitched and parked out front. You take our son's hand and let him walk to the carriage, and I'll carry our daughter. Is that fair enough?"

"I guess so, if I can hold on to a wiggling little hand." Sarah smiled.

"We'll stop by Remy's cabin and pick her up. She can handle Beau in the back seat."

"Thank goodness we've got Remy. I don't know what I'd do without her with two children."

Remy climbed in the back seat, and she lifted Beau over to sit with her. It didn't take long to get to Tom's house. When they arrived, Daniel knocked on the door, and Amy answered.

"Come on in. Papa and Miss Purdy are sitting in the parlor."

She led the way to the parlor. Tom stood and welcomed them. He and Daniel helped Remy and the children get settled in another play room. The girls quickly joined Remy to help entertain the children. Mattie was busy in the kitchen and getting the food on the table.

"Mattie hasn't cooked for guests in so long she may have forgotten how."

"Oh, I bet we can eat it. Tell me, how was church this morning?"

Sarah would've liked to have lightly kicked Daniel's leg when he asked, but she was afraid the others would see her.

Then he added, "I'd like to have been there to see you and Priscilla walk in together."

Sarah wanted to go through the floor.

Tom grinned, "There were some shocked people we could tell. Priscilla had a strange thing come up after church. You know ladies' man, Hines, from down at the wagon yard?"

"I know him."

"He comes up to Priscilla while twisting his black moustache and says, 'I see you finally made it to this church. How many times did I ask you, and you said you needed to attend your own church.' You know what she told him?"

Priscilla quickly spoke up.

I said, "Well, Mr. Hines, it was really Mr. Holder's two daughters who invited me. I teach the girls piano, and I wouldn't want to disappoint them, now would I?"

Tom was crying he was laughing so hard.

"She then turned her attention back to me. Hines stomped off in a huff. This lady is slick, I tell you. She can slide out of trouble quicker than a greased pig."

Daniel and Sarah were laughing, too.

"Priscilla, you haven't told us about all the invitation's you've gotten and you've turned down in this town."

"No, Sarah, and I'm not going to."

Mattie saved Priscilla from the teasing. She came to say that dinner was ready.

When the girls came in the dining room, Amy said, "We've never heard so much laughing. You grownups are really having fun."

"We *are* having fun. Miss Purdy and your papa are entertaining us with funny little stories of things that have happened recently."

The afternoon passed quickly with good friends and good food. Daniel and Sarah decided they needed to go and get the kids settled down before dark and bedtime.

"I think I better be going, too, Tom. I've been gone all day, but it's been incredible."

Daniel and Sarah offered to drive Priscilla back into town, but Tom jumped up and insisted he was driving her home.

Sarah hugged Tom and then turned to hug Priscilla.

"We've had a fantastic afternoon, and Amy is right, we've laughed a lot. Tell Mattie how much we enjoyed her meal. I told her, but hearing it again never hurts."

"Come by the factory when you have time, Tom, and are out our way."

"With Aaron gone, I'm driving the girls out to school every morning, so I'll come down and visit early in the morning."

On the way home, Sarah said, "Do you realize when Tom drives Priscilla home that will be the first time he's ever been alone with her?"

"I hadn't thought of that. I can see why he was so insistent that he wanted to take her home."

"I know he wants to hear the story of why Priscilla has never married. Perhaps he'll hear the story tonight. I think it would be good if he does. He'll know that he is very special to Priscilla already since she's even seeing him."

"I didn't tell him that I wasn't going to the factory that early since you're not teaching, and we have the new baby. I'll make an exception in the morning and meet him. I'm interested in hearing what he has to say. I'll go and then come back and have breakfast with you."

"That'll be nice. I'll be interested in hearing what he has to say."

Daniel got up early the next morning, quietly dressed, and left for the factory. Jetty was already in the kitchen.

"You're up early, Mr. Daniel."

"I know it, Jetty. I'm spoiled with these babies getting us up during the night and then sleeping late in the morning. Mr. Tom said he'd be at the factory early this morning. I want to go visit with him. I'll come back and have breakfast later with Miss Sarah."

"Would you like a teacake and a cup of coffee to take with you?"

"That sounds very good and would help stave off hunger. Thanks."

Jetty poured the coffee and set the honey and cream out for him. She put three teacakes on a saucer.

"I'll just take the teacakes in my hand, and I'll bring the cup back when I come home."

"You'd better get a jacket this morning. It's pretty nippy out."

"I've got one on the peg in the hall. I'll get it. Thanks for the warning."

Daniel put on the jacket, picked up his coffee, his teacakes, and started for the factory. The air was fresh, very

180

cool, and smelled as if it had never been breathed before. His jacket felt good, and the coffee was warm to his hands. Jetty's new coffee had been exceptionally good lately, and he wished he had a second cup.

He was in time to open the factory door this morning. The men would be surprised to see him this early. He would come to work early again as soon as Sarah started teaching again. He liked to set an example for the men and soon would once more. The other men started coming in, and Tom wasn't far behind.

"Let's go in the office, so we can talk without all the noise."

When they entered the office, the two took a seat.

"We did enjoy the afternoon yesterday, and the meal was very good," Daniel stated.

"I don't think Mattie cooks quite as good as Jetty, but she does all right. Jetty's bread, coffee, and cobbler are the best anyone could hope to make."

"Sarah taught her how to bake the bread and cobbler. The coffee is hers."

"You mean Sarah fed you like that before Jetty?"

"Yes, my father's cook, Dolly, taught Sarah to cook when we were first married."

"You're one lucky man."

"I know it better than anyone, and I thank the good Lord every day. Tell me, what do you think about Priscilla?"

"She's a very wonderful woman. You know, she's a few years younger than I am."

"What's a few years? You make a nice looking couple."

"Last night was the first time we'd ever been alone and just talked-serious talk. She told me about her life before she moved to Burkesville. She's had a hard time. She lost all her loved ones in one bad epidemic. She was engaged to be married and he died, too. She's never even dated since then. She's had offers, but she's spurned them all. I'm the first one that's even made it this far."

181

"Sarah has told me you're special to Priscilla."

"I know it. I kissed her last night, and I tell you this, I didn't want to leave her to go home. I did go home, but now I can't get her off of my mind."

"What're you going to do about it?"

"I'm going to try to see her a while longer, and then I'm going to ask her to marry me. We've got a lot of talking to do. Questions like your house or mine. My house is much larger, and with my family, that's probably not a problem for her, but we need to discuss it. I have three kids. One of them is almost grown. She's never had any. I'm pretty sure she's still young enough to have one now if she wanted to. Do I want to have another one, though? I've been through all of that. Do I want to start a new family at my age?"

"You asked the question, so what's your answer?"

Daniel could tell Tom was pondering the answer.

"I look at your beautiful babies and think-yeah, I'm not that old. I could certainly afford another one or two. I could get her some help, perhaps someone like Remy. You know, Priscilla is a busy lady like Sarah. I don't think she'd give that up. Shoot, I'm standing here talking to you, and I know as well as I know anything-I'm going to marry that lady if she'll have me. If she wants children, we'll have children or anything else she wants. Do you think she'll have me?"

"From what Sarah tells me, I'm pretty sure she will. You'd better be sure before you ask her. Don't lead her on long, though, before you ask. The lady's been hurt deeply once; don't do it to her again. She deserves happiness after what she's been through, and so do you. I'm predicting it's a lasting relationship. It's the real thing."

"The woman likes to fish. How can I ever beat that? I've got to get to work. I may have another family to raise," Tom chuckled to himself, shook his head, and walked out the door.

When he was out of sight, Daniel went back to the house to have breakfast. Sarah was up and ready for breakfast. Kate was still sleeping, and Remy was feeding Beau at the kitchen table.

"How was your visit with Tom?"

"I'll put it this way. I look for an early summer wedding, perhaps when Aaron comes home in the summer. Tom's even talking about more children. I'd say he's got it bad for her."

"Why don't we give them a wedding or wedding party at the school or in our back yard?"

"Don't get ahead of them, Sarah. Just play it quietly until they announce things, and *then* you can offer Priscilla our help. We'll see what they might plan."

"We're more like both their families. They'll need us."

"Yes, but let them settle things in their own way and time."

"You're right as usual. I'll show some patience even though I'm excited for them."

Daniel went back to the factory after they finished eating. He had two wagons loaded with furniture to take to the store. Susan met him, and he told them to unlock the back doors when he came in the front door.

"Noah and I have a bit of good news. We are expecting a baby next spring."

"That *is* good news. I guess George and Charity know about it since you're spreading the news."

"Yes, we told my parents and Noah's last weekend. Everyone's thrilled."

"So George is going to be a grandpa. I'll have to tease him. You'll be out for a while come next spring. We'll need to find Noah some help."

"I won't take off too long. I'll still keep books and come in off and on. I can do like Sarah and bring the baby in a basket to the store. It can sleep in the office. I'll look for someone and work out a schedule with them when time comes."

"I should have known that you have it all worked out. Do what's best for you and the baby, and I won't worry."

Daniel stopped by to see the Creel's while he was in town. Caleb was still selling the benches with good success. He still had them featured at the front of the store, and they were colorful and eye catching as you entered the door. Daniel stopped to talk to Caleb for a few minutes, and soon Molly and Sage came to the front of the store.

Daniel spoke to Molly, but the thing that caught his eye was Sage. She had thick chestnut color hair for such a little girl. She was talking, and her eyes fairly twinkled with life. Sage was born sometime a few months after Beau.

"Molly, your daughter is very pretty. She'll turn the heads of the young men in this town soon."

"Let's hope not too soon, Daniel. I have plans for her as she's our first."

"Sarah and I marvel at how well behaved she is at church. Our Beau is so full of life we have trouble getting him to be quite. He'd rather talk than listen right now. Sarah is working on that."

Molly laughed.

"I can tell he's one bright little boy. He's already tending to his little sister. He looks just like you, Daniel, with the exception of his blue eyes. They pop out at you."

"You're probably right. I'm afraid he's a great deal like me. Thankfully, I think Kate has more of Sarah in her. It's a little early to tell for sure but we can always hope."

"Give Sarah my regards, and let's get the children together to play before long."

"That sounds good, and I'll tell Sarah."

Daniel gathered a few items to buy, and he paid Caleb before leaving the store.

When he got to the house, it was time for his dinner, so he took the wagon back to the barn. He helped Ollie unhitch it, and they both walked back to the house.

"Ollie, I'm thinking about inviting Tom Holder, his girls, and Miss Priscilla to come out to fish Saturday afternoon. Would you be free to watch over us during the afternoon, and to assist anyone who might need help? I want to be sure everyone is catching a few fish and having fun. If you can help clean them afterwards, too, I'd appreciate it. We'll tell Jetty to be ready to fry up a big mess of fish, at least we hope."

"Mr. Daniel, that's not work for me. I'm happy anytime I'm around fishing. It doesn't matter to me if I'm fishing or I'm helping, it's all fun for me."

"That's good, Ollie. I know we'll catch fish if you're there."

Ollie smiled.

"Do I have your permission to fix Mr. Beau a little pole? I'd like to see if I can interest him in fishing? I'd just like for him to feel a fish on the pole soon as he can. I want him to love it as he grows up. Fishing is good for people. It's helps you relax and calms your mind."

"Beau's young, and his little mind's very quick. I was that way growing up, so I have hope for him. I'd love for you and him to become fishing buddies as he grows. Try to interest him in digging in the soil, too, Ollie. You can teach him a lot. I know because Toby, who Sarah and I speak of, taught me and Sarah a lot, also. What he taught Sarah probably is the reason she is with me today. I owe that man a lot."

Later that afternoon Daniel noticed that Tom's carriage was down at the school for piano lessons. He walked down to the school and stuck his head in the door.

"I hope I'm not disturbing things, but I saw all of you here, and I wanted to issue an invitation for that fishing date. Can you come this Saturday afternoon fairly early? That'd give us time to catch the fish and get Ollie to help clean them. Jetty can fry them up for our supper."

Tom looked at Priscilla and said, "We're free aren't we girls? What about you Priscilla?"

"I'm free and would love to come. What time would you like us to be here?"

"Come to the house a little after one, and I'll have the bait ready. Just dress for fishing and comfort."

"Priscilla, the girls and I'll get you shortly before one, then."

"If you'll come a bit after midday I'll have us a light lunch fixed. We'll eat and then drive out. However, I *can* drive myself out."

"Do you think the girls and I are going to miss an invitation to lunch? No, ma'am, no way, we'll see you a little after twelve o'clock at your house."

Daniel added, "That's settled then. We'll have fun. I'll get out of here so you can get on with your lessons."

Daniel walked up the hill to the house before he went back to the factory. He wanted to tell Sarah and Jetty about the invitation before they made other plans.

Sarah received the information with eager anticipation. She was looking forward to the outing even if it was just to their dock on the river. Ollie had previously mentioned it to Jetty while he was eating dinner. Now that she knew the invitation had been accepted, she started planning the rest of the menu. Jetty knew Ollie was looking forward to Saturday afternoon and was already making plans to be sure it was a success.

Ollie decided he could get Mr. Finley, the painter at the factory, to paint a cork bright red for him. He then got some white breast feathers that had fallen out of their duck's breast. He left one feather snowy white and he had Mr. Finley to lightly paint one bright pink and one a light green. He punched three small holes in the top of the red cork and stuck the feathers in the small holes. That made for a very colorful cork for Mr. Beau's fishing pole.

Ollie found the right size bamboo for a smaller pole down near the river bank. Mr. Finley painted the pole a bright red. When the paint dried, Ollie rigged up the little pole with a line and attached the colorful cork to it about two and half feet above the hook. This should hold Mr. Beau's attention floating on the river-at least, long enough for a fish to get on his hook.

Everyone claimed that Ollie had a secret for catching fish.

When asked his secret he always replied, "Well, sir, I jest spits on the worm."

Saturday afternoon finally arrived. Ollie and Daniel had dug some fat, juicy, red worms out of the compost piles. Daniel had a special wooden box with a lid to put the worms in. He and Ollie had dampened some of the rotted compost and put it in the box to keep the worms happy until they were used for bait. Ollie had found some white grub worms to put in a smaller box just in case the fish's taste wasn't for red worms that day. Ollie hauled both boxes of bait down to the dock and put them next to the bricks on the factory wall.

Sarah had fed Kate and told Remy to bring her in the big basket to the dock a little later. Beau would go down with them and the other guests. Sarah knew Ollie was planning a fishing lesson for Beau.

Sarah made sure she had her light weight leather gloves in her satchel as she liked to use them to bait her own hook. Priscilla bragged about baiting her own hook, and Sarah had wondered if her friend used gloves. That was a little trick she learned as a girl fishing with her father and brother, Ben.

Daniel, Sarah, and Beau were sitting on the back porch when the Holders and Priscilla arrived. Daniel knew that Tom was familiar with pulling to the back of the house so Ollie could put his horse in the pasture for him.

The Bordens walked out to the carriage to greet everyone. Sarah noticed that Priscilla had a leather satchel that looked much like hers. Sarah had hers since she was a young girl.

She made mention of Priscilla's satchel, and she replied, "I've had mine for years. I always carry it when I fish."

Sarah held hers up and remarked, "My father had mine made for me when I was a girl."

"The bait, poles, and all the fishing gear are already down at the dock. Shall we walk on down?"

"Let me get my wide brim hat from the porch, and I'll be ready. I see Priscilla has hers."

"Sarah, you lead the way, and we'll follow. The factory door is already open."

The two young girls were excited with the thought of fishing. They had been fishing before but so long ago they could barely remember.

Daniel had colorful benches for everyone to sit on. The railing around the dock was a nice height. You couldn't fall over but it was just high enough you could sit close and fish. Sarah watched and, sure enough, Priscilla reached in her satchel and took out a pair of thin leather gloves. They were just right for baiting a worm on a hook.

Tom turned to tease, "Now, that's cheating."

"Not for a girl. Look. Sarah has some, and your girls will, too, before long."

Daniel pointed out the worms. Priscilla went to the box and pulled out a long, fat one.

Tom came to stand and look over Priscilla's shoulder while she was baiting. Ollie was over in the corner of the dock doing something, and Tom's attention was half on Priscilla and half on Ollie. He was curious just what the older, black man was doing. Priscilla put the worm on her hook just right and dropped the line in the water.

Hardly had it hit the water than a big fish hit her line. She let out an excited squeal. Tom turned quickly to see what had happened. She jerked the fish in hard.

The big fish literally flew through the air, and it hit Tom hard right in the face and across his mouth.

Priscilla instantly realized what had happened, and she jumped up dropping pole, fish, and all on the dock. The girls and Daniel were laughing their heads off. Priscilla pulled her glove off and kissed the palm of her hand and

188

placed it on Tom's face. She, too, was holding back a giggle.

"I'm sorry, Tom. I'm so sorry. Does it hurt?"

"Go ahead and laugh, Priscilla. Everyone else is. It doesn't hurt, but how in the heck am I going to steal a kiss with cold wet fish all over my face?"

"Oh, Papa!"

The girls rolled their eyes.

All the laughing and excitement made Tom forget what he was saying. In haste he blurted out what was on his mind.

"You may as well know girls; I was planning on asking Priscilla to marry me this evening. I probably will kiss her at that time."

This statement sucked the air out of Priscilla's lungs. In amazement she crossed her hands over her chest. Then she felt her cheeks turning red, and put one hand on each side of her mouth.

The girls jumped up and rushed to Priscilla. They both put their arms around her.

"Please say yes, please."

"I didn't know the whole family was going to beg you. I'm sorry I'm so clumsy with all of this."

"May I answer later? I don't mean later—later."

Priscilla had thrust her arm out to show she didn't mean in the extended future. Then she measured between two fingers showing she meant just a little later.

"I'd like to answer sometime if we're ever alone."

"Oh, we'll be alone this evening. We'll drop the girls off before I take you home."

Priscilla cut her eyes up at Tom.

"I'll give my answer then if that's all right. One thing I can say, Tom Holder, this is an unusual proposal."

"Yep, none of us will ever forget it, including me. That's for sure."

Tom looked over at Daniel who visibility was getting the biggest kick out of all of this.

189

"Don't say a word, Daniel."

Ollie decided there needed to be a change of subject. He stepped out of the corner with Beau's fishing pole.

"Come here, Mr. Beau. I've fixed something for you. Let's show these folks how to catch a fish."

Sarah and Daniel couldn't believe Beau's fishing rig. Ollie had a little stool for Beau. The stool was just the right height so that Beau could comfortably reach over the railing without falling over. All fishing stopped to watch Ollie and Beau.

"See your cork, Mr. Beau? You hold the pole still and watch. When that bright, feathered cork goes under the water, you pull up on that pole to set the hook. I bet we'll catch us a fish then."

It was hardly a moment until the cork was pulled way under. Beau's little pole bent almost double.

"Pull it up, Mr. Beau. Like this."

Ollie helped Beau just a little. There was one excited little boy and older man, not to mention one proud mama and papa. Beau's eyes were as big as teacups.

"Fish," he pointed.

"See what you caught? Let's get him off the hook. You've caught a very nice bass. Not as big as Miss Priscilla's but big for a boy your age. Mr. Beau, I declare you a real fisherman."

Ollie patted him on the back and baited Beau's hook once more. The little boy was patiently watching for the feathers to go under the water. Then the real fun began when the girls began to catch fish, too.

Ollie was jumping from one child to the other helping bait and pull fish off the hooks. When they had three stringers full of fish, they decided to go to the house so the men could clean them for supper.

"Ollie has jumped all over the dock this afternoon. Daniel, I suggest we help him clean all these fish," Tom said.

"I think that's only fair, as he saw to it that my son will probably love fishing for the rest of his life. I doubted it with Beau being so young, but Ollie made it exciting for all of us."

"Well, I added to the excitement some myself. Do you think Priscilla will have me now that I've made such a mess of the proposal?" Tom questioned.

"Ah, it just adds to your boyish charm, Tom. She'll have you especially since the girls begged her, too. She wouldn't want to disappoint them."

Daniel slapped Tom on the back and had another hearty laugh.

With the fish cleaned and washed, the men washed up at the well so they wouldn't smell like fish. Ollie carried the fish in for Jetty to fry. The ladies were sitting in the parlor, and Remy was entertaining the children upstairs. When the men came in, they sat down on the settees.

Sarah went to sit by Daniel, and Priscilla took the seat next to Tom. Sarah noticed that Priscilla squeezed Tom's arm at the first convenient opportunity. It signaled to her that the answer would be *yes*. She hoped it signaled Tom, too, so he could enjoy the rest of the evening.

Jetty's meal was a great success, and the fried fish were delicious. It kept Sarah and Daniel both busy being sure that Beau had no bones in his fish. Daniel was beaming from the successful afternoon.

"Look, Beau likes eating the fish as well as he does catching them."

After they had eaten, and they had Jetty's tasty apple cobbler, the grownups had an extra cup of coffee. Daniel could tell Tom was getting twitchy to go. Old Tom had waited long enough for his answer. He wanted to be alone with Priscilla.

"I hope you folks don't mind, but I think we'll be going. Priscilla and I have a lot of talking to do this evening, and I want to drop the girls off while Mattie will be with them. We've had a very good time and a wonderful meal."

"We've enjoyed it so much, too. We'll do it again before too long. I think the girls had a good time."

"Oh, I could tell they did, Sarah. We all laughed a lot and that's good. I want to thank Jetty and Ollie for the delicious meal before we go."

Priscilla rose from the table.

"I want to thank Ollie for helping my girls *and* the wonderful meal. I'll get my girls."

Priscilla and Tom went toward the kitchen. Daniel and Sarah followed. Jetty was in the limelight receiving all the compliments on the food. Tom stepped to the bottom of the stairs and called up to his girls. They came down and thanked Sarah and Daniel for the afternoon. Beau hated to see them go. He loved the girls and their attention.

Ollie had their carriage waiting out back, and Tom helped all his ladies get settled. Daniel and Sarah could see Priscilla and the girls talking as they drove out to the road.

"They belong together. I sure hope Tom gets the right answer this evening."

"You aren't sure of the answer? Well, I am. You just have to observe them to know they're in love. Those girls are crazy about Priscilla, too. That puts her and Tom way ahead. Aaron'll be very pleased that his father found someone and will be happy again."

"*Miss Matchmaker*, now aren't we smug in our observations?"

Daniel reached and hugged Sarah.

"You had as much to do with this as I did. You're a bit of a romantic yourself."

Tom made the turn and pulled down his road to the front of his house.

"We'll let you girls out now. I won't be too late. If you have lessons you might work on them. You can wait up on me if you like and we'll talk."

The girls both leaned over the front seat and kissed their papa on the cheek. They then turned and kissed Priscilla.

"We had a very good time this afternoon. Thanks for going with us."

"I enjoyed it so much myself, girls. It was such fun."

The girls jumped down and gave another wave. Then they skittered in the door. Tom popped the reins and clicked to the horse.

As he was driving down his road to the main road, Priscilla said, "Will you stop the carriage?"

Tom turned his head to look at her.

"Would you pull to a stop, please?"

Tom obliged and Priscilla scooted closer to him.

"You've waited long enough for my answer."

She put her hands on each side of his face and pulled it near. She kissed him with a long lingering kiss.

"My answer is, *yes*. See, I love you enough to kiss you even after I've hit you in the mouth with a cold wet fish. In fact, I love your whole family very much, and I want them to be part mine."

Tom took a deep breath of relief.

"I love you, Cilla. May I call you that? Priscilla sounds so formal. I've had so much fun since you came into my life."

"I've had a lot of fun, too. You want to call me Cilla? Well, that's better than Prissy. My folks called me Prissy." Priscilla laughed and added, "That seems so long ago."

"Cilla fits you much better. It's what's in my heart. May Aaron and the girls call you that, too? I think they'd be comfortable with Cilla."

"I love it. I've kissed you. Will you kiss me now?"

Tom took her in his arms and almost took her breath away.

"When can we set the wedding date? I want everything to be proper but I hope it can be soon."

"Thank you, Tom. You can start the horse again."

They both laughed. She laid her head on his shoulder.

"I've told you about my life. I know I'm kind of old for this, but I want you to know that I'm still a virgin. I didn't think I'd ever marry, but I knew I couldn't think about a man without being married. I'm glad you won't push me. I think we'd both like for Aaron to be part of this. I do want his acceptance, too."

"You're right. I wouldn't want it any other way. Shall we set it for Easter? He'll have some time off then and can come home. I'll write him right away. He has very good grades and perhaps he can take a few extra days."

"There're so many plans to be made. I don't want a formal wedding-just a fun one. That is, if it pleases you."

"Cilla, everything you do pleases me. You plan it, and I'll love it. There is a thing or two I'd like, though."

"What would you like?"

She squeezed his arm.

"I like the way you squeeze my arm so don't ever stop doing that. The other thing I'd like for us is if we can have a honeymoon like we were young people at your house. Just a few days would make me happy. The girls can stay with Daniel and Sarah for a few days, if Aaron has to go back to school."

"I'd like a honeymoon. I do think we should plan on living at your house, though. It's much larger and better suited for a family."

"Okay, that suits me. There's one more question. Do you want a child or two?"

"I would like to have at least one of our own. Is that a problem for you?"

"That's fine with me. I can afford whatever you want. Before you even ask, *yes* you may redecorate my house to suit yourself. It will be our home, and I want you to love it."

"I'll want your help. I've heard it mentioned that you have very good taste, and I want you to be pleased with our home and comfortable. I realize my house is very full and feminine. The home I will make for both of us will have masculine things in it, too."

"Whew, that's a big relief. I'll build you a new privy if you want to decorate it and bring your sign."

They both laughed at that.

"That won't be necessary because I won't be Miss Purdy anymore. I'll be Cilla Holder and that wouldn't go good on my sign."

They pulled up in front of Cilla's house.

"May I come in for a while?"

"You're always welcome. Shall I make us some coffee? I really must find out Jetty's secret."

"No more coffee for me. I just want to sit and look at you. Maybe hold your hand and steal another kiss before I go."

Priscilla unlocked her door and lit a couple of lamps. The glow from the lamps made her look so soft and like a young girl again. She hung her hat on a peg.

"Let's sit in the parlor. I was just thinking that I may talk to Sarah, and see if we can have our wedding at the school or in their back yard. Ollie has their back yard looking like a real show place now. Some things will be blooming by the end of March. Easter falls on March the twenty ninth this year. Shall we have the wedding on Saturday, the twenty-eighth?"

"That date sounds very good to me. I'm sure Sarah will be happy to help you plan. Whatever you decide on will make me happy. This wedding is on me, so don't spare a dime. You pick out you're dress and whatever you want, and I want all the bills. Promise me."

"I can afford *some* things. What will people think?"

"You'll be my wife, and I don't care what they think. This will be your first and only wedding, and you should have what you want. Promise me."

195

"Okay, I promise. I can't get used to the idea that I'll have someone looking after me and someone who cares."

"Cilla, I not only care, I love you more everyday and our love will only keep growing. I will take care of you, and I'll make you happy."

"You do make me happy. I've never been so happy. I don't need money to make me happy. Just having you and your children makes me the happiest lady on earth. My cup runneth over! I'm stealing this kiss. You can steal yours when you're ready to go. Just hold me awhile."

They sat there a few minutes in total silence. Each was deep in their thoughts and in complete comfort.

"You know I don't want to go. That means I'd better go, so I'll steal my kiss and be off."

She walked him to the door.

"When will I see you again?"

"I'll probably see you almost every day now. Sometimes it won't be for long and other times we'll spend most of the day together. On those days, I'll keep the girls around for protection. That'll keep me out of trouble."

"It'll keep us both out of trouble. You know, I have my beliefs, and I want to deserve you and your love. I want this to be right and pure. I do love you so."

"We'll pick you up for church in the morning. Mattie will have dinner ready for us after church. Okay?"

"I'll be ready by ten in the morning." She blew a kiss and said, "Goodnight."

She closed the door and tears of joy trickled down her cheeks.

Tom arrived home, unhitched the carriage, and put his horse out in the pasture. Amy and Rachel were still up and waiting for him in the parlor. When he came in the room, they jumped up.

"Did you get her answer?"

"Yes, I did, and her answer was *yes,* she'll marry me. It seems she loves us all. She wants to belong to our family. We've made a lot of plans. We've set the wedding date for March twenty eighth. She wants Aaron to be here to be part of it all. Of course, I think she's right about that. I'll write him right away and see if he can come home then. Perhaps he can stay a few extra days. The other thing I talked to her about is that I want us to call her Cilla. Priscilla seems so formal for a family, and Prissy doesn't describe her at all."

"So we're all going to call her Cilla now?" the girls looked at each other.

"That's right. Do you girls like that idea? She won't be Miss Purdy anymore. She'll be Mrs. Holder soon. Cilla seemed right in my heart. I hope it does in yours."

The girls discussed it and decided that would be a good name for her.

"Aaron will like that, too. She's not all that much older than Aaron."

"Do you girls think I'm too old for her?"

"No, you're really nearer her age I guess than Aaron. You're just papa and that makes you seem older."

"One thing we've decided is that she and I are going to spend a few days after our wedding at her house. We need some time to ourselves to get to know about living with each other. Then this is where we'll all live and make our home. I've told her she can redecorate the house, so she'll feel it's more like her home. She'll probably help you girls decorate your room if you want to."

This thought excited the girls.

"Will she move her piano here with us?"

"We didn't talk about that, but I'm sure she will. That'll be an important thing in all our lives I'm sure. She'll teach you here at the house after we're married. There are a few other things she wants to bring. We'll have to talk about that."

"Having her and a piano here will be fun. I guess we'll put it here in the parlor."

The girls were making plans.

"That's probably what we'll do. We'll talk to Aaron and see what he might want to do with his room, if anything. You can see we'll be busy, but it'll be fun. I guess that's about all the news for now. We'll pick Cilla up in the morning for church. Then she'll have dinner here with us."

The girls were agreeable with all their papa had said.

"You'd better get on to bed now. We'll plan some more tomorrow, I'm sure."

Tom had trouble settling his brain down to go to sleep, but once sleep came, it was sound. He woke up refreshed and with a new lease on his life. His first thought was of Cilla, and how happy his life would be with her.

He chose one of his nicest outfits to wear to church and brushed his black slippers until they shined. He wanted to look his best when he entered the church with Cilla on his arm. Everyone would be watching, and the gossipers would be busy with their whispers.

Cilla and he hadn't discussed which church they would attend after they were married. He was hoping she wouldn't mind attending his, as he'd hate to leave all his friends, especially the Borden family and the Creels.

Tom would like for Preacher Kent to know about the engagement as soon as possible. He really wanted the whole town to know and to get used to the idea. Tom would start telling everyone this very morning, and it would spread fast over the town. Cilla and he needed to discuss church and a preacher right away. Everything should be clear from the beginning, so there would be no misunderstandings later.

Mattie was in the kitchen as he could smell breakfast cooking. He thought, *I'll get dressed and go have coffee. Mattie will be the first one I'll tell about the engagement today*. It'll be fun to see her reaction. I'll have time to write Aaron the news before we pick up Cilla.

Mattie was humming a hymn that could barely be heard.

"Good morning, Mattie. You sound happy this morning. I have a bit of news to tell you."

This got Mattie's attention.

"I proposed to Miss Priscilla Purdy last evening and she said, *yes*. We've set our wedding for March twenty eighth."

"Mr. Tom, this is wonderful news. I knew you were seeing her, but I had no idea it was getting that serious."

"She'll be coming to live here with us, but we want you to keep on with your schedule if you will. Miss Cilla is a very nice lady, and you two will get along nicely. She may want to do a little cooking for us, but I don't think she'll get in your way. The kitchen will still be your domain."

"Miss Cilla is what I'll call her?"

"Yes, my family decided to call her Cilla. Priscilla sounds so formal. I'm sure Miss Cilla will be all right with her."

"We'll get along fine I'm sure. I'll make her feel at home as best I can."

"Thank you, Mattie. She'll be having dinner with us after church today."

The girls came in and were already dressed for church.

"Mattie, did papa tell you we're marrying Miss Cilla?" Rachel asked. "I'm happy and excited."

"That's good, Miss Rachel. This house'll be coming alive again. That's a fine thing."

After they had breakfast, Tom went in his office to write Aaron. When he mentioned writing the news, Amy immediately said she would write Aaron about it, too. Tom told her he thought that would be good. He was curious what she would say, and he was even more curious about what Aaron would answer.

Tom looked at the clock.

"It's time to go, girls. I'll post both our letters to Aaron in the morning, if you'll put yours on my desk with mine."

"Thanks, Papa. I'll tell Aaron how happy we all are that Cilla said *yes* and that she loved us all. I'll tell him how happy you are now and what fun we're having. He'll laugh about the fishing trip and Cilla hitting you with the fish."

"It was funny. I'll have to learn to duck faster if she gets so excited when she catches a fish."

The girls laughed.

"You know everything's fun and exciting to her. I wish I could be such a happy lady when I get older."

"You can, Amy. Most of it is how you look at life. Life is what you make it."

Tom had hardly gotten Cilla settled in the carriage, when he said, "It came to me this morning that we didn't discuss which church we would attend after we're married."

"I guess I took it for granted that you and your children had attended your church all their lives. I wouldn't want to make them change. You all have so many good friends in your church and most of them are my friends, too. I think I'll grow to be very comfortable there."

Tom felt great relief with her decision. There was no need for discussion. She always seemed to reach a very reasonable conclusion. He thought, *This lady will be very easy to live with.*

When they parked at the church, Tom hurried to help his ladies out of the carriage.

"If you will this morning, you girls follow Cilla and me in."

As they walked down the aisle, everyone turned to look. Priscilla saw there was plenty of room to sit on the bench next to Sarah and Daniel. She was glad to see Sarah this morning. It gave her a sense of ease.

As she scooted in next to Sarah, she could tell Sarah was dying to know about last evening.

She leaned near and whispered in Sarah's ear, "The answer was *yes*."

Sarah smiled and squeezed her hand. Sarah leaned toward Daniel and passed the answer along. Daniel nodded his head. He had been confident all along.

After the service, Tom whispered to Cilla, "I'd like for us to go tell Preacher Kent about our engagement, and tell him you'll be joining this church."

She agreed. Tom then whispered to the girls.

"You talk to Sarah and Daniel while we go talk to the preacher."

When Tom shook the preacher's hand, he made the announcement about the engagement. Preacher Kent smiled and took Priscilla's hand. He welcomed her.

"I'm so happy for you both. I'd like to have more time with you. Can you and Tom come to my study one morning soon, and let's have a good visit?"

"That will be very nice. We'll look forward to it soon."

Tom smiled as Preacher Kent patted his shoulder. The happy couple walked back toward the girls. When they got near, Daniel rose and stepped forward. He was beaming at Tom.

"Well, I'm glad you didn't scare her off. Sarah tells me she said *yes* even after yesterday. That's a good sign it will last even if the girls had to beg her."

Daniel was still chuckling.

"She'll stay all right—forever—even though I have friends like you. Now I want to tell everyone I can that Cilla and I will be getting married the end of March."

Tom spoke and shook hands with James, then George, and on to the Creels. He was spreading the word as quickly as he could.

Sarah pulled Priscilla aside.

"Please, come have dinner with us tomorrow before my piano lesson. I'm dying to hear all about it and your plans."

"I'm dying to tell you and ask for your advice and help. I'll see you tomorrow. I guess I'd better catch up with Tom or he'll talk to everyone in the church."

Daniel was keeping up with Beau while Sarah was holding a sleeping Kate in the basket. When Priscilla finished talking to Sarah, Daniel went to join his wife.

"I'll trade with you and give your arm a rest. Are you about ready to go?"

"Yes, I've spoken to most of the family and nodded my greetings to a lot of other members."

Sarah grabbed Beau's hand and led the way to the door. Daniel had become quite adapt at helping Sarah in the carriage with one hand and arm while he held the basket. Sarah sat in the back seat most of the time when they had Kate in her basket. The basket rode on the seat beside her mama. Beau rode in the front seat with his papa, so Daniel could keep an eye on the boy.

Beau was curious about everything and battered Daniel with constant conversation. Whatever Daniel answered, Beau wanted to know-*why*. Daniel was a model of patience.

He would always remark, "They tell me I was the same way so perhaps there is hope for Beau. I've made it fairly well and I'm one thankful and happy man."

The next morning Tom came out to the factory.

"We didn't get to talk much at church. I want you to know that we've decided on March twenty eighth for our wedding. We're going to ask you and Sarah, Aaron, and Anna to be our witnesses. Cilla will talk to Sarah this afternoon."

"That sounds good, and I'm sure we'll do it."

"There is one thing Cilla has asked for. We'd both be more comfortable if we redo my bedroom before we're married. I've told her to go to your store and pick out new furniture and a mattress. I'm sure Susan will help her. I'll want it delivered and can your men help put my old furniture in storage in my warehouse? Aaron may have use for it one of these days."

"Sure. If I know when they'll deliver it, I'll come oversee the job."

"We'll probably want some more new pieces, as she's going to redecorate the whole house before long. Just the two of us are going to have a few days at her house after the wedding. I felt like we needed the time so we can get off to a good start. We haven't had that much time alone. If Aaron has to go back, I may want the girls to stay a few days with you and Sarah."

"We'd love having the girls so just speak up if you need us."

"We've decided we don't want a formal wedding, as Cilla says-just a fun wedding. She might ask Sarah about having it at the school or in your back yard. Of course, I'll pick up the cost of everything. If we have it in your back yard, I have some suggestions. If Sarah and Ollie will let me, I want to build a dance floor in the yard up and over some of the plants. What do you think about that? I'm full of good ideas. Do you realize how happy I am getting another chance at life?"

"I've got a pretty good idea. Just watching you and Priscilla together says it all by the way you look at each other. You ask Sarah and Ollie about that dance floor. Sarah and I are happy for both of you, and she'll probably let you do almost anything," Daniel smiled as he answered.

"We feel like you're both part of our family, you know. Priscilla and Sarah have become almost like sisters. They tell each other things like you and I do."

Daniel suddenly lowered his voice.

"I want to tell you something I think is important for you to know. Priscilla loves you. I mean deeply loves you or she wouldn't do this just for a home or security. She had decided to live her life alone until you showed up."

"That would have been a waste. She's got a lot of love to give to me and the children. Believe me I know what I'm getting, and will give her my heart. I'm so thankful. That woman is so much fun. Everything is exciting with her. Whatever she's involved in she gives it her attention and that's what's important at that moment. I love that in her. She gives my life a lot of joy and a new appreciation for everything."

Daniel had a nice visit with Tom. He was anxious to hear what Priscilla had to say at dinner. He knew she would be as happy about this marriage as Tom was.

Daniel could see Sarah and Priscilla in the back garden when he walked up the path from the factory. As he got nearer, he could hear they were already deep into the plans for the wedding.

"Hello Priscilla, it looks like you and Sarah might be making plans for a wedding already."

"How did you ever guess?"

Priscilla's face was lit up with a smile.

"Oh, I saw Tom this morning, and he was making plans. Did he mention that you two might want his men to build a dance floor in our back yard?"

"He mentioned if Sarah and Ollie would let him do it, that he'd like to."

"It might be fun, Sarah. What do you think and where?"

"I was wondering what if Tom took the rails off the porch, and we had a wooden arbor temporarily built along that section of the wall. The arbor could be painted white and decorated with vines, ferns, and flowers. Preacher Kent could stand under the arbor, and Tom with Priscilla could stand in front of him."

She outlined the arbor with the motion of her arms.

"Then Aaron and Anna could flank them on one side with you and me on the other side. People could step down one step from the porch to the dance floor."

She motioned with her hands how the step down would work.

"We can make two rows of benches with an aisle between them on the dance floor. After the ceremony, the men can quickly move the benches out to the yard around the fire pit and the big table. Boxes of bulbs and ferns could be placed along the edge of the porch. What do you think, Priscilla?"

"I can see it and I love it, Sarah. The garden should be very pretty with lots of blooms that time of year."

Priscilla thought for a moment as she visualized the dance floor and the decorations.

"The dance floor would only be over grass that way. Tom can build it out to the first row of boxwoods. That would keep people from falling off the dance floor."

"The musicians can stand on part of the porch to play. I like the plans, ladies, and I think Tom will be very pleased. It shouldn't take his men long to built the dance floor and arbor. I'll get the men at the factory to start building and painting the boxes for the plants."

Sarah asked, "Do you have a dress in mind, Priscilla?"

"I'm thinking I'd like a fabric like India muslin in a sky blue color. Maybe with a full skirt and the waist would be fitted and have a square neckline with puffed sleeves. I'd like white roses in my hair with ribbons. Would that look too young for me?"

Sarah could see in her mind how outstanding that would look.

"It'll be beautiful. We should have some early white roses by then. I'll help you fix your hair if you like."

"Oh, Sarah, this will be fun. What will *you* wear?"

"I think I'll make my own dress out of an indigo blue. That should help show up your lighter blue even more."

"I wonder what Anna will want to wear. Lucy and I'll probably make her dress. We can ask her when she comes to dinner since this is piano lesson day."

Jetty came to the door to say dinner was ready.

"Miss Mary and Miss Anna are here."

"Good, all this fashion talk leaves me out of it," Daniel jested.

After greeting Mary and Anna, the wedding talk continued at the table.

"Anna, I haven't asked you yet. Tom and I would like for you and Aaron to witness our wedding along with Daniel and Sarah. I'm planning on wearing a sky blue dress, and Sarah is choosing indigo blue. If you'll do it, what would you like to wear? Sarah says she and your mama will probably make both of your dresses."

"I'd love to be in the wedding, Miss Purdy. This is exciting. Is Aaron coming home?"

"Yes, the wedding is on Saturday, March twenty eighth. We're hoping Aaron can come a few days early."

"If it's all right, I think I'd like to wear a deep rose pink. Maybe a dress made of soft cotton or whatever Aunt Sarah thinks."

"A deep rose would look beautiful on you."

"Now, don't you two try to outdo the bride. I'll be struggling to keep up with two such beautiful witnesses. Oh well, never mind, I can never outdo the two of you."

Priscilla laughed.

"Tom will have to accept me as I am."

"Don't worry. He'll only have eyes for you."

Daniel broke in through all the giggling and teasing.

"Tom says you both want to redo his bedroom. He said you'd be in the store shopping soon. I'll tell Susan to be ready and make sure we have what you might want."

"I'd like new covers, too. Who do you suggest to make them?"

"Talk to Trudy Drake. She'll probably want you to choose the fabric but then she can make them if she has time. They make our good mattresses for us. You and Tom will want one of them. Have her make the new covers for it. Heck, don't skimp with Tom's money. You may as well get the best."

"Oh, Daniel, don't make me feel guilty about shopping with Tom's money."

"Daniel's teasing you. Tom wants you to get what you want, and he's used to good things."

"Enjoy it, Priscilla. Tom wants you to be happy."

"I'm so happy, but only with the thought of Tom and his family. His money is not important. I will contribute as I'm sure we'll either rent my home or sell it. I intend to keep teaching piano lessons, too. Teaching our girls at home will allow me to increase my student load."

"You'll still come teach at the school then?" Mary asked.

"Oh, yes. The students are used to it there, and that keeps my business separate from my home. Speaking of lessons, it's time for Sarah's and Anna's. I guess we should get down to the school."

The foursome rose from the table.

Daniel said, "I should get back to work. It's been very pleasant having dinner with four lovely ladies."

He went over and gave Sarah a kiss on the cheek.

"I'll see you later."

Sarah went to tell Remy she was going to the school for her lesson.

"Remy, if you need me. I'll be at the school. I think the children will be fine for that length of time, however."

The ladies rode to the school in the carriage.

Chapter Eight

Time had passed and March had arrived quickly. Priscilla had been busy choosing fabric for her wedding trousseau. She was having some new, fancier, undergarments made along with her wedding dress. In her search, she had found very pretty and unusual white slippers made from satin to wear with her sky blue dress. The shoes were not only pretty, but they seemed as though they would be comfortable for dancing.

Mrs. Drake was busy sewing new bedcovers and drapes for Tom's bedroom. Priscilla knew which mattress she wanted, but she had neglected shopping for the bedroom furniture. It was such a beautiful spring day she decided she would walk to the furniture store and shop. When she arrived at the store, she saw Daniel's fine-looking horse tied to the front rail.

Once inside, she told Daniel, "I'm glad to find you here. I've come to shop for Tom's new bedroom furniture, and you'll know what he'd like. I want our bedroom to look masculine. Mrs. Drake is making a very nice dark green bed coverlet for the top of the bed. She's monogramming the sheets and pillow covers. I'll be softening the dark green coverlet with a few smaller pillows of white with yellow flowers and dark green leaves on the fabric."

"Let's look at some of the furniture and perhaps you'll see something you like."

As they walked around the store, they continued to talk.

"Tom and I shopped for paint, and he chose and had the walls painted a cream color."

"We have a beautiful chestnut set that is stained dark. It has a very large armoire and a bed that fits our best largest mattress. There is a double waist-high chest of drawers that matches it. Let me get Susan to help us. She has such good taste and ideas. You go through the step down and start looking while I get Susan."

Daniel went to the office, and with Susan in tow, he went back to help Priscilla.

"This must be the one you were describing to me. I love it, and I think Tom will. The carving on the pieces is beautiful."

Susan got involved in the choosing. She was always very quick with good suggestions.

"Priscilla, we have two gold framed mirrors that would be beautiful over the double chest. We have two beautiful big round rugs that Mrs. Stewart just plaited and brought in for us to sell. If one of them will go with your colors, it would be beautiful on the floor in front of the fireplace. We also have two chestnut rockers that will match the bedroom furniture and a small round table that would go between them. Let me show you."

Daniel followed and let Susan do the selling. He was sure that Tom would love what the ladies were planning since he would like it himself.

"I'm so thrilled with this. Can you deliver it in the morning when Tom will be gone? The bedcovers will fit the largest mattress."

Susan spoke up saying, "We can deliver it, and Daniel and I will come with it and help you plan the room."

Priscilla was becoming even more excited.

"Okay, let's meet at Tom's house at nine thirty in the morning, if that's all right with everyone."

"I'll bring a couple of my men to move the old furniture out to Tom's storage warehouse and to move in the new. We'll even hang the mirrors," Daniel added.

"This is so much fun. Won't Tom be surprised when he gets home and sees what we've done?"

"Tom will love it. You can be sure of that."

"I'll go pick up the new covers and drapes this afternoon. You'll hang the new drapes won't you, Daniel?"

"For you and Tom, we'll hang the drapes."

Priscilla left the store a thrilled, happy woman.

"One more pleased customer. They'll be back for more furniture soon after the wedding, and Priscilla makes more of her plans," Susan predicted.

"Well, at least Tom won't have to live with a bunch of lace and ruffles. He'll be glad of that."

"Daniel, the lady does have good taste. Her house was decorated feminine but she lived alone. I thought for a lady it was neat and attractive."

The following day, Daniel, Moseley, and Latham were at the store before nine o'clock with two wagons. When they finished loading everything, Daniel led the way to Tom's house. They arrived right at nine thirty. Priscilla was already there, and she and Mattie opened the front door.

"Let's move Tom's old furniture out here on the porch, and then we'll carry in the new and set it up. When we finish with that, we'll load up the old and take it to the warehouse. Mattie, do you have the keys to the warehouse?"

"Yes sir. I know where they are. I'll get 'em. There should be some big old cloths out there to cover the old furniture. Mr. Tom thinks Mr. Aaron may want that furniture one of these days."

When everything was in place, they all stood back and admired the bedroom.

"I'm so pleased with how it looks. Thank all of you for your work. I think Tom will love it."

"He will, Priscilla. Go get Mattie and tell her to come and look."

Mattie stepped to the bedroom door.

"Oh my, Miss Priscilla, Mr. Tom is goin' to love this room now."

"See, I told you. Mattie knows what he likes. Let's load up everything and get the other furniture out of here. It's getting near dinner, and Tom will be coming for his meal. We don't want to get caught."

"Miss Priscilla, you'll stay for dinner won't you? That would be a nice surprise for Mr. Tom."

"Thank you, Mattie. I'd love to. Then I can see his reaction."

Daniel, Susan, and the men had not been gone thirty minutes when Tom came home. Tom saw Priscilla's carriage out front and wondered if something was wrong. He rushed in and Cilla was back in the kitchen with Mattie.

"Is everything all right?"

"It's wonderful, Tom. Just go look in your bedroom."

When he got to the bedroom door, he stopped and let it all soak in.

"Cilla, this is beautiful. I love it and *look* at that bed. There's one thing that it is missing to be perfect."

"What, Tom? I thought it was complete."

"Not quite yet-but soon, Cilla. The one thing it's missing is you. It'll be complete when you move in."

"What a lovely thing to say."

She walked over and gave him a tender kiss.

"I've been out spending your money. I'm afraid there is a bill waiting for you at the furniture store."

"Whatever it is, it's worth every penny. Are you pleased with it?"

"I love it! Daniel and Susan helped me with it. They assured me you'd like it."

"You deserve another kiss for having such good taste. I made a pun and didn't realize it until I said it."

He took her in his arms and hated to let her go.

"We'd better get to the dining room. Mattie will be wondering what's keeping us."

Tom had gotten a letter from Aaron and his son would be arriving home on March twenty fifth. They were all very excited and were getting ready for his coming.

His father had written Aaron to go have a tailor to measure him and send the measurements home. Tom and Cilla had taken Aaron's measurements to the local tailor and had a new waist coat and trousers made for him to wear to the wedding. Cilla had chosen a new white shirt for him, also. It was made of a fine silk. She and the girls had shopped and had new dresses made for both of them.

As a surprise for the girls, Cilla had gone in the silver shop and found two beautiful crosses on thin silver chains for their necks. While she was shopping, a gorgeous silver heart caught her eye. It had delicate engravings on the front that set it off. The heart opened and there were two engravings on the inside. One side had the silhouette of a young man and the other side a young lady. When it closed

211

it was almost as if they were kissing. She selected it and had Mr. Adler put it in a small, beautiful, ivory box.

Cilla was having supper at Tom's home on the evening of the twenty fifth. Aaron's new clothes were all laid out on his bed for him to see, and Tom had gone to meet Aaron in front of the tavern. Mattie was cooking a special meal, and Cilla was making sure the table looked just right.

The girls saw Tom's carriage coming down the road and ran out to meet them. They were so glad to see their brother. Tom got Aaron's bag for him as the girls walked their brother into the house.

"Look who we have, Cilla."

Priscilla smiled and stuck her hand out to Aaron.

He took it, but then she said, "I can't help it, but I'm going to hug you. You've just grown so mature since I last saw you. You're really a young man now. You're almost a full fledged doctor, and we're all so proud of you."

"Not quite yet, but soon. I hear you and papa are getting ready for a wedding."

"Yes, we're counting the days. I'm very excited and beginning to get a little nervous."

"I think we're all excited for you and papa. It's wonderful you found each other."

Tears formed in Cilla's eyes.

"Thanks for saying that. You don't know how much it means to me."

Mattie came to say she was putting dinner on the table.

"I fixed some of your favorites, Mr. Aaron."

"Good Mattie, I can smell them."

The supper was very pleasant. They listened to Aaron's tales of school and the friends he'd made. Tom suggested that after they had finished their meal, Aaron should try on his new clothes.

"If they don't fit just right, we still have a couple of days, and perhaps the tailor can alter them if need be."

After dessert, Aaron went to his room. When he returned, he had on the clothes and looked as if he was ready for the wedding.

"They fit perfectly. Thank you, Papa. I think they look very nice."

"Cilla helped me pick them out. She worried as she hoped they would fit and you'd be pleased."

"You look very handsome. Anna will melt when she sees you. You certainly favor your papa," said Cilla as she looked on approvingly.

"Does Anna know when I'd get here?"

"Yes, I talk to her often. She could hardly wait to see you."

"I'd like to see her as soon as I can."

"Tomorrow is her piano lesson after school. I happen to know that she'll be having dinner at Sarah's and Daniel's. Why don't the two of us go have dinner with them? I'll let you use my carriage, and you can take Anna for a ride after we eat. Tom, can you bring me home after the girl's lesson?"

"It'll be my pleasure. You can tell Aaron our wedding plans while you're at Daniel's. Show him where the dance platform will be."

"You don't mind me driving your carriage?" Aaron asked in surprise.

"My goodness no, I know you've driven your papa's a lot. Mine is smaller and easier to drive. I'll pick you up about ten in the morning. That way we'll get our name in the pot for dinner in plenty of time."

Aaron laughed.

"Thank you, and I'll be ready. I'll go change now and get more comfortable."

Cilla stood, reached for her handbag, and told Aaron, "I have something for you. May I come to your room for a minute?"

"Sure, you're welcome in my room. This'll soon be your home."

Aaron stood aside and let Cilla enter his room first. She reached in her handbag and pulled out the ivory box.

"You may think this is a strange gift for a young man, but I think you'll know what to do with it. I got the girls crosses, but I loved this when I saw it, and I think you know someone who will love it, too. It is yours so do as you wish with it."

She handed Aaron the little box. When he opened it, he was taken aback.

"This is beautiful, Cilla. I know a very pretty neck that it will set off or she'll set *it* off. This is one of the most thoughtful gifts I've ever gotten."

He kissed her cheek and gave her a hug.

"Thank you so much."

"I told you that Anna would melt when she saw you. Well, you'll do some melting yourself when you see her. May I say she's filled out in all the right places in just these past few months. She's become a beautiful young lady."

I've always thought she was very pretty."

"Oh, she was, but now she's beautiful. Her dark hair, her big, velvet, brown eyes and now she's filled out. You'll see tomorrow. She's still the sweet Anna we've all grown to love. She's very smart and more talented than most. She's been waiting for you. The young lady thinks you're special and you are."

"Cilla, I find you very easy to talk to. My mama and I never would have been having this conversation. I loved her, but we never just talked like this."

"Aaron anytime you want to talk to me about anything, I'll be here for you. I not only love your papa very much, I love all of you."

She gave Aaron a quick kiss on the cheek and left the room. When she returned to the parlor, Tom looked up toward Cilla's eyes.

"Is everything all right?"

"It's wonderful. Your son and I had a very good talk. We're very comfortable with each other and there'll be a special bond between us."

"Aaron's a smart young man. I'm sure he sees the special qualities in you that I see."

Cilla kissed Tom's cheek.

"I'd better be getting home. It's dark already."

"It is, and I'm not letting you go home by yourself. Leave your carriage. We'll take care of it, and Aaron can pick you up in it tomorrow for your dinner date. I'll drive you home. Let me tell him."

It didn't take long to get to Cilla's house. Tom walked her to the door.

"I'd better not come in tonight. I'll get back and spend more time with Aaron before bedtime. I'll take a goodnight kiss though."

With that, he gave her a passionate kiss.

"I'll see you tomorrow. Then it'll just be two days, and you'll be Mrs. Holder."

He gave her another quick kiss on the cheek and left.

About nine thirty the next morning, Aaron was knocking on Cilla's door.

"I came earlier since it's farther out to the Borden's from here. I want to be sure to get our names in that pot," Aaron said. "I hope I'm not too early."

"You're just right. Let me get my hat, and we'll be on our way."

As they got to the carriage, Cilla suggested, "You drive. I don't often get to be a passenger in my own carriage. I'll enjoy being a passenger today."

"I like your small carriage, and your horse is very well behaved."

"She *is* well behaved. I've had Pansy for a few years now. I bought her from Mr. Hines at the wagon yard when I first moved to town."

215

"Where do you keep her? When we returned you privy, your yard didn't look large enough to keep a horse."

Cilla couldn't help but giggle at Aaron remembering the privy incident.

"Oh, the neighbor across the back alley from me has a small pasture, and I keep her there. He has a small barn, too, and I keep my carriage in it."

"You hitch and unhitch her yourself?"

"Aaron, when you live alone, there's a lot of things you have to do for yourself. I've been alone for a few years now."

"You've never married?"

"I was engaged to be married once, but the young man died from fever about three months before we were to be married."

Cilla looked off in the distance as if looking for a long lost dream.

"I'm sorry. I didn't know."

"That's all right. You can ask me anything. I have no secrets. There was a bad epidemic, and I lost him and my parents within two weeks of each other. A few months after that, I moved to Burkesville. It was a new town just getting started, and I needed a new life. I must say I never thought I'd get married, that is, until I got to know your papa."

"I know he built your privy for you. Did you get to know him then?"

"My goodness, no. That was business for both of us. When your sisters started taking piano lessons from me at the school, he would bring them. He just left them at first and would come back to pick them up. Then he started visiting, and we would talk for a few minutes. He started staying a little longer. I began to know him a little better when the Bordens gave a dinner party, and I came with Susan and Noah. I guess that's when we became friends."

"I see."

"You may not see. Aaron, I'll just be frank with you. Your papa and I have never been together in that way. Not even now. I guess I'm old fashioned about such things. Tom knew my feelings, and he's always been very much a gentleman with me. We're going to have a honeymoon at my house after the wedding, though. I hope you don't mind since you're visiting. We hoped you'd have time to stay with the girls for a few days. They can stay with Daniel and Sarah if you can't."

"I can stay until the following Wednesday, but then I have to start back."

"Tom and I haven't discussed how long we'll stay at my house. I was leaving that up to him. We'll work it out, so you don't have to worry. We're just so glad you could come."

"I am, too. I feel like I've gotten to know you, and I'm proud of that. I'm really glad to be here to welcome you into our family."

Cilla patted his shoulder just before they turned onto the Borden's road.

As they passed the school, Aaron said, "I'd just like to walk through that school door and see Anna, but I won't. She'll be surprised to see us at the Borden's for dinner."

Jetty was surprised, too, when they knocked on the door.

"Come in, Miss Priscilla and Mr. Aaron Holder. My goodness, I never thought about seeing you today."

"Aaron couldn't wait to see Anna, so I just invited us to dinner at Daniel's and Sarah's," Cilla said and giggled.

"I wanted to get our name in the pot. I've also wanted to watch you make coffee. I plan on surprising Tom the first morning after our wedding with my spectacular coffee. After I watch, I want to show and tell Aaron about our wedding plans."

Cilla went on to the kitchen with Jetty. Aaron followed and watched Jetty make coffee, too.

"All right, I can make that fabulous cup of coffee now. I just have to get some linen scraps and the right glass pot to put it in. Aaron, after we eat, why don't you take my

217

carriage and you and Anna go shop for me a glass coffeepot? Now that you've watched Jetty making coffee, you know what I'll need. Here, let me give you some money now before I forget."

Cilla dug in her handbag and handed Aaron money. The young man thought, *She's already treating me like a son.* He rather liked the idea.

"Let's go out to the garden, and let me show you how things will look."

Aaron and Cilla walked out in the back yard. Ollie saw them and came to speak.

"Does the garden please you, Miss Priscilla?"

"Ollie, it's beautiful. It looks like an artist's painting."

Daniel came walking up the path from the factory. He was surprised to see Cilla and Aaron there. When Sarah, Mary, and Anna came from the school, they just came in as usual and went right in the dining room. They were talking and never looked up to see who was coming in.

"Anna, aren't you even going to speak to me?" Aaron calmly asked her.

Anna gave out a little squeal and threw her arms around Aaron's neck.

"Aaron Holder, what are you doing here?"

"I thought you knew I was coming home for the wedding."

"I did, but I wasn't expecting to see you here for dinner."

"Cilla invited us for dinner. She wanted to show me and to tell me about the wedding plans. I understand we're supposed to be two of the witnesses. I wanted to learn what I'm to do."

"You look so good."

Anna could not take her eyes off of him.

"So do you. Cilla told me you were even more beautiful than before, and she's right."

Anna's cheek's flushed a bit.

"I want to hear all about your school and your plans."

218

"After we eat, Cilla has asked me to take her carriage and to go to town to shop for her a coffee pot. I was hoping you could go with me."

Anna turned, "Aunt Sarah, may I go with Aaron to shop?"

"You may. I think your music lesson can wait for another time."

The conversation was lively around the dinner table. Aaron told a tale or two. They discussed the wedding and the new bedroom Cilla had done for Tom. As soon as dessert was over, Aaron suggested he and Anna start for town.

"Dad's bringing the girls out for their lesson?"

"Yes, I'll be at the school until about 4:30."

"I'll take Anna home and be at the school by that time. Is a coffee pot all you need?"

"Get me a yard of white linen while you're at Creel's Store if you will, please. Just leave the packages in my carriage and don't mention them to your papa. I want my coffee to be a surprise."

"Okay, I understand."

Aaron walked around and gave Cilla a kiss on the cheek.

"Thanks for everything."

After Aaron and Anna went out the door, Sarah smiled and said, "I'd say you're already making a hit with all the Holder family."

"I'm very fortunate there. Aaron and I are very comfortable and find we can say anything to each other. He has really matured. He's responsible and thoughtful. I find him to be everything anyone could want in a son. Tom and Dorcus did a fine job raising him."

Aaron and Anna pulled up in front of Creel's store. He hurried around to help Anna out of the carriage. As they stepped in the door of the store, Molly Creel looked up.

"My goodness, if it isn't Aaron Holder. We haven't seen you in quite a while. I know you've been off at school. I guess you're here for the wedding."

"Yes ma'am. I'm here to see it well done," he smiled and then continued, "Priscilla has sent us to shop for her a coffee pot and a yard of white linen."

"The yard of linen is the secret to the kind of pot she wants. I found the right kind of pot and ordered them shortly after Jetty learned to make her coffee. Let me show you."

"Here's a pretty one. It's white and almost like thick pottery more than delicate porcelain. It has pretty bright flowers painted on each side. It has a lid and comes with a higher trivet to sit above the hot coals. It'll keep the coffee hot without changing its taste."

"That looks like Cilla. Don't you think, Anna?"

"She'll like it very much."

Molly walked over and cut the yard of white linen.

"Will there be anything else?"

"No, I think that's it for today. How much will that be?"

Molly figured and told Aaron. He pulled out the money and paid. Molly wrapped the linen around the glass pot and then wrapped and tied brown paper around both.

"That should help to get it home safely. I guess we'll see you both Saturday at the wedding and party?" she asked rhetorically.

Anna spoke up.

"Yes, ma'am, we're both witnesses along with Aunt Sarah and Uncle Daniel."

Aaron took the package and opened the store door for Anna. When they got to the carriage, he handed her the pot.

"I'll let you keep this safe."

He put a hand on Anna's arm and one on her waist and lifted her up in the carriage.

"Thank you, Mr. Holder."

"Anna I want to talk. Do you know where we can go for a while?"

"There's a nice ford and meadow out along the river just north of town. People stop there for picnics under the trees. It's not far."

"Do you go there often?"

She quickly wheeled in her seat and looked Aaron right in the eyes.

"If you're implying I've been there with other young men, never."

"I'm sorry, Anna. I didn't mean to upset you. You're just so darn pretty now I'm sure you've had a lot of invitations."

"There have been a few. I've not been the least bit interested in any of them. I've been too busy plus I've been waiting for your invitation. I do wish you could get that through your thick head. I've trusted you to write if you found someone else. I haven't gotten that kind of note, so I've kept my faith in you."

"I've kept my faith in you. It's just almost unbelievable to me that a beautiful girl like you would wait around on me."

"Aaron, I happen to think you're handsome, charming, and very smart. I also see all the wonderful qualities in you that seem to be absent in most young men. If you're interested in me, I'm not such a fool that I would throw that away on a fling of some sort. I'll wait on you until I hear differently."

"Point me toward the place by the river. I have something for you, but I want to wait until we're stopped to give it to you and express my feelings."

"Just go out the North River Road for a short distance. It's not far, and I'll show you when we get there."

They hadn't gone far when there was a turnoff with a short trail to a little meadow and some trees along the river.

"This is a beautiful place. I don't think I've ever been out here."

"Eli and I came once with Aunt Sarah and Uncle Daniel when I was younger."

Aaron stopped Pansy, put on the carriage brake, and wrapped the reins around the brake handle. He reached under his waist coat, into his breeches pocket, pulled out the little ivory box, and handed it to Anna.

She took the box and looked at it.

"This box is beautiful."

"That's not the gift. Open it. I'm anxious to see what you say."

Her hands slightly shook.

"You can breathe, Anna. It's not a ring. I wouldn't do that to you after our understanding. I've had my time at school, and I want you to have your year to study and meet new friends. While you're gone, I'll be here getting a practice set up and getting things ready. If we both still feel the same way, there'll be a ring then. I won't wait too long for an answer or for a wedding after that."

Anna took a deep breath and opened the box. There lay the beautiful silver heart on dark blue velvet.

"Oh, Aaron, it's beautiful."

"Open it and then tell me you'll wear my heart."

Anna gently opened it.

"Of course, I'll wear it. Is that us inside the heart?"

"I hope it is, Anna. I hope it with all my heart. May I kiss you?"

"Please do Aaron. I can tell you something now. I'll take my year, but I will come back to you. I think a doctor's wife needs to be smart and accomplished. I hope to be both when I return, so I can deserve your love."

After the kiss, Aaron asked, "May I fasten it around your neck?"

"Yes, of course you can."

Aaron laughed when he suddenly remember that day with Garrett Adler.

"You have to remember I heard you that day Garrett Adler asked you to wear his cross."

"You're not Garrett Adler. Just wait until you see it with the dress I'm wearing to the wedding. Our heart will look beautiful with it."

"I believe that. Anna, you're smart enough and plenty accomplished enough for me already. I want you to fulfill your dream though, and I'm willing to wait."

"I know, I see what your studies have done for you. You have self-assurance now, and you can talk to anyone about anything. That is-you have self-assurance with and about everyone except me."

"I can tell you why. I love you so much already. You're so special to me, and I still have problems believing I'm the one that's caught you."

Anna took his face in her hands.

"Look at me. You've caught me, so relax. I'll be back. I've decided I want to study music now. I love the piano, and I'm good. I've found out I have the special gift, plus now I read music, too. I've found my voice is very pleasant when I sing. I want to teach voice and playing more than one instrument if my instructors deem me good enough."

"Wow, you don't only have self-assurance already, you have spunk. You remind me of your Aunt Sarah and my nearly step-mother, Priscilla."

Anna began to laugh.

"You couldn't have given me a nicer compliment."

She still had her hands on his face.

"I'll just be forward and steal another kiss without even asking."

Anna continued to hold his face and gave him a very tender kiss.

"Sometimes you surprise me in the most astounding ways. We better go and get you home. I'll be picking my sisters up after school tomorrow. Can you join us for dinner at our house tomorrow?"

"Will you be able to drive me home afterwards?"

"Sure, my sisters will probably be with us."

"I don't mind them. Amy and I are friends. I visit with them occasionally while you're at school."

"That's good. I think you know that Amy keeps me up on what's going on, especially at school. Let me offer Pansy a drink of river water before we go."

When they pulled up in front of Anna's home, Aaron walked her to the door.

"Thanks for helping me shop."

"Thank you for the beautiful gift. I'll cherish it always."

Anna brushed his cheek with a light kiss. Aaron headed back to the school. As he arrived at the school, he could hear the piano. He went to the door and stuck his head in. Tom motioned for him to come and to sit by him. Rachel was playing the piano, and Cilla was watching her.

"That's very good, Rachel," Cilla said as she turned around. "Don't you think so, Tom?"

"No doubt she's improving more all the time."

"You're back, Aaron. Did you and Anna have a nice drive?"

"Yes ma'am. Thank you for the use of your carriage. Anna loved the heart, and it's beautiful around her neck."

"What heart did Anna love?" One could see the surprise on Tom's face.

"Oh, I helped Aaron select a gift for Anna. You'll see it around her neck at the wedding. He chose a beautiful silver heart for her. We better close up the school. I have a dozen things to do this evening."

Cilla locked the school door, and Tom kissed her cheek and helped her into the carriage.

Tom suggested that Aaron go with him to carry the girls to school the following morning.

"My men will be working on the dance floor and putting the arbor up this morning. Cilla will be out at Sarah's helping choose the flowers. We won't put the finishing touches on everything until in the morning."

The two prepared the carriage and Aaron herded his two sisters on out to get in. The conversation continued as they headed for the school.

"Since Anna and Cilla are going to have dinner with us today, you can pick the girls and Anna up after school, and I'll drive Cilla in her carriage. Anna's folks will probably be coming and going from Daniel's this morning. I think you might win some favor if you pitch in to help."

"Do you think Anna will be at her aunt and uncle's later this afternoon?"

"I wouldn't doubt it if she thinks you'll be there."

"Okay, count me in. I can gather firewood for the fire ring if nothing else."

"Now that's the spirit."

"Papa, you know I'm really happy that you're marrying Cilla. I like her very much, and I consider you a very lucky man."

"Aaron, thanks for telling me. That's very important to me."

By this time they had arrived and Daniel's back yard was buzzing all day with everyone working. After dinner, Aaron and Anna returned to Daniel's to help gathered firewood and kindling. They piled it up near the fire pit. Daniel walked out to talk to Aaron.

"Sarah and I've been talking. Why don't you and the girls bring your things tomorrow and stay with us until you're ready to go back to school. There's no need you staying at your house with just you and the girls. They'd be convenient for school, and perhaps Anna can have dinner with us while you're here. I'll speak to James and get his okay. You could spend more time together strolling along the river and visiting."

"Thank you, Mr. Borden. The more I think about it, the more I like the idea if we won't be too much trouble. I'll accept and thanks so much for the invitation."

"We'll plan on it, then."

"Will you tell papa about our plans?"

"I'll tell him, and he'll feel better if he thinks you all are having some fun. Heck, we might even have time to go fishing."

When Daniel walked off, Aaron said, "I'm proud of the invitation. We'll see so much more of each other the next few days. We'll take walks and sit in the swing. We can go down to the school, and you can play and sing for me. This is going to be great."

"I'm glad you accepted their invitation. We'll have fun."

Late that afternoon, everything was ready for the ceremony except adding the fresh flowers to the arbor and placing bouquets around. Tom had hired Mattie, Ollie, and Jetty extra to tend to serving and to make sure food and drink was available at all times after the ceremony.

That evening after they got home, Tom told Aaron, "Daniel told me you and the girls have decided to stay with them for a few days. I think you'll enjoy your time at their home more than here. Cilla will go out in her carriage in the morning, and we'll go in ours. After the party, Cilla and I'll slip off in her carriage and leave mine behind for you. You can handle it can't you?"

"Sure, Papa, I can handle it. I've had plenty of experience with it now. Ollie will help me if I need anything."

"Cilla and I'll be at her house in town until the next Friday. We'll want to see you off on Wednesday though. You can come pick us up in my carriage on Wednesday."

"Papa, you know I'll be moving back the end of May. I'll be an apprentice to Dr. Wade for a while and then he wants me to be a full-fledged partner. I'll be making my home here then. I'll be Dr. Holder and I'll have to make plans for my own home."

"Dr. Holder, you've made me very proud. Your mama would have been, too."

"I know, Papa."

Early the next morning Cilla gathered her wedding clothes and went to Sarah's. She would help put on the finishing touches with the flowers this morning. Sarah had tied Cilla's hair up in rags when she first arrived so it would curl. Sarah had Ollie put Cilla's things in the bedroom where the girls would be staying. She'd get dressed for the wedding in that bedroom. Later this morning they would have a big, late breakfast. Cilla was looking forward to a bath in Sarah's bathing room.

Late in the morning, Sarah went to the garden and chose several small, perfect, white roses. She placed them in water so they would look fresh. She had white ribbon to intertwine with Cilla's hair and the roses.

Cilla had brought a string of white pearls and pearl earrings with three diamonds hanging down from the pearl to wear. They had been her mother's. Sarah had a pair of fingerless, white, lace gloves that came above the elbows. Priscilla was going to wear them for the ceremony. Sarah was also going to lend her an old sixpence to wear in her shoe.

Sarah and Cilla were upstairs when Tom and his family got there. The girls slipped upstairs to put their bags in their room. They laughed seeing Cilla's hair up in rags.

"You wait until we comb her hair. She'll look like a fairy princess."

Ollie had the back yard looking like a picture. Everything and everyone was ready. Tom was waiting with Preacher Kent at the arbor. Sarah and Daniel came out the door first, followed by Anna and Aaron. The bride was next. She was on the arm of Dr. Wade who had agreed to give her away. The Wades had become close to Tom because of Aaron.

The ceremony was beautiful and went smoothly. After Tom kissed the bride, the men quickly cleared away the

227

benches and the musicians stepped to the hallway and got their instruments. The music and dancing began. The big table between the trees began to fill with food, cider, and a fruit punch. People stayed late into the evening.

Ollie slipped Miss Priscilla's carriage out to the front road. Cilla and Tom slipped out the front door with only Daniel and Sarah realizing it. Their plans had all worked perfectly.

The young couple had spent all of Tuesday afternoon together saying goodbye. Wednesday would come all too quickly for Aaron and Anna.

"I'll see you again in May. We'll have some time together before time for you to head for school. We'll have a busy year, and I'll have things ready for you to become my wife when you return. Do you want a big wedding?"

"I don't think so. We can plan it later. People may expect more from a doctor. We'll see how the year goes. There *will* be a wedding. I can assure you of that and just a simple ceremony will be fine with me."

"Anna, you're very talented. You'll get offers for a career in big cities. Cilla said if you were a man, you could become a conductor of a big symphony orchestra."

"I don't want a career in a big city. I want to be happy. You and my family make me happy. My dream will be fulfilled if I can marry you and teach right here in our little school."

They said their goodbyes, and Anna walked home through the woods.

It was now Wednesday morning, and Aaron was packed and ready to leave. He'd said goodbye to his sisters before they went to school. Ollie had his papa's carriage waiting behind Daniel's house for him. Daniel had said goodbye and went on to the factory. Sarah was to ride as far as the school with him, so Aaron helped her into the carriage.

"We enjoyed having you so much. Take care, and we'll see you in May."

He waved one more time as he drove the carriage down the road. When Sarah walked into the school, Anna knew that Aaron was on his way back to school.

The week passed quickly. Tom and Cilla started moving her clothes and other personal things to Tom's house on Friday morning. Friday when school was dismissed, Tom and Cilla were there to pick up the girls. They had to go to Sarah's house to pick up the girl's clothes. Jetty answered the door and asked them in.

"Miss Sarah and Miss Mary haven't come from the school yet."

"We know. We were there to pick up the girls, but we need to get their things. They've enjoyed their visit with the Bordens and especially playing with Beau and Kate."

"We enjoyed having them. You all are going to stay for lunch, aren't you?"

"We'd had no plans to."

"Well, you make plans right now, and I'll set four more plates. I always have plenty of food. If no one's here to eat it, we have it for supper or sometimes the next day. Nothing much goes to waste."

Tom told Jetty, "Well, set those plates then as I won't turn down one of your meals. Mattie won't be back until tomorrow to cook, so I'm sure Cilla is not looking forward to finding us something for dinner."

Tom squeezed Cilla's shoulders. About that time, Daniel came in the back door.

"Do I hear voices?"

"You hear the Holders. They're here begging another meal."

Tom tried to disguise his voice.

"Now Mr. Daniel, don't you believe that. I insisted they stay and eat with us. They're here taking two of our girls off and with nothing to feed them."

"Well, I'm glad you made them stay then, Jetty. We don't want any girls going hungry."

Amy and Rachel went and hugged Daniel around the waist.

"You did feed us well all week," Amy said.

"I would keep you, too, if they want to give you away."

"No way. Just as I'm getting two girls and a boy, I'm not giving them away to anyone," Cilla laughed. "I can cook. I just haven't had time at Tom's house. If there's any food at Tom's house they'll have a reasonably good supper."

"Trust me-she can cook, at least, for two."

The girls then went to hug Cilla.

"See, they know how to play the game. Whoever offers food is the winner of their hearts." Tom joked and continued, "I have them trained well."

Sarah and Mary came in the door.

"We didn't know people were waiting on us. The day's so nice we were walking slowly and enjoying it."

Then Sarah went to Cilla and gave her a hug.

"I'm glad to see you, as we haven't talked since the wedding."

"We've had such a lazy relaxing time. We knew the girls were in good hands, so we just enjoyed our time together. Not a worry in the world. Tom and I are so happy. Thank all of you for such a wonderful wedding and week."

Cilla put an arm around each one of her new daughters. Jetty finished putting the food on the table, and everyone set down to eat.

Cilla was settling in very nicely and was beginning to redecorate Tom's house. Tom was very supportive with whatever she wanted to do. They moved her piano to his house and that made the girls very happy. Also, they moved a few other pieces that were dear to Cilla and relocated some of Tom's things to the warehouse. Then Cilla had ordered a few new pieces to be delivered.

The house was becoming more her domain every day. Tom showed the signs of being a very happy man and laughter reigned in their household now.

One morning while having early coffee in their bedroom, Tom asked, "Have you given any more thought as to what you want to do with your house?"

"I guess we'll either rent it or sell it. What do you think?"

"If you want to sell it, why don't you sell it to me? I was looking at it the week while we were staying there, and it could easily be remodeled. It could be made into a very striking two story home. Aaron mentioned that he was going to need a home of his own when he comes back. I was thinking it'd make a very nice wedding present for him and Anna."

Cilla was mulling it over in her mind. Something did not seem quite right about that offer.

"Why would I want to sell it to my own family? I might give it as my share of a wedding gift if you'll remodel it. Tom, things work both ways. What's mine is now yours, too. You're always telling me what's yours is mine now."

"That's a very big gift on your part, Cilla."

"I would only join my money with yours. There's no difference in my mind. Besides I love Aaron and Anna, too. I have no doubt they'll marry. Aaron gets a little unsure about her feelings toward him occasionally, but I'm never unsure about either of their feelings."

"You *are* reassuring. Then let's do it. Will you help me plan? We can spend evenings in my office for a while drawing up plans. We can pretty well furnish it with what I have in the warehouse and some of your things."

"Let's start tonight. Won't Aaron be surprised? Anna will see some of the beginnings before she leaves."

Cilla got up from her rocker and plopped down in Tom's lap. She put her arms around his neck.

"This project excites me."

Tom placed his arms around her waist.

"You make me very happy. I thank the Lord every morning for you."

"I'm glad to hear that, Tom, as I have a bit of news to break to you. I'm pretty sure you are about to have your fourth child."

"Cilla, I shouldn't be surprised, but I am. I'm also very excited with this news. You know how to make a man feel young again."

"You are young and very good-looking. I'm a very lucky woman to have caught such a wonderful man."

"I'm going to tell Sarah today about the baby. She'll be so thrilled for us. Daniel's going to tease you so be ready."

"I'll tell Daniel that I'm just twice as lucky as he is with four children to his two."

They could hear the girls up.

"Shall we go join the girls for breakfast? Should we tell them our news?"

"Let's do."

The prospects of having a new baby in the family made the girls very happy. They immediately started planning.

When Sarah and Cilla met for their piano lesson, Cilla couldn't wait to tell Sarah her news.

"Cilla, this is wonderful news. Your first child-I know what you're feeling. There is no other feeling like it. I have news for you, too. I'm expecting my third child. I told Daniel last week. You're the only other one we've told."

Comparing notes as best they could figure, their babies would be due very near the same time.

"Won't it be fun raising them together? Sarah, can I come and make little things with you? I know you can sew, and I've never done much sewing. I can learn a lot from you."

"Why don't we have Amy and Rachel sew a few simple things for your baby, too?"

"That would be fun and exciting for the girls. Just think-sewing for their new sister or brother would make them feel a big part of it. I like that idea. My other news is that I'm giving my house as a gift to Aaron. Tom is going to remodel it and make it a two-story. We think it'll make a wonderful wedding present in case Aaron gets married in about a year. It would be ideally located for a doctor living in town. It would be close to his office."

"I'm sure Aaron and Anna have discussed it. It'll happen, and I think soon after she returns from her studies. They have that look in their eyes."

"I feel the same way, Sarah. We both can't be wrong. Tom and I are starting to make plans, so it'll start taking shape soon. We're both excited about this project."

Anna came in the school door. Quickly Cilla and Sarah changed the subject and never mentioned babies or the house project.

Chapter Nine

It was the end of May and Sarah's school had been closed for a few days for the summer months. Mary was going to run a summer program for the girls again but Sarah was going to take the summer off. She wanted to spend more time with her two children before the new baby came. The infant was due around the first of the year.

The Holders were expecting Aaron to arrive home today. The whole family plus Anna were in town to pick him up when he arrived. Anna spent the rest of the afternoon with them and had supper. Aaron drove her home after supper in Cilla's carriage. They finally had some time alone on the drive to Anna's house.

"Anna, I'm going to take a week off before starting my apprenticeship with Dr. Wade. Do you suppose I could come out to visit some in the afternoons? Perhaps we could take some carriage rides or just sit in the parlor?"

"Yes, and we can walk along the river and sit out in our swing and talk. My parents know I want to be with you as much as possible before I leave. They are even aware we've discussed marriage when I return. Aaron, they like you, and Uncle Daniel told my papa that he could put his complete trust in you to be a gentleman."

"I didn't know your uncle had done that. I appreciate his recommendation. I'd never do anything to even chance hurting you or your reputation, Anna. I want you to be my wife. I love you too much to chance hurting you. I want our relationship to be perfect when it happens."

"I want that, too. However, I do wish you would kiss me before you get me home."

"How did you know that was what I was thinking? I'll just stop right here in the road."

Aaron stopped, he kissed Anna, and they both had a good giggle.

"Here, hold my hand. I can hold the reins in one hand, and Pansy is not going to run away. Did you know Cilla and papa are remodeling her house for us?"

"I'd heard they were making a home for you."

"They know it will eventually be ours. In fact, we'll go see it several times before you leave. I'm thinking of moving in as soon as the house is ready."

"It's funny how things change. I'm the nervous one knowing you'll be a young, single doctor with a beautiful home. Do you realize every young female in town will be chasing you?"

"Anna, I'll be busy. They may chase, but I won't get caught. Trust me-I feel like you do. Why in the world would I throw away what I'll have with you for a meaningless relationship?"

Anna stretched to kiss Aaron on the cheek.

"I do love you. Can you pick me up to see the house tomorrow afternoon? Then you can have supper with my family."

"I'll pick you up when school's out, but why don't you have dinner with us? Then we can go see the house. I'm anxious to see it, too. I know from what papa says it's a mess now but will be very nice when he's through with it. I hope it'll be far enough along before you leave that you can tell something about it."

"That sounds like a good plan. Let's do it that way."

Cilla and Tom knew exactly how Aaron's house would look when Tom finished with the remodeling. He had already emptied the whole house and had torn off the roof and had beefed up the ceiling joists. All the walls in the house were bearing walls, so he wouldn't do anything to the foundation but it was still very sturdy and in great shape.

Tom had decided the lower half would be bricked and the upper would be clapboard. A local brickmaker and his men were already making the handmade bricks. A few of the bricks had an impurity in them that didn't weaken them, but it made their face look smoked with black. Cilla liked the looks of them when they were mixed in with the orange-red color of the other bricks.

A light yellow paint was chosen for the clapboards. She planned black shutters and a black front door with a small, gabled porch over the front door.

The white picket fence would be left around the house and there would be a large, covered back porch. Cilla was leaving her swing to hang on the porch, as that would make a private, comfortable place for the young couple to sit.

Cilla was already planning how she would redo the front garden to show off the house. Tom would hire a couple of men to do the work. He wasn't about to let Cilla lift anything and didn't want her digging in her condition. However, the garden would have to wait until Tom's men finished with the outside carpenter work.

Aaron pulled near Anna's front porch and hurried to help her out of the carriage.

"I'll be at the school tomorrow to pick you and my sisters up. Be sure your folks know you'll be eating dinner with us tomorrow and supper with them tomorrow evening."

"I'll tell them exactly what we're doing. I don't keep secrets from them or you, Aaron."

"Good, I want them to know where I stand, too. I'm not kidding about a wedding a couple of weeks after you return home from your studies."

Aaron tilted her chin and kissed her right at the front door.

It was dark when Aaron got back to his father's house. He took care of Pansy and Cilla's carriage and went into the house.

Cilla and Tom were in the study.

"Am I intruding?"

"Come on in. We're just going over the drawings of your home. Come look at them. We hope you approve."

Aaron looked over Tom's shoulder while his papa explained the plans.

"It's going to be a very nice home."

"I'll be a proud owner, thanks to both of you. This is much more than I'd ever expected. Cilla, I know your part in this, and I think it's wonderful that you think this much of me and Anna. I've invited Anna for dinner tomorrow, and then we want to go see the house. I know papa'll be there after dinner, but will you ride over with us? We'll bring you back home after we see the house."

"Oh, I'd love to see you and Anna when you first see what your papa's doing. Tom's work shows he's a master builder. He's really an artist at his work."

Tom felt proud of his work and rightly so.

"I'm enjoying this project. Usually I'd rather build a new house, but I'm enjoying seeing what I can do with

Cilla's old home. Aaron, it strikes me it's in a prime location for a new, young doctor to live."

"You're right, and it'll be great. Cilla, do you think your neighbor would let me keep a small carriage and horse at his place? I'd pay him a monthly or a yearly rent."

"We'll go talk to him. I think he will, as he'll like the idea of having a doctor as a neighbor."

"If he'd take care of my horse, I'll take care of him and his family when they need medical care."

"Bartering for your horse's care is a good idea."

Aaron was parked at the school when Anna came out with his sisters the next afternoon. He jumped down to help them all into the carriage. He put his sisters in the back seat and Anna up front beside him.

"Are you ready for dinner?"

Rachel answered even though Aaron was looking at Anna.

"I sure am. I was hungry by mid morning."

Anna smiled and answered, "I'm hungry, too, Rachel. I wonder what we're having."

"I think I smelled chicken baking before I left. I don't know what else," offered Aaron.

"Anna, I have about three long division problems I need help with. Could you help me sometime this afternoon?"

Rachel liked Anna's attention. Before Anna could answer, Aaron butted in.

"Rachel, Anna and I are going over to the house papa's working on after we eat. Maybe Amy can help you."

"I'll help you, Rachel, while they're gone. You don't have to bother Anna."

"But you're not as smart as Anna."

"I know, but maybe she can check your work at school in the morning to see if we have them right."

"Hey girls, has Anna been doing your school work for you?"

237

"No, but she sometimes helps me understand things and checks what I do. She's a good teacher."

"Thank you, Rachel. I'll let you explain to me how you arrived at your answers before you hand them in. Then next time *you'll* know how to work them."

When they arrived at Tom's home, they could smell the food while Aaron tied Pansy to the rail.

As they were eating, Cilla said, "Aaron, I want you and Anna to know that Tom and I are having a baby around the first of the New Year."

Anna got up and went to hug Cilla and Tom. She told them how wonderful she thought it was. Aaron was a little more reserved.

"A tiny new brother or sister? That'll be exciting for all of us. Congratulations to both of you."

The meal was very good, and when they finished, Anna told Mattie, "That was a wonderful meal, Mattie. You outdid yourself on this one."

The cook felt proud of her ability.

Tom started back to work soon after he ate.

"I'll see you lookers in a little while, I guess."

He kissed Cilla on the cheek as she said, "Yes, we'll be right along, but first I'll quickly show Anna your drawings of the house."

She led them to Tom's study and spread the plans out on Tom's desk. The three of them looked and discussed what was being done.

"I can just imagine the front of the house, but the inside plans are harder for me to visualize. I know that if you are planning them and Mr. Holder is building it, it will be very nice."

Anna expressed confidence that she would be pleased.

"Anna, I'm like you," Aaron continued, "I'm not sure what I'm seeing for the inside. We'll just wait and be surprised." Then he added, "Pansy's waiting. I'll go offer her a drink before we go. Come on out as soon as you're ready."

The ladies walked out and Aaron was patiently waiting.

"Would you like to drive your own carriage, Cilla?"

"No, you drive. I'll just sit in the back and talk."

Aaron got them settled, and he headed Pansy toward his new home.

When they pulled up in front of the house, Anna said, "I love these bricks. Everything is looking much larger than I imagined. Aaron, it's going to be a beautiful home. I can see why you'll be anxious to move in."

"Cilla, I'm impressed, too, and very pleased with it."

"Tell your papa. He's the one doing most of the work."

Tom saw them and walked out to meet them.

"Papa, I'm very impressed and pleased."

"Thank you, Aaron, but now I want to hear what Anna thinks."

"I love it Mr. Holder. The bricks are beautiful. I didn't realize it would look this large."

"We plan to put clapboard on the top part. Cilla has planned for it to be painted a light yellow with black shutters and a black door. If anyone objects or has a better idea, let me hear it now."

"I like the yellow very much, but it's really Aaron's to say."

"That wasn't my impression, Anna. I thought you would very much have a say in this house."

Anna's cheeks began to turn pink. Aaron couldn't help but tease her.

"Papa, she's embarrassed."

Then he explained their feelings to Tom and Cilla.

"She knows I think of it as hers, too, but it's not official yet. Our understanding is that she'll have a year to study with no strings attached. If we still feel like we do right now, it'll be official very soon after she returns. I had two years, and now she deserves a year to be sure what she wants."

Anna spoke up saying, "Since Aaron put it that way, Mr. Holder, I think Cilla's plans are perfect, and I wouldn't

239

change a thing. I love Cilla's taste. I trust her to decorate it and have it ready when I return."

"Okay. I love a lady who can make a definite decision. It'll be waiting on you when you return," Tom said as he hugged Anna.

After they had finished looking, Aaron told his father, "We'll take Cilla by the house and then I'm going to have supper with Anna's family. I'll be a little late getting home."

Tom turned to Cilla and asked, "Is there a lantern in your carriage?"

"There's one and plenty of fuel. Remember? We used it when we slipped off after our wedding."

"Okay, make sure the lantern's full, and you light it before you leave Anna's. Stick the flintlock under the carriage seat before you leave the house just in case you run into trouble and need one."

"I will, Papa, don't worry. It's not that far."

"Strange things can happen. Get Daniel to tell you the story about the dark and the wolves. He won't even go to his brother's house after dark now without a flintlock rifle."

"Are you ready, Cilla?"

Tom walked them to the carriage and helped the ladies in.

"Cilla, you watch that Aaron minds me."

Cilla smiled sweetly and said, "He'll mind you, Tom. He wouldn't want you worrying."

Tom waved goodbye as they rode down the street. When they got home, Aaron helped Cilla from the carriage.

"I'll double check the lantern and offer Pansy some water. Are you sure you don't mind me using your carriage?"

"No, I don't mind. I'll bring the flintlock out and put it under the seat in case Tom asks."

"Well, I'll go to the privy while you two are busy."

Aaron hurried to help Anna down.

When everything was ready, they waved goodbye to Cilla.

"Poor Pansy-we've been up and down this road a lot today."

"We'll give her some oats when we get to my house."

"That would be nice. She's a patient horse."

When they got to Anna's house, Aaron helped her out of the carriage.

"I'll go tell mama that we're home, and we're going to give Pansy a few oats."

After they fed and watered Pansy again, she was set for the evening. They washed up and went in the house so Aaron could speak to Lucy.

"Hello, Mrs. Borden. Something smells very good."

"We're having pot roast this evening. I hope you like beef."

"Yes ma'am. I eat about everything. Where's Mr. Borden?"

"He rode over to check the cattle that he keeps on Daniel's property. He should be back any time now. In fact, I think I hear him on the porch washing up."

Sure enough, James came in the back door and spoke to Aaron.

"What did you two do this afternoon?"

"We went over to see the house Cilla and papa are remodeling. Cilla went with us to show us around."

"Papa, you and mama will have to go see it. It's going to be beautiful and much larger than I had imagined. Mama, can I set the table for you?"

"Please do. The food'll be ready soon. Call Eli and tell him to wash."

James said the blessing, and in his prayer, he asked that Aaron be a wonderful doctor and that Anna would realize her dreams.

"Aaron, are you a full-fledged doctor now?"

"Well sir, I'll be called Dr. Holder, but I still have to work a year's apprenticeship under Dr. Wade. He's offered me a partnership in his office after that year. I'm taking a week off just to relax before I start on my apprenticeship."

"Congratulations, I know the work it takes to become a doctor. You're father must be very proud of you."

"Yes, sir, he is. Mr. Borden, Anna spoke quite frankly to my father this afternoon. I'd like to be up front with you, sir. Anna and I had an understanding before I went away to study."

Aaron explained how each had agreed to write the other if they found someone else of interest.

He then added, "If she still feels the same way about me when she returns, I'll warn you now, I'll want to marry her shortly after she returns. I hope we'll have your and Mrs. Borden's blessings."

Aaron smiled at Lucy and continued talking, "Mrs. Borden, I'm saying probably an October wedding so you and Anna can plan whatever she wants."

"Aaron, you'll have our blessings if Anna still feels the same way in another year."

"Sir, while I'm speaking, I'd want to say I'd like to see Anna as often as I can before she leaves. I want you to know that I love her, and I wouldn't do anything that might jeopardize her future. I hope she'll be my wife, and we'll wait for that."

"Aaron, Daniel told me quite awhile ago I could trust you with Anna. After this evening I know I can. While she's gone, we'd like for you to still come out, visit, and have a meal whenever you can."

Anna got up, put her arms around her papa's neck, and kissed him on the cheek.

"Thank you, Papa. I think you'll see the qualities in Aaron that I've seen for years."

Aaron grinned at Eli and mentioned, "You haven't gotten to say much tonight. You've grown a foot or more since I've seen you. How did your school go this year? No more grasshoppers in class?"

Eli laughed when he thought about the grasshoppers he let loose in the classroom.

"No more ever again. I'd get killed for sure next time. While Anna's gone, you'll have to come out, and we'll go fishing on Uncle Daniel's dock. I might even teach you some of Ollie's fishing secrets."

"That's a date Eli. We'll hopefully get to fish often."

The summer had gone by too fast for Anna and Aaron, and now Anna had been gone a couple of weeks. Aaron had received a letter from her telling all about school and how she missed him and everyone. Aaron answered telling her about the house, his work, and that he couldn't wait for her to get home.

Tom had the outside of the house completed but was still working on the inside. The outside was beautiful, and Priscilla was having two men working on some fall planting.

Aaron went on every call with Dr. Wade now. He was even setting bones and stitching people up. They had a few bad colds to doctor, and they even delivered a couple of babies.

Sarah's school was going full force. There were a few students still there that had started with her, such as Eli, Nancy, and Rachel. They had been among her youngest students back then, and now they were among her oldest students.

Sarah and Priscilla both were well showing they were expecting babies. They got together some afternoons and on Saturdays and made baby things. The girls were excited to be invited to help with the sewing.

Daniel and Tom sometimes went fishing while the ladies were sewing and sometimes the two played their instruments. It was a relaxing, leisurely winter.

Aaron moved into his house the middle of December. He had it feeling very comfortable and was pleased with the way it had turned out. The young doctor had also purchased a small, second-hand carriage much like Cilla's. He bought a good-looking horse from Anna's Uncle George that was trained to pull a carriage. The horse was a majestic gray with a few dark spots on his rump.

Aaron decided a good name for his horse was *Cloud*. The horse had some spirit and could run if Aaron needed to get to a patient in a hurry.

The new doctor had made a deal with his elderly neighbor to keep his carriage in the old man's barn and to have his horse tended. In return, he gave the man and his wife medical attention when needed.

It was the second day of January, and Cilla woke up when it was almost daylight. She shook Tom.

"I think the baby's coming. Perhaps you better get Dr. Wade and stop back by and tell Aaron. He may want to go get Lucy Borden just in case. Sarah suggested she's like a nurse, and Lucy said she'd come."

Tom never dressed as quickly as he did that morning. He rode his horse into town and decided to stop at Aaron's first. It was too early for either Dr. Wade or Aaron to be at the office. He knocked on Aaron's door. A sleepy-headed young man answered the door.

"Aaron, sorry to wake you, but our baby is coming. Can you get Dr. Wade and then go tell Anna's mother? She said she'd be glad to come assist Dr. Wade with Cilla. Cilla knows you can assist, but under the circumstances, she thought it might be better if Lucy comes. I'm going back home to be with the girls and Cilla."

Tom got back to the house and Cilla was still in bed.

"I thought it would be better if I lay still, but I'm having contractions fairly regularly."

"I know a little bit, and I'll get the bed ready."

Under his breath Tom said, "Dear God, help Dr. Wade hurry. I don't know much about this sort of thing. Let him get here soon. Take care of Cilla and the child. Amen!"

Tom heard someone at the back door and rushed to see who it was. It was Mattie.

"Come in, Mattie. Forget about breakfast. Miss Cilla is having the baby, and the doctor isn't here yet. I know you're not a mid-wife, but you've got to be better than I am. The doctor should be getting here soon."

"Mr. Tom, I'll do what I can, but I pray that doctor gets here soon."

"I've already said a prayer, but it won't hurt for you to say one, too."

Tom heard someone else coming in the back door. It was Dr. Wade.

"She's back here, Doctor. She's having contractions fairly close together."

"Have you timed them?"

"No sir."

"Let's see how close together."

A contraction came, and the doctor looked at his pocket watch and waited. In a while, another one came.

"You can relax for now, Tom. It will be a little while. I suggest we have breakfast. Sorry Priscilla, nothing for you just yet but perhaps some broth."

Mattie said, "I'll start cooking. I'm better at that than birthing babies."

Tom heard Mattie talking to someone in the kitchen, and then he heard Aaron's voice. He quickly went to the kitchen because he knew Lucy would be with Aaron.

"Oh, Lucy, thank you so much for coming. Dr. Wade's back with Cilla, but you go on back and check. If you need to know where anything is, call me or Aaron."

"Mattie, the coffee smells very good this morning. I'd like a cup when it's ready. Someone got me up early this morning, and I'm hungry, too."

"I'm cooking, Mr. Aaron or should I say-Dr. Aaron?"

245

"Mr. Aaron's fine. You've known me most of my life. Are my sisters up?"

"I haven't seen them."

"I'll go check with papa and see if he wants them to go to school today. I'll get them there if he does."

Aaron found Tom in the study and asked, "Do you want me to get the girls to school this morning?"

"So much is happening, I hadn't thought. It won't hurt for them to miss this morning. James'll see that Daniel and Sarah know that the baby's coming. Sarah may not teach today, anyway, as she's due at any time, too. Let the girls sleep."

"Are you doing all right, Papa?"

"I'm fine. I just don't like the waiting."

"I'll go check and see how things are going."

Aaron was back in a minute.

"She's doing fine. I talked to her, and she said for you not to worry."

The girls were up now and were dressed. Aaron went in to tell them the baby was coming, and papa said they could stay home today. When Aaron saw how excited they were, he knew they felt the baby being born was part theirs. All of a sudden, he felt that it was his brother or sister, too. He hurried back to be with his papa.

Mattie served Dr. Wade and Lucy their breakfast on the small table in the bedroom. She had a little beef broth for Miss Cilla. She called the others to the dining room. While they were eating, Daniel stuck his head in the dining room.

"Do we have a baby yet?"

"Not yet. Dr. Wade said it'll be awhile."

"Sarah says she's sorry not to be here but you'd understand. She's scared to leave home for fear ours will come anytime. Kate came so quickly, even before Dr. Wade could get there. You better go tell Cilla to hurry up. Sarah may need Dr. Wade any minute, too," Daniel quipped.

"I'll wait awhile. I'd love to tell Sarah what it is and how they're doing before I go."

Mattie appeared at the door.

"Mr. Daniel, would you like a cup of coffee and breakfast?"

"I'll take the coffee, but I've had breakfast."

Tom suggested they all move into the parlor where they could be comfortable while waiting. Aaron got up and went to the bedroom to check on things. He reported when he came back.

"It's getting nearer. Dr. Wade said not too much longer."

About midmorning they heard a cry.

"No doubt it's here."

In just a few minutes, Lucy came to the parlor door.

"Tom, you have a beautiful little girl. It seems mother and baby are doing fine. You can come back in a few minutes."

Tom grinned and said, "I guess I'll pace now. I can hardly wait to see them."

The new father walked down the hall and stuck his head in the doorway.

"May I come in now?"

Dr. Wade said, "Yes, come on in. We're just finishing up with things."

Aaron gave Tom a few minutes and then he walked down the hall. He lightly knocked on the door.

"Am I allowed in?"

Dr. Wade looked up.

"Surely, come on in and see your new sister."

"May I take her out for the others to see?"

"She's just about ready. Cilla requested she be put in one of the little dresses her sisters made for her. Let me wrap her in a blanket, and you may have her."

Aaron was watching how tenderly Lucy was handling the baby. Her touch was soft and kind. She picked up the little bundle and placed her in Aaron's waiting arms. When he walked in the parlor, the girls jumped up.

"Let me sit down on the settee, and we'll have a better look at her."

He sat in the middle with a sister on each side. He laid the baby on his lap and pulled back the warm blanket.

"Look, Amy, she has on our little dress. Isn't she cute in it?"

Rachel was so proud.

"She looks like a big doll, but she looks so red."

Aaron chuckled at that remark.

"That's because she was just born. She's had a hard journey. The red'll begin to fade in a day or so."

"Her hands are so tiny. Can I touch her, Aaron?"

"Sure. Hold her hand and look at her tiny fingers. Her fingers are long and slender. She may be a piano player like her mother."

"What's Cilla going to name her? Well, let everyone see her, and I'll take her back to her mama and ask."

Aaron pulled the blanket back around her and stood up. Daniel came to have his look.

"She's pretty according to some I've seen. I'll find out her name because Sarah will want to know, and then I'll go so I can report."

Mattie had to peep at her. All she could say was, "Another girl, Mr. Aaron. You're surrounded by women."

"You can't get much better than being surrounded by women, Mattie. Let me go check on her name and leave her with her mother. I'll be right back."

Aaron was back in a minute.

"The decision is Julie Anne Holder."

"That's a pretty name, and I like it," Rachel said.

"That's good, Rachel. I'm glad you approve," Aaron teased.

"I'm off and I'll check back tomorrow."

Daniel left out the back door and headed home. He went by the house to tell Sarah the good news about Cilla and the baby.

Two days had passed and Ollie hurried down to the factory.

"Mr. Daniel, Jetty said it's Miss Sarah's time. She sent me to get you, and now I'm going for Dr. Wade. She sent Remy after Miss Lucy."

"I'm on my way to the house, Ollie. Please hurry. Last time it happened so quickly. Saddle and take Honey. She's the fastest horse we have. You be careful."

"Yes sir, but I'll ride like the wind."

Ollie got to Dr. Wade's office very quickly. He ran in the office, and Aaron saw him when he came in.

"Mr. Aaron, it's Miss Sarah's time. Tell Dr. Wade to hurry. I'm going to the livery and make sure his carriage is ready."

"I'll be shortly behind him, Ollie."

Aaron and Dr. Wade both got their bags and hurried to get their carriages. Aaron's horse was faster than Dr. Wade's so they got there at the same time.

Daniel let them in and could hear Lucy coming in the back door. Remy took Beau and Kate upstairs. Jetty was helping in the bedroom, but when Lucy got there, Jetty took her place back in the kitchen.

Sarah was in labor for about two hours. When the baby arrived, it was a wonderful little boy.

He was perfectly healthy, and Sarah had done wonderfully well. There was one problem.

Sarah's milk was not coming, and she was an experienced mother. The baby tried and tried to suckle to no avail. The baby cried, tried, and fussed. Dr. Wade called Aaron in to consult.

"Dr. Wade, it looks like we need a wet nurse, and I know one. Lucy,-excuse me-I mean Mrs. Borden, bundle

249

the baby up good. We're taking him to Cilla. She has enough milk for two babies until I can try something else. I'll talk to Sarah and Daniel and explain what we're doing."

"Aaron, I'm turning the baby over to you. You work with him and I'll tend Sarah," Dr. Wade told Aaron.

The new doctor called Daniel to the bedroom and explained the situation to both Sarah and him.

"I'm taking the baby to Cilla. She has enough milk for two babies. I'll find another way, Sarah, so hopefully you can have the baby back in a couple of days. Dr. Wade will work with you and maybe your milk will come. You've never had a problem before, but right now the baby's my main concern. Have you chosen a name for him?"

"Yes, he's Andrew Steven. We'll call him Drew. Take care of him, Aaron."

"He'll have my full attention; I promise you. I'm taking Lucy with me. Daniel, you let James know. I may need Lucy for two or three days. Tell him to bring her some clothes. Daniel, you can come and stay as long as you like at papa's house. However, Sarah may need you more right now than Drew does. Sarah, I promise you, I'll find a way and have Drew back with you as soon as I safely can."

By this time, Lucy had the baby in the basket and ready to go. Daniel helped them out to Aaron's carriage, and they were off. The baby was crying, and Lucy was trying to soothe him. Aaron kept Cloud at a fast pace.

"Be sure the baby's warm."

Aaron turned down the road to his father's house. He pulled to the back door and jumped down. He rushed around, took the basket, and gave his hand to Lucy to help in her descent from the carriage. Aaron rushed to the bedroom.

"Cilla, you have a hungry guest for dinner."

Cilla looked up in surprise.

"Sarah's milk isn't coming, and her son is in distress and needs to eat. I can't be delicate about this. I need to watch him suckle. He's my patient and right now he's my

250

main concern. Let's put him to your breast and see what happens."

Cilla pushed up on the pillows and pulled her shift back. Aaron placed the baby in her arms.

"You know what to do now."

Cilla offered her nipple to the baby and he instantly latched on.

"There's nothing wrong with his suction," Aaron observed.

Cilla asked, "You said he. Sarah had a boy?"

"They named him Andrew Steven but they'll call him Drew."

Cilla rubbed his little head, as the baby settled down to his task ahead. Tom came in.

"What's happening here?"

"This is Sarah and Daniel's son. Sarah doesn't have any milk to offer him, and he was in distress from needing to eat. I knew he needed a wet nurse, and I thought of Cilla. She has plenty of milk for two. It's kind of like having twins. It'll keep her busy for a while feeding two, but I'll think of something, and get him back to Sarah as soon as I can. Cilla's in good health, so this shouldn't be a problem for her or Julie."

"I guess you know what you're doing, Aaron. We all have to trust you."

"Dr. Wade knows what I'm doing. He's tending Sarah, and the baby's my patient."

"Cilla, let me explain what I want you to do. Before you feed either baby, I want you to clean around you nipples thoroughly with vinegar and then warm water. I want you to use clean scraps of linen to wipe with. I don't want any germs to pass from one baby to the other. This is very important so don't forget."

"The baby seems to have had enough."

"Are you full, Mr. Drew? You look like you feel much better. Aaron, called Lucy, "If you'll put him in his basket perhaps he'll sleep now."

The young doctor hesitated to explore the situation in detail.

"I have an idea. I want to go to town to see if I can find what I need. If Drew cries and won't rest, you might try cuddling and rocking him. Try to feed him again if it becomes necessary. Don't forget about cleaning the breasts."

Aaron got in his carriage and went to Creel's General Store. Caleb was at the counter.

"Hello, Aaron, can I help you find something?"

"I hope so. My request is strange, but I need it badly. There's a thing on the market called a Bubby Pot. It's for feeding babies whose mothers can't feed them for one reason or another."

Caleb thought and then answered, "I don't think we've ever had one of those in stock."

"It looks very much like a small teapot. It has a shorter, straight spout. The end of the spout is closed with the exception of small holes in it so the baby can suck the milk out."

Molly happened to be listening to Aaron's description.

"I think we have one. I ordered it when we first opened the store. Let's look in the storeroom."

Aaron and Caleb followed Molly to the storeroom.

"Last time I cleaned, I think I saw it on the back of the shelf in this section."

Caleb looked, and way back on the very top shelf was a little ceramic pot. Caleb pulled it down.

"Could this be one?"

"That's it! I could hug you for this, Mrs. Creel."

And he did.

"Is someone having problems feeding their baby?"

"Yes, it's Sarah Borden. She had a little boy this morning, but Sarah's milk didn't come with this one. At least, not yet. This little pot may save the baby's life. How much do I owe you?"

"We've had it so long I don't even know. Take it as a gift for Sarah and her son. She's a good friend, and I would give her anything I had to help save her baby."

"Thank you so much."

Aaron took the little pot and hurried back to the house.

Tom came to meet him and asked, "Did you find what you need?"

"It was a miracle but the Creel's had one in stock and didn't know what it was. Thanks to Mrs. Creel, we found it. Now, Papa, I need two nanny goats that are giving milk. That's your job."

"I know a few farms around here that have goats. Maybe they'll sell me a couple or I'll steal them if I have to," Tom jested.

"Just get them, and I won't ask questions."

Dr. Holder headed for the kitchen to give additional instructions for cleaning the Buddy Pot.

"Mattie, I want you to pour boiling water in this little pot and let it set for a few minutes. Then pour boiling water all over it, especially around the spout. Each time it's used, wash it in hot water with soap and then do the boiling water again. Please do this every time the pot's used and don't forget. Then dry it with a clean cloth, and cover it with another clean cloth."

Aaron hurried back to the bedroom.

"Where's my patient, and how's he doing?"

"He's been asleep every since you left. Lucy has him in the parlor, so the babies won't wake each other up."

"There's nothing wrong with that boy, and I think I've found a way to feed him."

Then Dr. Holder went to the parlor.

"Lucy, I found what I think we need to feed Drew. Come into the kitchen, and I'll explain it to you."

Aaron showed her the little pot and explained how it was to be cleaned.

"Papa's gone to find us two nanny goats that are giving milk. We're going to try goat's milk. I want Cilla to feed him one more time and then let's try the goat's milk."

"Aaron, you're amazing me for such a young man."

"I've learned and studied about these things, Lucy."

All of a sudden it dawned on Aaron that he had been calling Anna's mother Lucy. He turned a little red and started to apologize.

"I'm so sorry; I was speaking to you like my nurse. I meant no disrespect. I'll try to do better."

"Aaron, I thought nothing of it. Please, call me Lucy, and I only wish I was a nurse."

"Do you really mean that?"

"That was my dream when I was a young lady, but it was not to be. That's why I've been so intent on Anna following her dream."

"It's not too late, Mrs. Borden-Lucy. I've watched you with Dr. Wade and now with me and the babies. If I could call on you to assist me in some cases, I would love to have your assistance. I can't pay you much right now, but I can train you."

"I'm so flattered. Let me speak to James, and I'll give you my answer soon. I'm going to stick with you night and day with this case, that's for sure. James will want me to."

Julie had been fed and was back asleep. Now Drew was awake wanting to eat.

"You've got another customer, Cilla."

Aaron had Drew in his arms.

"Lucy will help you clean your breasts. I won't need to watch this time. You know what you're doing, and I think Drew does now."

Aaron heard Daniel's voice in the kitchen and went to meet him.

"Good news, Daniel. The baby's eating from Cilla. In fact, she's feeding him now. He's been sleeping and doing well."

"That *is* good news. Sarah wanted me to come and check. She's beside herself, as she still has no milk. Dr. Wade has given up on it coming."

"I may have our problem solved."

Aaron told Daniel about the Bubby Pot.

"Papa's gone to find us a couple of nanny goats. I hoping their milk will substitute for Sarah's and Cilla's."

"I'm going to keep Drew here overnight and try the goat's milk. If it doesn't work, we'll need to be near Cilla. If it works overnight, Lucy and I'll bring the baby home tomorrow."

"Thank you, Aaron. You don't know how much we thank you. Dr. Wade said to tell you he'll be by soon to check on things. You seem to have everything well in hand."

"I'll check and see if Drew has finished feeding, and then you can hold him."

Aaron went to check and came bringing Drew out to Daniel.

"Let's go sit in the parlor, and you can have a good look at him."

Daniel tenderly carried the baby to the parlor. Lucy came in to see him.

"How's Sarah doing?"

"Physically she's feeling fine. She's beside herself that our son can't be with her."

"He'll be with her soon because our Dr. Holder has everything well in hand."

Tom came in.

"I got the two goats, and I didn't have to steal them. I'll milk them, Aaron, when you give the word."

"The baby just ate, so let's wait a while."

Daniel looked up at Tom.

"When I've teased you about paying me back, I never thought it would be your wife feeding my son, and you out milking goats."

"Well, Aaron and your son just came in, and they nudged my new daughter over. They said he was hungry and wanted to share. Cilla is thrilled to death she could help. Now she has a tender spot in her heart for him already. Daniel, don't worry. Aaron is giving this all he's got. He's going to make sure Drew makes it. Tell Sarah to relax. Everything's going to be all right."

Tears came up in Daniel's eyes.

"We thank you all so much. I better go now and give Sarah my report."

Daniel kissed the baby on the forehead and handed him to Lucy.

"We'll see you tomorrow."

Tom milked the goats and placed the crock of milk in the well to keep it cool. When Drew was ready for the next feeding, Aaron supervised the fixing of the Bubby Pot.

Mattie warmed the milk and poured it in the pot. Aaron carried the pot in the parlor and had Lucy to try it. At first Drew made a face and screwed up his little mouth.

"Let me tie a square of linen around the spout and see what happens. The spout might be too hard for his liking. He's had two soft meals."

Aaron went to the kitchen.

"Try this and let's see what happens."

Lucy let the linen get damp with the goat's milk and then she stuck it in his little mouth. It set there a second and then he tasted the milk. He started to suck. It was a little hard at first, but before long he was getting the idea.

"I kind of like this. I can measure and see how much he's getting now."

Drew drank all of the milk that was in the pot. Aaron picked up his little hand.

"You kind of like that old goat's milk, don't you?"

He carried the empty pot back to the kitchen.

"You make good milk, Mattie. He emptied what we gave him. Better get the pot ready for the next feeding. That one went really well."

Dr. Wade knocked on the front door. Aaron let him in to see the baby and gave him a report of what he'd done.

"Aaron, you've done an excellent job. I'm not sure I would have remembered the Bubby Pot. I've never used one before."

"I read about it at school and saw a picture of it. To be honest, I was desperate and searched my mind. I was willing to try almost anything. How's Sarah doing?"

"She's well, but she's anxious to have her son with her."

"If things go all right tonight, she'll have him back by tomorrow. If you don't mind, I'd like to stay at Daniel's for a couple of days and nights to oversee things. This case is special to me."

"It's special to me, too. Do whatever you think is best. I'm very proud of you, Aaron. You're making an excellent doctor."

Little Drew, Aaron, and Lucy made it through the night. Drew was now taking every feeding on the Bubby Pot and goat's milk. The household rejoiced with the good news.

After breakfast, Aaron told Tom, "Lucy and I'll take Drew home to his folks if you'll bring the goats. I'm sure Ollie will help you get them settled in. This'll be a happy day at the Borden's."

Lucy went in to thank Cilla for all she had done and the hospitality.

"Sarah'll be indebted to you." She hesitated and then added, "We all are."

"I'm so glad I was here at a time when I was needed most. Think of the wondrous things that happen in life and work out just as they're needed. It's amazing."

Lucy walked to the bedside and gave Cilla a kiss on the cheek.

"I'll be checking on you and Julie again. She's a beautiful baby."

Aaron already had Drew bundled up, and the carriage was waiting.

When they drove up to the back of Daniel's house, Ollie gave out a shout, "Glory Hallelujah!"

He hurried to the back door.

"Jetty, tell Mr. Daniel and Miss Sarah that Mr. Aaron is here with the baby."

He then went to help them out of the carriage with all their belongings.

"This is a great day, Mr. Aaron. Seeing you and Miss Lucy with our baby makes our hearts sing."

"Aaron, you take the basket and get the baby on in where it's warm. I'll get out of this carriage."

"Here, take my hand, Miss Lucy. We don't want you falling with all this good news. I'll get this other stuff for you."

"Ollie, Mr. Tom is coming with two nanny goats that we need for the baby. Would you be sure he has a place to put them? They'll probably need milking."

"I'll tend to it, Miss Lucy. Don't you worry none."

"Let me have the little pot. That's very important to the baby, too. I want to show Jetty and Remy how it must be cleaned for every feeding."

Lucy took the pot and went in the house. She showed Jetty and Remy how to clean it after every use.

"Handle it as you would a precious jewel. It's the only one we have. I'm sure another one will be on its way soon."

Lucy then went to the bedroom. Aaron had the baby in Sarah's arms with Daniel sitting on the edge of the bed.

Lucy told Aaron, "Doctor, the feeding pot is clean and ready for the next feeding when it's needed. Ollie will help your father with the goats."

"Lucy, is Tom here with the goats yet?" Daniel wanted to know.

"Not yet, but I know he will be here soon."

"I'll go and make sure they're taken care of. Those goats are precious right now. I want a warm place for them

258

out of the weather, and a place for them to gaze. We'll need goat feed, too."

Daniel kissed Sarah on the cheek and Drew on the forehead.

"I'll be back when I can."

Sarah snickered as he rushed out the door.

"I'm glad you found something for Daniel to do. He has hovered over me night and day. It's all kind of funny when I think about it. He can help feed this baby and rock him, now. This may not be as bad as I first thought."

"It's good that you're laughing, Sarah. There *will* be some good things to the baby feeding without your every attention. Daniel can get up some at night, feed, and change the baby as needed. There's no reason he can't. We'll teach him about all of it while we're teaching the rest of you. I'm spending a couple of nights with you. I'll go tell Jetty to put my name in the pot and get my room ready."

Lucy smiled at Sarah.

"Aaron is very much at home with you, isn't he?"

"Yes, after all these years, we consider him and the girls as part ours."

Lucy began to whisper to Sarah, "I hope our Anna will have the good sense to come back home when she's finished with her studies. That's the young man for her. He'll be an excellent husband. I've watched him with little Drew. He feeds, changes, and knows how to love a baby already. Just think about having him right there if someone gets sick."

"Lucy, don't worry. Anna will be back. She's seen things in him much earlier than the rest of you did. I saw them, too, when I was teaching him. She loves him with all her heart."

"Sarah, he's asked me to assist him on cases, especially with babies. I hope James won't mind. I would love to do some nursing."

"If that's what you want to do, we'll all talk to James. He'll come around."

A knock came on the bedroom door, and James stuck his head in.

"May I come in? I heard sawing and hammering out by your barn and came to see what was going on. Daniel told me Lucy and Aaron brought that boy home this morning."

Sarah told him to come on in.

"Drew's sleeping, but you can look at him. Is Tom here with the goats yet?"

"Oh my, yes. They're out there building them a palace," James retorted, and then went to give Lucy a kiss on the cheek.

"I've missed you the last couple of days."

Lucy smiled and said, "You mean you and Eli missed my cooking. James, I need to talk to you about that. Young Doctor Holder has offered me a position as his assistant nurse."

Lucy looked at James to get his reaction and then continued.

"He won't need me every day-just at certain times. And he'll train me. I'll be making a small salary and will get a raise a little later when he can afford it."

Lucy glanced at James again for a reaction. Nothing.

"I would like very much to do it-at least for a while, anyway. We can afford to hire a cook, can't we?"

"I'm going to have to talk to that young doctor. I think he's taking all my women."

"Yes, I think he's very partial to the Borden women," Lucy was smug with self-satisfaction.

Aaron walked in the door.

"What is this about me and the Borden women?"

"I was telling James that you had asked me to assist you on certain cases. He says you're trying to take all his women and I told him, you seemed to be very partial to the Borden women."

Aaron walked over and kissed Lucy on the cheek and then Sarah.

"That's right, Lucy. He just doesn't know how partial I am. Well, Mr. Borden, can she work with me?"

James put his thumb up to his lips as if he were thinking.

"You've been off a couple of nights together. You're calling her Lucy, and now you want her to work for you? Not only that, but you want to marry my daughter. I don't know about you young doctors. I guess if that's what Lucy wants to do, I won't stand in her way."

James couldn't help but to play this to the hilt. Lucy came and threw her arms around James and kissed him right on the mouth.

"James, you know that's been my dream. Just to get to nurse a little is all I ask."

Daniel walked into the bedroom and observed, "My new son is sleeping with all this going on?"

"I'm a nurse now or soon will be, Daniel." Then she asked, "Are the goats taken care of?"

"Yes, and Tom brought plenty of food for them. He and Ollie are putting the finishing touches on their new home. I milked them and the milk is cooling in the well."

Lucy took command of her hasty training and ordered, "It's about time for the baby to be ready for his next feeding. Dr. Holder and I will be giving lessons in the kitchen now on the preparation of the milk and then in the bedroom for actually feeding. I want Daniel, Jetty, and Remy present at this first lesson."

"Good gosh, Aaron, you've created a monster, and it scares me," James teased.

"I'll report to the kitchen right now, Colonel," Daniel said.

Lucy giggled.

"Oh, I want to watch you change the baby, too. I want to be sure you can do it correctly."

Daniel went toward the kitchen shaking his head.

The lessons all went well. Lucy did watch Daniel clean the baby's little bottom and change him. She decided he did it well enough.

Aaron told her to go home for the night. He and Daniel could take care of the feeding and changing.

Lucy continued in command, "Now, Dr. Holder, you let Daniel fix the milk, do the changing, and the rocking if any needs to be done. When you leave, the nights will be his for a couple of weeks until Sarah is able to do it. We want to be sure he can handle it."

"I will, Lucy. You rest tonight for you deserve it."

Aaron lit his lamp, closed his bedroom door, and read some that night. Before he went to sleep, he opened the door so he could hear the baby if and when Drew cried.

He suggested, "Daniel, leave your door open, too, so I can hear if Drew cries as well."

Aaron was sleeping in the bedroom at the head of the stairs. He'd been asleep about two hours when he heard the baby fretting. He jump up and hurried down the stairs. Daniel's bedroom door was open.

Aaron whispered, "Daniel, the baby's waking. Let's go fix his milk."

Daniel dragged up, and Aaron told him, "Get the milk out of the well and then warm it some. Make sure it's not too warm and put it in the pot. You're lucky this time for the pot's clean. After you feed him, you'll have to come back, wash it in soapy water, rinse, and then put boiling water in the pot. Since it's night, you can let the hot water set in it until the next feeding."

"The old way was much easier. I just handed the baby to Sarah."

"I know, and she can help you in two weeks, but now it's entirely your job at night."

Aaron followed Daniel back to the bedroom.

"Check to see if Drew needs changing. Then hold and feed him. When you can get him back down, take the pot to the kitchen and wash it. Leave the boiling water in it until the next time you get up. I'm going back to bed. I'll see you next feeding."

The next morning Daniel was worn out.

"This being a mama is hard work."

"I'm finding that out, too. I've had a couple of more nights of it than you. I'm getting tougher from it though. I hope that encourages you."

Aaron teased.

"When Beau gets up, slip up to his bed and take a nap. You'll find you need maybe a couple of naps a day to keep going. Even twenty minutes will help you."

He wanted Sarah to sit, feed, and interact with the baby during the day and later she and Daniel could split this time up.

"I want him to have an attachment to you and Daniel. I think babies may grow a lot of their ties while feeding. I know animals grow the fondest of the people who feed them. Why not babies? I have no way of knowing this for sure. It's just my feelings."

Aaron stayed one more night and things were going very well. The goat's milk was agreeing with Drew, and Sarah was gathering her strength. Aaron had given permission for Sarah to lift the baby and change him. He didn't want her to lift him from the cradle while she was lying down. That put too much strain on her back.

The household was beginning to return to as normal as possible with a new baby.

Almost two weeks had passed, and Aaron got a letter from Anna. It told him she had received letters from several members of her family praising his doctoring skills to the upmost.

My Dearest Aaron,
They all consider you saved Drew's life.
Even my mama wrote that she was afraid
I might not realize what a wonderful
young man you are. She told me if I had
any sense I would not give a second look
at any other young man while I'm gone. I
think this is very funny, as they are all
seeing what I had seen almost three
years ago. I am so glad that they finally
realized it. I want you to know that both
of my hearts are right where they
belong. I'm enjoying my studies, but I
can't wait to get back to you and
everyone I love.
Always yours,
Anna

He folded the letter and placed it in the drawer. He felt proud of his profession and his first true patient. He would answer the letter right away.

It was May twenty-fourth, eighteen hundred and ten, and Anna was arriving home that afternoon. Lucy had invited Aaron to their home for supper. They were all so happy with the thought of Anna being home to stay. James and Eli had driven out north of town to pick her up. She had caught a ride with another family whose daughter had studied at the same school as Anna.

Anna was so excited to see James and Eli. They unloaded her things and put them in their wagon and started home.

"Where's mama?"

"This was her afternoon to work. She and Aaron had a few patients to see and then they'll both be at our house for supper."

"I can't get used to her being a nurse. I'm thrilled you asked Aaron, as I can hardly wait to see him. Who's cooking supper?"

"Mama's surely told you we have a cook now. Winnie will be cooking, and she's a good cook. Aaron likes her cooking. He eats with us fairly often. We've been fishing some together, too. I've taught him some tricks to catching fish that Ollie taught me."

Eli smiled a smug little grin with that remark.

"Mama told me about Winnie. Since I've been away a few months, things have really changed. I'll have to get used to it. I'm glad you and Aaron had some fun."

"Aaron and your mama have become very good friends. He's almost like a son to us now."

"That pleases me so much. I knew when you got to know him, you'd love him."

They got to the house and unloaded Anna's things. Anna went to the kitchen to introduce herself to Winnie.

"Supper smells really good, Winnie. I've been told what a good cook you are."

"Thank you, ma'am. Miss Lucy asked me to fix a pot roast this evening. She knows how you love it and so does Dr. Aaron."

"That sounds good. I have to unpack, so I'll see you later."

Anna unpacked, freshened up and changed her clothes. She put on a dress that showed off her silver heart really well. It seemed like a long time since she had seen Aaron. Of course, they wrote regularly.

Anna looked out her bedroom window and saw Aaron and her mama coming down the road. She checked her hair, went down the stairs, and was sitting in the parlor when they entered.

As they got to the parlor door, Anna stood up and instantly rushed to hug her mother. Then she turned to Aaron, hugged him, and kissed his cheek.

"It's so good to be home. I know I haven't been gone all that long, but so many things have changed."

She looked at Lucy.

"You're a nurse now, and we have a cook. Eli's grown a foot. He's taller than me now."

Then she turned to Aaron.

"You're a young, good-looking doctor now with your own nurse," as she said that, she smiled. "I'm really glad it's my mama. I couldn't have rested if it had been a pretty young thing."

"Well thanks, Anna."

"Oh, Mama, you know what I mean. I knew you wouldn't flirt with him."

"No, I've managed to keep all the women beat back while you were gone. I'm going in the kitchen. Aaron, would you please give my daughter a proper kiss while I'm out of the room and settle her nerves?"

"Yes, ma'am, Mrs. Borden, I'll be more than glad to oblige."

Aaron and Lucy laughed. As soon as Lucy got out the door, Aaron took Anna in his arms and kissed her.

"I guess mama was right. I needed that."

"I'll do even better if you'll walk down by the river with me after supper."

"I wish we didn't have to eat."

"Quick, let me kiss you again because I'm starved, and maybe that'll hold you through supper."

The conversation never lagged during the meal as everyone had something to tell. When they finished supper, they commented on how delicious it was.

As soon as they had finished dessert, Anna looked at Aaron and said, "I'd like to take a walk perhaps down by the river. Would you like to come with me?"

"Just try to get off without me. Do you need a wrap or is it warm enough?"

"I'll be fine."

James spoke up.

"Be sure you're back at the house before dark. We'll clear out and let you visit in the parlor."

"Yes, sir. I'll take care of her. Don't worry."

They walked toward the river holding hands and talking. When they got to the river bank, Aaron kissed her with a long passionate kiss.

"Have you given any thought to a wedding date yet?"

"Not yet. Everything seems so different since I got home. Give me just a little time. There's no doubt, I do want to marry you."

She put her arms around Aaron's neck and returned his kiss. They walked and talked about what had gone on in their lives.

"We better get back, Anna. I've missed you so, and things aren't easy seeing you now. It's been so long since I've seen you, and you get more beautiful all the time. Don't take too long to set a wedding date."

"I promise I won't."

"Will you have dinner with my folks tomorrow? I want you to see our house, but I want Cilla and Julie to go with us when we look at it."

"Will you pick me up? I've never seen Julie. That's something else that's new. I haven't seen Drew, either. "

"Well, you have a treat on both counts. Both babies are beautiful. I'll get you about eleven thirty. I'll stop by and tell Cilla to be expecting us. I really should be going if I'm going to stop by papa's house."

He went in the house to thank everyone for supper and lightly kissed Anna one more time.

"I love you, and I'll see you tomorrow."

About ten o'clock the next morning, Preacher Kent rode up to Anna's house and knocked on the door. He had heard she was home. Anna answered the door and invited him in.

"You're the very young lady I want to see. I heard you were back. I know you've been off studying music and voice. Would you honor us by singing in church Sunday morning? I'll talk to Cilla Holder and ask her to play for you."

"I'd be the one who's honored to sing at church. I'll see Cilla in a little while. I'll ask her to play for me."

"That's wonderful, Anna. We'll all be looking forward to hearing you. I won't keep you. I know you're busy."

Anna saw Preacher Kent to the door and spotted Aaron coming down the road. The preacher and Aaron met, and they waved to each other.

When Aaron got to the door he asked, "Was Preacher Kent here to talk about a wedding?"

"No, he didn't mention one. He asked me if I'd sing in church on Sunday, and if Cilla would play for me. I told him, yes. You're early."

"I know. I couldn't wait to see you."

She gave him a light kiss.

"Sit down in the parlor, and I'll finish getting ready."

They talked all the way to Tom's house but never mentioned a wedding date again. When Anna saw Julie, she couldn't believe how cute she was.

"Cilla, I think she looks like you must have at this age. Her smile just bubbles. I just want to squeeze her. May I hold her if I don't squeeze too hard?"

Cilla handed Julie to Anna. Anna took her and sat down on a settee. Aaron went to sit beside them.

"Oh, look, she wants her big brother to take her."

"Oh, she loves him. She thinks he's the greatest thing."

"She's not the only one."

Anna cut her eyes at Aaron.

"Oh, Cilla, our preacher was at the house this morning and asked me to sing in church Sunday. Will you play for me?"

"I'd be delighted. Do you know what you will sing yet?"

"No, will you help me decide?"

"Let's meet at the school tomorrow and work on it. That way we can practice without an audience. Let's meet about one thirty."

"That sounds good. Aaron you stay away. No audience."

"I haven't heard you sing since you've been studying."

"I know, and I think you'll be surprised, as I've improved some."

Tom came in for dinner, and Mattie had it ready. After they had visited at the table, Tom had to go back to work.

"Aaron said you and Julie would go with us for me to see his house," Anna told Cilla.

"Yes, he asked me to go. Between you and me, I don't think he trusted himself alone with you in his house. I hope you didn't mind me going with you."

"Oh, not at all. It might be the best for everyone. Anyway, you can probably give me a better tour than he can. I'll be interested in the plants, and he probably couldn't answer my questions."

"Anna, I'm a doctor-not a gardener."

That prompted a laugh from all.

When they arrived at Aaron's house, Anna thought the gardens were outstanding, and she loved the house. It was even prettier than she imagined.

Aaron carried Anna home later that afternoon.

"I won't see you tomorrow, but I'll see you in church on Sunday. Can you eat with us Sunday afternoon?"

"I'll plan on it."

Aaron kissed her goodbye.

269

"I can hardly stand not coming to the school tomorrow."

"Don't you dare. I'll see you Sunday morning."

Sunday morning came, and Preacher Kent gave Anna and Cilla an introduction. Anna stepped up on the rise near the piano. Cilla played a few introductory notes, and Anna opened her mouth to sing. If you closed your eyes, you would have thought an angel had come down from heaven to sing. Silence fell over the church. Not one thing could be heard but the music and Anna's beautiful voice.

When Anna finished, the audience rose to their feet and gave her a standing ovation. Some eyes had tears welling in them, for her song was so touching. Aaron was amazed at how some training had improved her voice. Only now did he realize how good she really was.

When she finished, she smiled and took a slight bow. Then she raised her hands to hush the crowd.

"I have an announcement I'd like to make. Aaron, would you come up and join me?"

Surprise was written all over Aaron's face. His cheeks flushed a little, but he had no idea why she was asking him to come up there with her. He stood beside her, and she continued.

"Dr. Holder and I would like to invite all of you to our wedding on June ninth. It will be held here at the church on that Saturday afternoon at two o'clock. Afterwards we'd like for you to come to a pot-luck meal in the back yard of my Uncle Daniel's and Aunt Sarah's house. They didn't know this was happening since I've been gone so long. That's why I'd like to make it pot-luck. They weren't expecting this."

The congregation laughed at that remark.

"It will be a party, refreshments, and dancing. Aaron is there anything you'd like to say?"

She caught Aaron completely unaware.

270

"Anna has left me a little weak-kneed. All I have to say is I'm one of the happiest men in the world. I do hope all of you can come."

Everyone just roared.

Even the preacher got up and said, "I think Anna has caught us all in her little surprise. Luckily, she and I knew, and the church can be ready by June the ninth. We're all very happy for this wonderful, young couple."

After church was dismissed, Aaron told Anna, "I can't believe you surprised me like that."

"You did want a date didn't you? If you've changed your mind I can announce it's all off next Sunday."

"Not on your life."

"While I was singing, I remembered a young man sitting at my papa's dining room table. He was promising my papa he would marry me two weeks after I returned from my studies. I consider the two weeks up June the ninth. I wasn't going to give you a chance to back out."

Aaron reached and kissed her right there in front of the church, God, and everyone. James walked up.

"You're supposed to save that for after the ceremony. Anna you've surprised us all with this. Your mama hasn't planned a thing."

"I thought I'd wear the dress I wore for Cilla's and Mr. Holder's wedding. Aaron looked handsome in what he wore. We haven't worn those clothes since then. No one will have to worry about food if everyone brings something. Two weeks will give Uncle Daniel and Mr. Holder time to put up the dance floor. Family musicians will take care of the music. It'll be just like a family and friend get-together and it'll be fun. Trust me. I knew what I was doing."

"Aaron, son, you've got to live with her. Good luck."

James just shook his head.

"You know, Anna, now that you've explained it, it makes perfectly good sense. I agree with you whole heartily." Aaron squeezed her hand.

Chapter Ten

It was the summer of 1815, and a gorgeous Sunday afternoon. The Bordens had attended church that morning, and Jetty had left the family plenty of food for a good dinner. Sarah and Daniel had the kitchen straight once again. Daniel suggested that they get ready and take a swim in the river. The water should be plenty warm.

They hadn't been swimming this summer, and they always had such fun in the river. Daniel wanted to see how much he could teach Drew this year. The boy had grown into a sturdy, almost-six-year old, rambunctious boy. Beau, who had turned ten this summer, was becoming an excellent swimmer like his papa.

Kate, who was now eight and would soon be nine, was a graceful swimmer, but needed to improve her strength. Daniel was sure that would come with age.

"Beau, why don't you invite Eli to join us while we swim? He's probably looking for something to do this afternoon. We'll wait for you at the factory."

The water was nice and there was a lot of laughing. After getting used to the water again this year, Sarah was swimming very well. Daniel was pleased with her progress. Kate was going to be a better swimmer than her mama, but then she had started learning much younger than Sarah. That made a big difference in how good she could swim.

Daniel had worked with Drew, and he was becoming more comfortable in the river. Drew watched Beau now and wanted to copy him. There was beginning to be a little competition between the two brothers. Eli helped Drew a lot as he looked up to his older cousin.

The family had a fun afternoon. Eli walked back as far as the factory with them and then continued down the path to his home. After the family dried off and dressed, Sarah fixed the food Jetty had left them for supper.

Then she suggested, "It's such a pretty evening, why don't we all go outside and build a fire in the fire pit."

"That's a great suggestion. Come on kids and let's go out and get the fire started. Last one out is a rotten egg."

With that challenge, the children were off like a shot with Sarah dragging up the rear. There were benches built around the fire pit that made sitting very comfortable.

"Grab up some of those limbs and let's get a fire started."

"You're a rotten egg! You're a rotten egg!" they all yelled at their mama, when she stepped out the back door.

She acknowledged that she was indeed the rotten egg and that delighted the children. Sarah had been the only one thoughtful enough to bring hot coals from the fireplace. Besides, she knew that she had chosen not to participate in the mad dash to the fire pit. She was smart and not really the rotten egg. She wouldn't have to help gather the wood and kindling, so really, the joke was on them.

When she arrived with the shovel full of coals from the fireplace, the others had a nice pile of dry wood and leaves stacked in the fire pit. It was ready for the hot coals. She poured them in the center of the pile, and it soon began to glow.

Each took a seat and Sarah asked, "What shall we talk about? Who'll be the first to start an intelligent conversation?"

She laughed because she knew the kids would think that the way she asked the question would be funny to them.

Sure enough, Beau said, "Mother, you talk just like a school teacher."

That got it started, and the children began to giggle and laugh.

"So you think that's funny, do you?"

Daniel grabbed little Drew and began to goose and tickle him. That just made the others laugh more.

"Listen! What was that?"

Daniel pretended to cock his ear first in one direction and then another.

"Oh, Papa, you're hearing things. It wasn't anything," said Kate confidently.

"Okay, I guess you're right."

Sarah took a stick and poked at the fire.

"Let's play a game."

"I know a good one. It's called *Tell On?*"

Beau was proud having thought of it.

"I don't know how to play that," remarked Kate.

"It's easy. I start telling a story, and then I suddenly stop and say 'Tell On" and the person on my left picks up on the story and starts to tell on. They tell a little and then they say "tell on." It's easy but lots of fun."

"I don't know. I don't think I like that one," remarked Drew.

The conversation of trying to select a game to play continued with laughter and, "No, I don't like that one."

Unnoticed to the group, the sun had set, and it was beginning to turn twilight. Somewhere off in the distance they heard a coyote's lonesome howl, then came a second.

"What was that noise, Papa?" Kate asked. "We all heard that."

"It was just a coyote howling. About this time of evening they seem to get lonesome and start to howl for company. If you listen, you'll hear an answer to his call soon."

Sure enough, in just a few minutes, a second coyote answered from another direction.

"See, I told you there would be an answer to his howling."

Sarah thought back to a time when she was the same age as Drew and how her older brother and sisters used to scare her and her sister, Polly, with ghost stories. One in particular she fondly remembered.

"When I was your age, my brother and sisters told your Aunt Polly and me ghost stories and tried to scare us with them. I remember one they told that would just scare us to death."

"Mama, tell us about it."

"Oh, I don't know. It used to scare me, and I'm afraid it'll scare you, and you won't be able to sleep tonight."

Drew snuggled up next to Sarah and then he looked up at her and said, "Please tell us. We won't be afraid."

By this time the sun had long since disappeared below the horizon, and it was becoming dark. Another lonesome howl sounded in the distance and a second responded. Then more howls were heard in other directions.

"The coyotes are really active tonight. Throw another stick on the fire and build it up a little."

Sarah sensed that the time was ripe for a ghost story, and against her better judgment, she began to tell the one her siblings had scared her and Polly with years before.

"It seems that ghosts lurk in the most unsuspected places. We had not one but two in our house when I was growing up."

Six eyes got as big as saucers, and even Daniel didn't know what to expect next.

"Mama, you're just joking aren't you?"

"I know they were there because my brother and sisters told Polly and me they were. I grew up in a big two story, log home but it also had an attic that we never used. They told us that the ghosts lived in the attic, and if Polly and I weren't good, they would come down, and we would see them and they might even kidnap us."

Sarah hesitated to give the coyotes time to sound another chorus. If eyes could have gotten larger, they would have popped out of their sockets.

"What did they call the ghosts, Mama?"

"The worst one was named Sanko and the other was named Bloody Bones. In my mind, Sanko was all black with no color at all. He was an ominous fellow, and he was very menacing with very sharp fingers and a big head. No one knew where they came from—they just showed up one night. Bloody Bones must have been a prisoner at one time because you could hear him dragging a chain behind him. Sometimes it would slap on a rafter and bang."

"Mama, what did you do?"

"Well, if I was in bed, I pulled the covers up over my head until the noise stopped. Sometimes on a windy night the noise would go on for a long time."

"Then what did you do?"

"I would try to go to sleep as soon I could. My brother said sometimes they could hear Sanko and Bloody Bones arguing. And they said sometimes they could hear them sword fighting because they could hear the swords clanking."

"Did you ever see them?"

"No but my brother said they had seen them. They were always telling me which part of the attic Sanko and Bloody Bones were in. The worst place was back out in our kitchen, and it got so that I didn't want to go in there. And I never would have gone into the attic."

Sarah could tell the story was beginning to sound too real and thought her little ones were getting drawn up in it. Another coyote howl was heard, and Sarah decided it was time to bring her ghost story to an end.

"You know, Polly and I never did see those ghosts, and, after my older brother and sisters married and left home, we never did hear from Sanko and Bloody Bones again. Maybe they moved on with one of them. Now, I think it's time we call it a night and head into the house for bed, don't you agree? I know our home doesn't have any ghosts or your papa would chase them out if they came."

Kate said, "Mama, sometimes I hear noises in our house."

"I know, Kate, but that's just the wind blowing a shutter or something. Believe me, our papa wouldn't put up with any ghosts. Would you, Papa?"

"Never. I'd grab them by their ankles and pull them out of the house."

The children laughed with the picture in their minds of their papa pulling ghosts by their ankles.

"This was a fun day for all of us. Don't you agree? I'll remember it always. But we have so many days to remember."

Everyone was soon tucked into their beds. The boys shared a room but little Kate had a room all to herself. Sarah hoped she hadn't scared her so badly that she

278

couldn't sleep. If so, Kate never got up and nothing was ever said about being scared.

———————————

When Daniel went into town the next day, he went by Creel's Store to check their mail. There was a letter waiting for them from his brother, Joshua and his wife, Polly. The letter told that they were coming out for a visit. Daniel could hardly believe what he was reading. They hadn't seen them in over fifteen years. He knew Sarah would be excited with the thought of seeing her sister, Polly, again. All the family would be excited about this visit.

Sarah was at the school this morning, so he waited to tell her and Mary at dinner. He thought he'd go by and tell James and George this morning. The letter said Joshua and Polly would stay for six weeks.

Daniel was expecting them to stay with him and Sarah because Polly and Sarah would want to be together as much as possible.

Daniel checked the date on the letter closer. They were already on their way. They should be here in about a week. Daniel knew the road had improved so much since they had made the trip. There would be some bridges or ferries over most of the rivers now. There would be more towns and people and travel would be much faster. A sense of excitement and urgency hit him when he realized how soon they would see each other.

He went to James' house first and found his brother out at the barn. He showed James the letter and then they discussed the visit. Next, Daniel rode down and told George and Charity.

George said, "This'll mean lots of family get-togethers. Let's do throw one big barbeque in your back yard for the family and some of our friends. We'll all pitch in and help with it."

"Let's start with you, me and James along with our wives getting together and really plan all these things. Ya'll come for supper tomorrow night, and we'll start making plans. I'll run back by and tell James."

"That sounds good. We'll see you tomorrow night."

Daniel was getting more and more excited. He decided to walk down to the school and escort Sarah and Mary back for dinner.

It was summer school, and Sarah and Mary were only teaching the girls their cooking class. School hadn't dismissed yet so he sat on the edge of the porch and checked his pocket watch periodically. When Sarah dismissed the girls, Kate was among one of the first out of the door. She stuck her head back in.

"Mama, papa's waiting out here on the porch."

"Kate, you walk on to the house if you like. I'll walk with Mary and your papa."

Sarah knew when Daniel was waiting for her to dismiss school, something important had happened.

As she and Mary walked out the door, she asked, "What's wrong, Daniel?"

"It's nothing but good news, Sarah, so relax. We got a letter this morning from Joshua and Polly. They're on their way out for a visit. They'll be here in about a week as best I can figure. Travel will be so much faster and better than when we made the trip."

"Joshua and Polly are coming to see us?"

"That's right. I've already told James and George. They, along with Lucy and Charity, are coming for supper tomorrow night to make all our plans. The letter mentions they are bringing us a big surprise, but they'll be in a wagon so I can't see too big of a surprise."

"Are the kids coming with them?"

"No, just the two of them are coming. Making this long a trip with the kids would be too much, so the kids are staying with their grandparents. Don't you know Joseph and Carolina are excited having those kids for over a month? Carolina will be entertaining them every minute

280

with picnics and fishing. They'll make trips into town and no telling what else."

"Daniel, I'm so excited that my head is spinning. They'll be here in about a week?"

"That's what I figure, Sarah. They said they were going to visit for about six weeks."

"Mary, I'll want to take some time off. Can you and Anna teach the school for six weeks?"

"Yes, Sarah, we can do it. Like Daniel says, you just relax and let things happen. You need to enjoy this time with your sister."

"Oh, Daniel, this is unbelievable, and I'm so excited. Won't it be wonderful to see family?"

"Yes, it certainly will. Do you realize we have a lot to do and not much time to do it?"

That night family members came to make plans. Jetty and Remy cooked up a big pot of greens and a big pork roast was still cooking in the Dutch oven. Jetty cut up some small, fresh onions around the roast and put in some carrots to brown in the juice. Some big yams were in the coals to bake. With a big skillet of cornbread, this along with some peach cobbler would be enough. She had cold cider with the meal and plenty of coffee to go with the cobbler.

The food was a great success. They all sipped coffee and sat around the table to make their plans.

George volunteered, "I've been thinking. I'll bring one of my horses and saddles down here for Joshua to ride while he's here. You don't want to hitch up the carriage every time both of you want to come visit with all of us. No doubt you'll want to show him around town and introduce him to friends."

Lucy added, "Sarah can drive the small carriage. She and Polly can run around in it while they're here. They'll want to see all their nieces and nephews, their houses, and their children."

281

Sarah said, "They'll attend church with us. I'll want them to hear Anna sing at least one Sunday."

George chimed in with, "Clay and I'll roast the meat for our barbeque if you and James will furnish the rest of the food."

"You've got it. We can use one of my cows in James' herd."

"I'll furnish the piglet and a few chickens. We can all bring vegetables, breads, and desserts," James added.

"We'll ask everyone that's kin to us. We'll also include the Wades, Holders, and Stewarts."

"Whoa, stop. They're all kin to one of us through marriage now anyway."

"I see what you mean."

"That means that if Joshua has his own horse while he's here, he can come and spend time with both of you. You can come spend time with him and fish off the dock. I'm sure there'll be times when you'd like for just Polly and him to come for a meal. That'll be fine. We want this visit to be fun for all of us."

The brothers got to talking about old times back when they were boys in North Carolina. The ladies got up from the table and moved to the parlor so they could talk undisturbed. They all had a good evening reminiscing. Plans were made for a wonderful, whirl-wind visit.

The next few days were busy for everyone. They were planning meals and scheduling their families for meals with just Polly and Joshua. Daniel spoke with Jetty and Remy explaining that knowing when and how much to cook might not be easy the next six weeks.

"You'll just have to do the best you can as it might get wild around here."

"Mr. Daniel, you and Miss Sarah just enjoy your family all being together. Let us worry about the meals and serving them. We'll handle it. The two of us has got to where we can handle almost anything that's throwd at us."

Jetty laughed thinking how true that was.

"Ollie will do his part planning and helping, too."

"I know, Jetty. You and Remy always come through with the best meals ever."

The anticipated day finally came, and Ollie came running to the house.

"Miss Sarah, a strange wagon is coming up our road, but a black man is riding a horse following the wagon. Could this be your sister and Mr. Daniel's brother?"

"It could be, Ollie. Let's step out on the front porch and I'll see. I don't know who the black man could be, though."

Jetty and Remy followed them out on the porch.

As they watched, Sarah hollered into Beau, "Go to the factory and tell you papa we think Uncle Joshua and Aunt Polly are here. Hurry, run!"

The wagon pulled up in the turnaround at the house.

"That looks almost like Mr. Daniel getting out of that wagon," Ollie said.

"That's them," Sarah said. "Let's help them in."

Sarah almost ran to the wagon. Joshua picked her up and swung her around. Then he turned to help Polly down, and both sisters were squealing for joy.

Daniel, running with an out of breath Beau behind him, came from around the house. Both brothers grabbed each other and clung like they didn't want to let go. Polly was jumping up and down.

"Let me hug Daniel."

Joshua finally let go and then Daniel grabbed Polly and swung her around.

Joshua said in amazement, "This has to be Beau. He looks like Daniel spit him out except for those light blue eyes."

About that time, Kate and Drew appeared. They had heard all the shouting and squealing. They were a little timid with the goings on. Sarah put an arm around each child and introduced them.

"This is our Kate and this is Drew. Kids, meet your Aunt Polly and Uncle Joshua."

Polly stood and looked at each child. Kate was standing there with her papa's dark hair, but with green eyes that would put any cat to shame. Her eyes were what caught your attention. They were almost iridescent or translucent.

Then there was Drew. He had his mother's blond hair with his father's hazel eyes. They had the same yellow flecks that looked like sparks when he smiled. Both boys had Daniel's dimples.

Polly turned to Sarah and said, "Sarah, your children look as though you had an artist to plan each one separately."

"Our artist was the good Lord from above. Wait until you get to know them. Each one has their own personality."

Kate asked, "Is this the Aunt Polly who knew Sanko and Bloody Bones."

That brought Polly to attention.

"Sarah, what have you been telling these children?"

"We were just telling stories about growing up and our childhood."

"Aunt Polly, did you ever see those ghosts?" said Drew as he continued to press.

"No, Drew, I never saw them."

"My papa said if we had any ghosts in our house, he'd pull them out by their ankles."

"I'll bet he would, Drew. He wouldn't allow them to stay in his house."

Polly smiled at Sarah with pleasant memories.

All of a sudden, they remember their surprise.

Joshua said, "Can you guess who we've brought to you?"

Both Daniel and Sarah stood and looked.

Daniel said, "It looks a lot like Toby if I didn't know better. It can't be Taylor. It's got to be little Hector."

Daniel went to hug him.

"Welcome, Hector. It's good to see you."

"Father freed him and gave him a horse. Hector always said he wanted to come live with Mr. Daniel and Miss Sarah, so we told him he could travel with us. It's an answer to his dream."

Sarah said in shock, "Hector isn't so little anymore. You do look like your grandfather."

"Welcome, Hector. We can always use one more in our family."

Hector was grinning from ear to ear.

"Mr. Daniel, I'd know you and Miss Sarah anywhere. You haven't changed a bit since I was a little boy."

"Ollie, I guess we'd better see about getting our new family member settled in. You take him around back and get his horse fed and settled in. I'll start getting things that need to go in the house."

Beau said, "Papa, I can help."

"You surely can. Joshua, show us what goes inside, and then we'll put your wagon in the barn and get your team settled."

"Polly, this is Jetty and Remy. That's Ollie, he's Jetty's husband. Jetty is our head cook, and Remy is a very good cook. She helped raise the children and cleans. Really, all of them helped to raise the children, and all of them do whatever needs to be done. We just all pitch in around here and help take care of each other."

The two sisters walked up the path to the house holding hands with their arms swinging like little girls. They were chattering away like they had just seen each other yesterday.

"Mr. Daniel, can I talk to you?"

"Certainly, Ollie. What's on your mind?"

285

"Well, me and Jetty was talking. Hector can stay with us. We're not using that loft in our cabin and it's all furnished."

"I was going to fix a place up in the loft of the barn for him temporarily. I'll get another cabin built as soon as I can."

"Yes, sir, but our space is going to waste. Jetty and I were noticing that Hector is of marrying age. We'll take him to church, and he'll meet young ladies there. If he finds someone he wants to marry, then you can build him a cabin. I just wouldn't be in no big hurry."

"You do have a good point there. I know Hector's from a good family. If you and Jetty don't mind sharing your cabin, we can wait a while and see what happens. I appreciate you taking him to your church, and so to speak, under your wing."

"I can tell by talking to him that he's a good, young man. We'll make him feel part family."

"Okay, Ollie let's try it, but if you or Jetty want a change, you come tell me."

"I will, Mr. Daniel."

This certainly helped Daniel's worry as to what to do with Hector.

The visit with Joshua and Polly was going wonderfully well. George had brought a good-looking horse for Joshua to ride. Sarah was driving the small carriage, and she and Polly were going all over town shopping and meeting people.

They had gone to see where Dr. Aaron Holder and Lucy worked and to meet Dr. Wade. Polly loved the Creel's store and really liked Molly Creel. She thought their young daughter, Sage, was a very pretty girl. Polly noticed that Sage had beautiful green eyes, too.

"Sage's deep green eyes are beautiful with her chestnut hair. They don't compare with Kate's. Kate's eyes are just striking. They are such clear green and so big. That's what you see first when you look at her. Then her beautiful black

286

hair just sets them off. I tell you, Sarah, she's a real beauty."

"Polly, you'd think my daughter was pretty if she had a big wart on the end of her nose."

"That's not true, Sarah. If she had a wart on the end of her nose, I'd be the first to encourage you to see if Dr. Wade or Aaron could cut it off."

Polly thought that was funny after she said it. So did Sarah. They stopped on the sidewalk and laughed until they almost cried.

"Polly, we're so glad you and Joshua got to come out to see us. I wish you didn't have to leave."

"I know, but we belong out in North Carolina, and you belong in Kentucky. I'm just glad I got to come and see what a wonderful life you and Daniel have made for yourselves. I can't wait to tell everyone back home. Oh, I forgot to tell you. Carolina has invited our parents for a few days while we're gone. She's planning for both sets of grandparents to be with our children. Isn't that great?"

"Leave it to Carolina; she knows how to make people happy. She's a great lady."

Daniel planned dinner and an afternoon of fishing off the dock for just the four brothers. The wives came to the dinner, but then Sarah and the ladies visited on the back porch. Ollie and Hector kept the brothers supplied with cool cider and plenty of bait. Ollie reported back to the wives that he had never heard so much jesting and laughing in all his life. And still, they were catching fish through it all.

After they fished, they decided to clean their catch and ask Jetty to cook them for supper. They all had a wonderful day together.

Another afternoon, the four brothers decided to ride into town to the Palace and have some ale. The three brothers who lived in Burkesville had never been in the tavern either. When they told Joshua about Cilla's privy and the sign, they decided that was one place Joshua needed to see while he was in Burkesville.

They stopped by to get Tom to go with them. George and Daniel knew Tom could embellish the story and make it even funnier.

After they visited the Palace, they rode over to Aaron's and Anna's and slipped into their back yard to look at the privy and the sign. The sign was still hanging on the privy just like it had been when it was on top of the Palace. It provoked an unbelievable hardy laugh from all.

Time was going all too quickly. The big barbeque and dance had been a huge success. The afternoon before Joshua and Polly were due to leave, only the family members and all their children had one more gathering in Daniel's back yard. There was music and plenty of good food.

Just before it was time to say goodbye, the four brothers gathered in Daniel's dining room. The three brothers who were staying behind all had written letters to Joseph and Carolina.

They told of their lives since they had left home. They told of their children and grandchildren, and what it had meant to them that Joshua and Polly had gotten to visit.

Sarah had gotten every grandchild and every great-grandchild who could write, to write a little note. The ones who couldn't write, drew pictures. Sarah gathered all the letters and tied a ribbon around them. She put them in Polly's good care to be sure that Carolina and Joseph received them. This was better than any gift they could think of to send their parents.

The next morning was met with mixed feelings. They hated to see their guests go, but they were so grateful that they had gotten to come. Many wonderful memories had come with the visit and would remain with them the rest of their lives. They said their goodbyes, and Daniel's family stood in the turnabout and watched them drive down their road.

Chapter Eleven

Hector had been in Kentucky for two months now. He stopped Daniel one evening when he was coming from the factory.

"Mr. Daniel, do you have time to talk to me?"

"Hector, I'll take time. What can I do for you?"

"I've been living here a while now and have gotten to know Ollie, Jetty, and Remy. I'm very happy here."

"That's good to hear, Hector."

"Well sur, I've gone to church with Ollie, Jetty, and Remy. Ollie has introduced me to any number of young ladies my age."

"That's good."

"To tell the truth, there's none that catches my eye or that I like as well as I do Remy."

"Remy you say?"

"Yes, sur, Remy and I've talked. She loves living here and loves your family. She says she never wants to leave here."

"We think a lot of Remy and would hate to see her leave. She's lived with us a long time."

"Yes, sur. I wouldn't want to leave here either even though I could now that I'm free."

"We'd hate to see you go, too, Hector."

"Remy and me, we've decided we'd like to jump the broomstick, Mr. Daniel."

"You mean get married?"

"Yes, sur."

"Now, Hector, we are talking serious business here. I would want you and Remy to be sure of what you're doing. I don't want either of you getting hurt. You said you liked her."

"Oh, yes, sur."

"Can you stand there, and look me in the eye, and tell me that you love her and want to live the rest of your life with her? You'll take care of her and be a good father to any of your children?"

"I promise, Mr. Daniel. She's the only girl I'll ever look at."

"I believe you, Hector, but now we're going to do a little more than just jump the broomstick. You can jump a broomstick if that's what you want to do. I'll even supply

290

the broomstick, but you go to a church now. I want you to ride over and talk to your preacher. You get him to perform a wedding ceremony in your church for you and Remy. Jetty and Ollie can be your witnesses."

"I'll do that, Mr. Daniel. I'll tell Remy we need to plan that."

"Okay, you do that, and I'll talk to Jetty and Ollie. If they agree, you can plan a small wedding party down by their cabin. I'll see the dance floor is put up and I'll supply the food if Remy and Jetty will fix it."

"That sounds good, Mr. Daniel. Will you ask Ollie and Jetty if they want to help?"

"I'll talk to Jetty when I go in the kitchen. She and Ollie will let you know what they think."

"Thank ya, Thank ya, and I'll tell Remy."

"I'd ask her to marry me, if I were you."

"I'll do that later this evening."

"Tell her you love her."

"I'll do that, and thank ya, again."

Daniel went on in the house to talk to Jetty.

"Jetty, can you come in my study? I want to talk to you about something."

"I'll come right away, Mr. Daniel. Have I done something wrong?"

"No, no, not a thing. It's about something else."

Daniel began to tell her about his conversation with Hector.

"Have you seen this coming?"

"Well, yes, I have. I could tell by the way he looks at her, and she returns his looks. He's very patient and kind with her."

Do you think it's something that will last and won't just pass?"

Daniel searched Jetty's face to determine how sincere her answers were.

"If I don't miss my guess, I'd say it's a lasting thing."

"That's all I need to know, Jetty. I'll supply everything for this wedding, if you all will do the planning and the doing. I told Hector I'll want him to have a church ceremony and then he can have a small wedding party down by your cabin. I'll have the dance floor put up, and you all can make some fire rings. You can find some musicians, and I'll furnish the food if you'll let me know what you want and need. We'll see that Remy has a new outfit, and Hector has a new suit."

"That's very nice of you."

"Miss Sarah and I may even come down, and offer congratulations and dance two or three dances with you."

"That would please Remy and Hector. We'll tend to it all."

"Let me know as the plans come together and when it'll be. I guess Ollie was right, and I don't need to worry about another cabin. Hector will be moving in with Remy."

"Yes sir."

Daniel was anxious to tell Sarah what was happening in the lives of Remy and Hector.

A couple of days later, Hector stopped Daniel again.

"I visited with our preacher, and we're going to have our ceremony at the edge of the trees down by the cabin. Is that all right with you? We'll have it on Saturday after this next."

"That's fine as long as there's a preacher, and you say the vows, and mean them."

"Oh, we mean them, Mr. Daniel."

"I'll take you to town and find a new suit for the wedding and maybe some new shoes. I'll get Miss Sarah to tend to what Remy will wear."

"We appreciate that very much."

———————————————

Hector and Remy's clothing needs were taken care of, all the arrangements were made, and the day finally arrived. Their guests started arriving around one thirty.

292

Daniel could see several guests with instruments so he knew music was no problem.

The workmen from the factory had built a nice table for the yard. He was sure there was plenty of food as Jetty and Remy had been cooking for three days.

Beau announced he could see the ceremony taking place from one of his bedroom windows. Daniel and Sarah slipped up and took a peep out of curiosity. Daniel had even supplied a new broomstick. He wanted to see them jump it. He didn't know if they used it before or after the preacher, but if that was part of the custom, he didn't mind.

After dark and he had heard the music going for awhile, Daniel suggested to Sarah, "Let's go dance about three dances. I want us to offer our congratulations, and I have a little gift for them."

"That's nice of you."

Daniel went to his study and got a sheet of parchment. It was folded with a seal on it.

"This is a document I had Rice draw up. It's Remy's paper saying she is a free woman. I figured that would be one of the nicest things we could do."

"Daniel, this will please both of them so much."

"Are you ready for our dance?"

"I'm ready. Do I look all right?"

"You're beautiful as usual to me."

Daniel and Sarah walked down to the party. They went to the bride and groom, and shook hands.

Sarah kissed Remy on the cheek and whispered, "I'm so happy for you."

Daniel presented Remy with the document. She broke the seal and looked at it.

"It looks official, Mr. Daniel."

"It is official, Remy."

Daniel turned to Jetty.

"Can you read it to her?"

"Yes, sir, I can."

Jetty held the document in her hands and looked at it.

293

"Why Remy, this says you're a free woman, as of today."

"She may be free of Mr. Daniel, but now she belongs to me."

Hector hugged Remy, and then he shook Daniel's hand.

"Thank you, this means so much to both of us."

"Well, Miss Sarah and I came to dance, so let's have some music. How about a jig?"

The music started, and Daniel spun Sarah around the dance floor. Everyone else backed off to clap and watch.

When the jig had finished, Hector stepped forward, "Mr. Daniel, I remember seeing you and Miss Sarah dance when I was a little boy."

"That was a long time ago."

"You can still dance just as good. That's what I want's for me and Remy-to dance the rest of our lives together."

"That's the right attitude. You make it happen. Can we have a waltz now, and then finish up the last one for us with another jig? Then Sarah can carry me to the house."

Daniel laughed, wiped his brow, and then took Sarah in his arms. She still looked as stately as she always had when she waltzed.

As they walked away from the dance, Daniel was holding Sarah's hand. They went in the parlor, and Beau came down the stairs.

"I was watching you dance together from the window. You both are good. Mama, could you teach me to dance that well?"

"I can only try, Beau. Maybe we can go to the school soon, and papa can play the piano for us, and we can dance. I think that would be fun."

Kate was listening.

"Papa, could you dance with me?"

"I'd love to, Kate. You can never start learning too young."

"Daniel, I want to know, how did you know Jetty could read?"

"I knew she and Ollie had some education, as they speak so well. Ollie had told me once that Jetty's cousin from New Hampshire was a statesman. You can't be a statesman without education. I thought that if the cousin was educated, then probably Jetty was."

"They'll be good to help with Remy's and Hector's children. I'm glad Toby's grandson will have above average people helping to raise his children. I wouldn't mind helping some, as Toby was so good to teach me."

"You can do a lot of teaching on the back porch and enjoy being at home and outside, too."

"You're right. I'll give that some thought."

Two years had passed and Hector and Remy were about to have their first child. Jetty was almost as excited about it as they were. It was February and the winds were cold. Remy and Hector had come up to the big house for breakfast. Remy was helping clean the kitchen when she bent over with her first pain. Jetty turned to Hector.

"Put her coat on her and get her home. She's starting to have the baby. I'll tell Miss Sarah where we are."

Jetty found Miss Sarah in her bedroom.

"Remy's having the baby. I've sent her home, and I'm going to help."

"Do you need me, Jetty?"

"No, ma'am, I can handle it. I'll send Ollie to the school to tell you what it is, and how they're doing."

"Now be sure to let me know."

Jetty hurried to Remy's cabin. Hector had her in the bed. He had a nice warm fire going in the fireplace. Jetty got everything ready, and she could tell by the contractions this one wasn't going to be as long in coming as some first babies were. An hour passed.

"You take one deep breath when the pain starts and as it grows, you take short shallow breathes. I know this helps some. You'll have to push some. I'll knead on your stomach some and help you push it down. It's coming keep pushing."

The baby popped out.

"We have us a baby boy, Remy. Let me finish up here and then I'll clean you both up. Are you all right? Here take a sip of water."

Hector and Ollie were sitting up in the loft. They could hear Jetty talking so kindly to Remy. They heard the baby let out a cry when it arrived.

"It has strong lungs," Ollie said.

It wasn't long before Jetty called up.

"Hector, come and get your baby boy. Rock him while I make sure his mama's all right."

Jetty had the baby all wrapped up in a little warm blanket. She called up again.

"Ollie, come and go tell Miss Sarah that we have a baby boy. Tell her mama and baby are doing fine."

It wasn't long before the baby acted hungry, and he started to cry and fret.

"He's trying to gnaw his fist."

"He's hungry. Mama, let's see what you can do about that."

Jetty took the baby and put him in Remy's arms. She helped get the baby ready to suckle. He just took it right up, and Remy had no problem supplying the baby with his needs. She smiled up at Jetty.

"Thank goodness, I'm not going to have to use that Bubby Pot thing."

It was a cold morning, and Beau saw his friend, Marcus, already down at the school standing in the cold. Beau was dressed warmly and walked on down to join his friend. Sarah was still dressing to come to the school, and neither Mary nor Anna had gotten there yet.

Marcus suggested to Beau that they play a prank on the class this morning.

"I heard my older brother telling about the school he went to once playing a joke and smoked the class out of the school room."

"How do you do that?" Beau inquired.

"You take some evergreen branches and stuffed a bundle in the chimney and then spread a few on top. The first thing you know the chimney is stopped up, and smoke pours out in the room."

"My mama will catch us. I can never fool her."

"Oh, she'll never suspect anything. Women don't know about such things."

"I know there's a hatchet out in the shed back there. I also know there's a ladder hanging on the back of the shed. We can cut the branches now and put the ladder up back here. No one'll notice the ladder. Let's put the branches up on the roof now."

The industrious boys grabbed the ladder, cut some big branches, and Beau passed the branches up to Marcus.

With everything ready, Beau said, "No one knows you're here yet and won't miss you until later. Wait and when you hear Miss Anna playing the guitar and us singing, stop the chimney up."

"I'll watch and holler "fire, fire" when I see the smoke coming out. You come join us outside, and no one'll notice."

Marcus agreed this was a good plan. Beau went out and hung around out at the bell tower until his mama came.

"May I ring the bell this morning, Mama?"

"Yes, Beau, you're tall enough now to reach it by yourself. Give it five pulls and that'll do."

Beau obliged and then wrapped the rope back around the pegs that held it. He followed Sarah as she unlocked the door. Then, as usual, he stuck his mittens in his coat pockets and hung his coat, scarf, and cap on a peg.

"Shall I stoke the fires up, Mama?"

"That would be good. Add more wood to both, as it's cold this morning, and this room is still a little cool."

Sarah went on about her business suspecting nothing. Mary and Anna arrived almost at the same time. Then the children began to arrive a few at a time. When they had settled down a bit, Sarah called them to attention.

"Let's say our prayer, and then we'll sing a hymn."

They all bowed their heads. Sarah started the prayer, and they all joined in unison. Anna stepped forward with her guitar.

"Let's sing an old hymn this morning, *Let's Plow the Fields and Scatter.* The words are on your hornbook, if you can't remember them."

Anna began to play, and everyone began to sing. Beau was watching the fireplace. He was waiting for the smoke to really pour out.

He could tell his mama was sniffing the air, so he shouted, "Fire! Fire!"

The smoke was really pouring into the room by this time.

"Quickly file out, everyone."

The children didn't panic. They filed out orderly as they had practiced so many times.

It was cold outside, and no one had a coat. Sarah had left the doors open. The smoke was pouring out of them now. Sarah began to suspect something. One thing she noticed was that Beau was laughing under his breath and getting a kick out of all of this.

She said to Mary, "It seems as though the chimney is stopped up. That's not unusual. I'll send one of the boys to get Ollie or Hector to come check it."

Marcus volunteered to climb up on the roof to check. Sarah thought, *He's my second suspect.*

"Wait, Mary, we have a volunteer. There's a ladder behind the shed, Marcus. I'll help you get it so you can climb up."

Beau stepped forward and volunteered, "I'll help him, Mama."

"No, Beau, I'll go as I want to supervise his climb."

The boys knew they were caught.

Beau sidled up to Marcus, "I told you she was too smart and would catch us."

Sarah heard the whisper, too. She smiled a smug little smile to herself. *Beau knows I'm not the usual woman, and now Marcus knows it, too.*

"Beau, if you'll come help Marcus, please. I think we'll have this problem solved in a few minutes everyone."

When they walked to the back of the building, Sarah saw the ladder leaning up near the chimney.

"Which one of you stopped up the chimney?"

"I did, Miss Sarah," said Marcus sheepishly.

"I helped cut the branches and put them on the roof, Mama."

"Okay, Marcus you climbed up there the first time, so you can climb up again and unstop the chimney. You boys will have to be punished for this. The very idea, driving everyone out in the cold. I've got to think about your punishment. Beau, you go open up all the windows, and then you bring everyone their coats."

The smoke was now rising through the chimney again. It took a few more minutes to get it clear enough to go back in the school room.

"I don't mean this as punishment, especially for the innocent, but you've just had your recess."

"Beau and Marcus, would you come to my desk."

When the boys came near she whispered, "I've decided on your punishment. I want three pages written as to why it was not a good idea to stop up the chimney. Have it on my desk by tomorrow morning."

Sarah knew Beau didn't mind reading, but he hated writing stories. She decided she would let this subject go and say no more. She was pretty sure that Kate or Drew would tell their papa, and it wouldn't be necessary for her to tell Daniel.

Anna did pass by Beau's desk, and she whispered, "How dumb, Beau Borden. You knew your mama would catch you."

That evening at supper, Kate couldn't stand it any longer. She had to tell her papa what Beau and Marcus had done that morning.

Daniel listened and didn't say a word while at the table. Sarah didn't say a word about it either. Beau wondered what was going on.

After everyone had finished their meal, Daniel looked at Beau and said, "Beau, would you join me in my study?"

Neither Daniel nor Beau said a word. Daniel rose from the table first, and Beau followed behind him. Sarah knew Beau thought he was about to be killed. She wasn't sure herself what Daniel was going to do. Daniel closed the study door

"Have a seat, Beau. Can you tell me what made you think of smoking out the class today?"

Obviously uneasy, Beau started his tale.

"Well, I saw Marcus down at the school this morning, and I was dressed and ready to go. I walked on down to talk. He told me about this happening at his older brother's school, and we thought it was funny. I knew where the hatchet was to cut the limbs. I knew you kept a ladder out behind the shed. Everything was just so handy. I told Marcus that mama'd catch us. She seems to catch me in everything I do."

"You do realize that your mama is a very smart woman?"

"Yes, sir, I told Marcus that."

"Still you blindly pulled the prank?"

"Yes, sir, he stopped up the chimney, and I hollered fire."

"Did it ever dawn on you that your mama has taught school for a long time? She knows just about every trick in the book. You can't put anything over on that woman."

300

"I know. Anna told me I was dumb and that I knew mama would catch me. Deep down I knew it."

"Well, I believe from now on I'd study harder and just forget about any pranks."

"I've got to write a three-page story tonight about why I shouldn't have done it. Mama wants it by in the morning."

"I think you'd better get up to your room and get it done then. It better be good or she won't accept it from you."

"I hate to write, Papa."

"I know. I have a feeling that is exactly why that is the punishment."

After they went to bed that night, Sarah asked, "Did you kill him? Kate, Drew and I kept listening for him to cry, but we never heard anything."

"We just had a good talk. After I reasoned with him how smart his mama is, I don't think he'll ever try to pull anything again."

"Good, that was better than a spanking. You know," she said reflecting back on the incident. "It took me a minute to catch on to what was happening."

Daniel reached for Sarah. "Miss Sarah, you know I love you even if you are slow."

Chapter Twelve

Beau Borden was a young man of almost twenty years now. When he finished studying at his mother's school, he started working in his father's furniture factory. Beau seemed to have a special feel for the wood. When he was younger, he had hung around his father's factory. He loved watching and learning. Occasionally one of the men would let him try his hand at a task.

Beau decided this is what he loved and wanted to do from a young age. Daniel had loved the craft from a young age also, but his son had the touch and a talent that didn't come natural to Daniel.

Beau had learned how to carve from Si and Rich, but he had surpassed even their skills. This pleased Daniel very much.

Now that Beau was older, Daniel was teaching him the business side of the factory. One day Beau would take over and run the business.

This morning Daniel asked Beau to go in to town to check the mail at Creel's General Store. He was expecting a sizeable order for a load of furniture that was to be shipped to Nashville, Tennessee.

Beau saddled his horse, Tar Baby, and started to Creel's Store. When he went inside the store, he looked for Mr. or Mrs. Creel. He didn't see either of them. Instead a pretty young lady stepped forward and asked could she help him.

"I'm Beau Borden, and I'd like to get my family's mail."

"Beau, I thought I recognized you. You look so much like your father. You don't remember me, do you?"

Beau looked a curious look and still was unable to recognize her.

"I'm sorry. I can't say that I do."

"I'm Sage Creel. We probably haven't seen each other in three or so years. I've been off studying in England for two years and have just returned."

"Sage! Of course. We used to play together when we were kids. It's been a long time. So you've been studying in England? That's very interesting. May I ask what studies you've pursued?"

"I went to study styles and fabrics, but I got a little side tracked. I've stayed longer than intended and studied design of furniture along with the fabrics."

"Furniture design? That's interesting. Do you remember my father owns a furniture factory, and I've been studying how to make and carve furniture? I guess we have something in common even though we haven't ventured out into settees or overstuffed chairs at the factory."

"I'd love to see some of your carving, Mr. Borden."

"Oh, please, call me Beau. You've always called me that even though it *has* been a long time. Will you be at church this Sunday with your parents?"

"I'm sure I will be."

"Why don't you plan to ride home with my family and have Sunday dinner with us? I'll take you down to the factory and show you what we're doing now. That is, if you're interested. I'm sure my folks would love to see you again."

Sage smiled and accepted the invitation.

"Our families have always been such good friends. We've been in the process of remodeling and updating our equipment in the factory. We still build a lot the old way by hand, though."

"The process and your carving would all be of interest to me."

"Then I'll see you Sunday. Oh, I forgot, would you check the mail for me?"

"Of course. That's why you came in."

She flipped through the pile of letters.

"Yes, you have a small stack."

She handed Beau the package of letters all tied together.

"Thank you, I'll see you Sunday."

Beau returned to the factory and handed Daniel the letters.

"Let's go to the office and have a look at these."

Daniel began to open the mail.

"Here's that very nice order I was looking for. We'll have to start to work on this order tomorrow. It's a large one."

Daniel wanted Beau to get interested in the business end of things, but he was teaching him a little at a time.

The morning had passed quickly. Daniel looked at his pocket watch.

"Let's go to the house for dinner."

As they were walking up the path toward the house, they could see Sarah, Mary, and Drew coming up the road from the school.

Drew was finishing up his last term at Sarah's school. He had been working as an apprentice in John P.'s law office. Drew loved the work and was planning to attend William and Mary, as his cousin, Rice, had done. Rice and he would take over the law office when John P. retired.

All arrived at the house about the same time. The table was set, and Jetty had dinner almost ready. When they sat down, Sarah and Mary began to discuss the rumor going around that a new, larger school might be built near downtown Burkesville.

"Since I almost have my last child educated, I just may retire. I'm going to think about it."

Beau spoke up.

"Something interesting happened to me this morning when I went to get our mail."

Everyone looked at Beau and were anxious to hear more.

"I ran into Sage Creel. She's been off studying in England for a couple of years. I probably hadn't seen her for three years. She's really filled out in the right places and is a very pretty young lady. She has beautiful chestnut colored hair and green eyes. They are a dark, emerald green, and Kate's are lighter and more translucent."

Drew had to tease.

"You certainly must have run into her noticing all that. I thought you went to get the mail?"

Drew had to rib him a bit more, but Beau continued to ignore him.

"I asked her what she had been studying, and she told me she studied about fabrics and furniture design. That interested me, so I asked her if she was going to be in church Sunday."

Beau reached for another serving of meat.

"She said she was sure she would be. I invited her to ride home with us after church and have Sunday dinner with us. I'll take her and show her the factory. She said she'd be interested and would like to see my carvings. I hope you don't mind, Mama. I forgot Jetty and Remy were off on Sundays."

"I'll work it out. I'll be glad to see Sage again. I haven't seen her in a long time."

Drew teased again. "Are you sure she's just interested in your carvings?"

"Drew, this is strictly business. If she's studied fabric and furniture design, I want to see just how much she knows. I was thinking I might want to talk to papa about us expanding into making upholstered pieces."

"Beau, that's interesting. I've been thinking I'd like to expand some. Upholstered pieces might be just the thing. You check it out thoroughly, and then we'll talk."

Sunday arrived, and Sage came to dinner. After Sarah had served the meal and all had their fill, Beau suggested that he and Sage walk down to the factory. He got the keys. Sarah watched out the kitchen window as they walk down the path.

"This might be business, but it might not be all business. This'll be interesting. I saw the way they looked at each other."

"Don't be matchmaking, Sarah."

She just smiled and looked at Daniel.

After Sage and Beau looked at the factory and some of his carvings, they walked along the river. She was impressed with his carvings.

They were gone about three hours. Sage came in to thank Sarah for the tasty dinner and said Beau was going to drive her home.

Beau wasn't gone long when he took Sage home. When he returned, he came in the parlor and announced they were going to meet at her house tomorrow afternoon.

Their son announced, "We wanted to look at some of the furniture books she's had shipped from England along with some fabric sample books."

Sarah mentioned to Daniel, "They must be getting along very well."

Daniel just smiled.

"Oh, Anna told me that Aaron was interviewing a new young doctor for his office. Aaron's been running the office since Dr. Wade retired, and he needs help. The new doctor is from Philadelphia and wants to live in a small town. I believe Anna said his name is Scott Sims."

"If Lucy retires when Kate finishes up her nursing studies, Kate will be working for two doctors, I suppose."

"Lucy may stay just to work with Kate for a while. She'll want Kate to have a good start in the office. Lucy has loved her work."

"I'm tired, Sarah, let's go to bed. The boys are settled in their rooms. I'm very pleased that Beau is thinking about the business and expanding it. It'll be his someday, you know."

The next afternoon Beau went to meet with Sage. He was gone far into the evening. Sarah and Daniel were still up when he finally got home, and he came in the parlor.

"I had a wonderful afternoon. Sage and I have so much in common. I stayed and had supper with the Creel's. I've always liked them very much. You know, Papa, this just may work into something with this expansion."

Beau took a seat next to the settee and continued his discussion of a proposed expansion.

"Sage is a very smart lady. She'd be interested in overseeing the upholstering. She could even order and choose the fabrics for the pieces, and she has very good taste. We'd like to carve part of the arms and upholster the other part of them. The legs would also be carved."

"You sound excited about this project."

"I am, and she is, too. Do you think we have room to have Mr. Holder build another whole section on to the building?"

"We could talk to Tom about it. We just might build another building down close to the original."

"I want to confess something. After seeing Sage and being with her for a couple of days, it might be more than business here. I believe we are attracted to each other. Let me restate that. I know we are attracted to each other. I'm pretty sure her parents approve. I hope you do."

"Beau, if you're serious about her that would be wonderful. We've always loved her and her parents."

"I don't plan on rushing it. I just wanted to let the two of you know."

A few months had passed, and Tom's crew was almost finished with the new building for the upholstery division. Beau and Sage were working with Tom on the project.

Kate had come back from her studies to become a nurse. She took off a week and then reported for work at Dr. Holder's office. Lucy was thrilled to death that Kate was working with them.

Aaron made Kate the new assistant nurse to Dr. Scott Sims.

One morning Kate and Dr. Sims had gone out on a call to the sawmill. There had been an accident. A piece of lumber had slung from a saw and had cut a gash in one of the sawyer's forehead. It required some stitches, but the man would be all right.

Now it was almost dinner time, so Kate invited Dr. Sims to meet her family and have dinner with them.

When they came in the front door, Kate hollered, "Mama, we have company."

"Kate, what are you doing home this time of the day?" Sarah asked as she came down the hall.

"There was an accident at the sawmill, and Scott, -eh- Dr. Sims and I've been out there. It's time for dinner so I'd thought we'd stop and eat with the family. I'll go tell Jetty to put our names in the pot."

Kate headed for the kitchen.

"I hope this isn't inconvenient for you, Mrs. Borden."

"Not at all, Dr. Sims. We're used to people dropping by at anytime. Jetty, bless her, always seems to have enough food. We've wanted to meet you, as we hear Anna and Kate both mention you."

"I've wanted to meet Kate's family, too. She and Aaron are forever mentioning you."

"I hear Daniel and Beau coming in for dinner."

Sarah and Dr. Sims could hear all the bantering and laughing in the kitchen.

"You're a close family, and I hear they're having a lot of fun with each other."

"Oh, yes, you should come to one of our family's get-togethers. When we all get together, the laughter, music, and dancing livens this place up."

"Mrs. Borden, I'm going to take that as an invitation to your next get-together. I'll be here."

"Mama and Scott, dinner's on the table."

Kate did the introductions of her papa, Beau, Drew and Dr. Scott Sims.

"Dr. Sims, are you enjoying living in Burkesville?"

"I love it here. I've rented a small home in town, but one day before too long I'd like to have a home built here."

"One of my best friends, Aaron's father, is the best builder around. He built our house. I'm sure you've met him," Daniel said.

"Yes, he's a very nice fellow. Aaron was telling me he builds and even remodeled his house and made it the home it is. He does do good work."

The doctor looked at Beau and addressed him.

"Kate tells me you help run your father's factory. She says you carve beautifully. One day, when I have time, I'd like to see the factory."

"Why don't you meet us for church this Sunday?" Sarah asked. "We'll plan on having dinner, and Daniel and Beau can show you the factory."

"Well, I'll do that, Mrs. Borden. Thank you for the invitation. Kate can tell me all about the time and directions to the church."

"Do you fish, Dr. Sims?"

"I like to, and I do occasionally, but it's been a long time since I've had the time."

"Kate, we'll have to make a date to invite him out to fish."

"Yes, Papa, we will. He doesn't know what he's missing until he's had Jetty's fried fish."

When the meal was over and Dr. Sims and Kate were on the way back to the office, he said, "Kate, I've never been around a nicer, friendlier, family. I'd like to get to know them better."

"Don't worry, Scott, I'm sure you will. Didn't you get about three invitations today to return again? This is the first time you've met them. Another time or two and you won't need an invitation. You can just show up. Ask Aaron. He'll tell you that you'll just be one of our family before you even know it."

Dr. Sims reached and took Kate's hand. "That's not a bad idea."

Kate blushed, "Are you saying you're interested in calling on me?"

"I'd very much like to if it would please you."

"Let's take it slow, and we'll just see what happens."

It was a beautiful afternoon. Everyone but Sarah and Daniel was busy. They decided to sit on the back porch and just talk.

They were swinging when Sarah remarked, "I've been thinking, Daniel. I'm going to retire. I've offered the school to Anna for a music school. She was thrilled with the thought. She said Cilla would help her. Together they can have a marvelous school. Anna needs to utilize her voice more."

"That's fine with me, Sarah. You've taught for a long time. I'm going to start slowing down myself. Beau's surprised me. I didn't think about him taking to my business like he has. It's going to grow and prosper under his helm. We're thinking about offering Susan and Noah a partnership in the furniture store. Beau and I feel that they've deserved it."

"That will please them and George. Dr. Wade and Flora will like the idea, too."

"Just what will we find to do?" Daniel was thinking out loud.

"We'll be planning weddings and be expecting grandbabies. I'll have a lot of back porch teaching to do."

"We know who Beau has chosen. I'm pretty sure Kate and Scott will marry soon. I can tell by the way they look at each other."

Daniel laughed and kissed Sarah on the cheek.

"Who do you suppose Drew will find to bring home?"

"I don't know who she'll be, but she'll be special and smart. I wouldn't think a good-looking young lawyer in town would have any trouble attracting the ladies."

"We'll always be busy with all our extended family members. Then there'll always be a lot of family get-togethers."

Watch for this author's other books:

George's Creek to Georgia

The Borden Family Series—
Carolina Calling
With Sarah Beside Me
The Bordens of Burkesville

Children's Chapter Books—
Little Man:--A Little Girl's Dream
Sadie, the Goat Lady
Stranger, the Miracle Dog
The Ghost of Coalville

www.ingramcontent.com/pod-product-compliance
Lightning Source LLC
Chambersburg PA
CBHW062126280526
45788CB00001B/70